A POST-PATRIARCHAL CHRISTOLOGY

American Academy of Religion Academy Series

edited by
Susan Thistlethwaite

Number 78
A POST-PATRIARCHAL CHRISTOLOGY

by
David W. Odell-Scott

David W. Odell-Scott

A POST-PATRIARCHAL CHRISTOLOGY

Scholars Press
Atlanta, Georgia

A POST-PATRIARCHAL CHRISTOLOGY

by

David W. Odell-Scott

Library of Congress Cataloging in Publication Data

Odell-Scott, David W.
A post-patriarchal christology / David W. Odell-Scott.
p. cm. — (American Academy of Religion academy series ; no. 78)
Includes bibliographical references and index.
ISBN 1-55540-657-2 (alk. paper). — ISBN 1-55540-658-0 (pbk.)
1. Jesus Christ—Person and offices. 2. Feminist theology.
I. Title. II. Series.
BT202.03177 1992
232—dc 20 91-37534
CIP

Printed in the United States of America
on acid-free paper

For Lauren

CONTENTS

ACKNOWLEDGEMENTS

An acknowledgment commonly is the means by which one notes/traces some debt to person(s)/institution(s) for support or direction which made possible the accomplished work. To acknowledge is to play upon the double meaning of the term "knowledge" as "to know mentally" and "to beget." Thus, to acknowledge is "to-thank" those named "in-knowledge" of their contribution to the "production" of the text. There is an intimate knowing which is shared by those who labor in the production of a text. It is a labor which results in something which has a life and a death of its own.

I acknowledge my gratitude to Charles Scott of Vanderbilt University for his continued questioning of the text and author. His involvement in the project provided occasion for thinking which he neither dominated nor was absent from. I also wish to acknowledge my gratitude to Daniel Patte, also of Vanderbilt University, for his painstaking labor with me on the Pauline epistles. Many of the subtler insights of this text are the outcome of questions or queries raised by Scott and Patte. I am also grateful to many others in the community of scholars at Vanderbilt University, especially John Compton, Michael Hodges, Don Sherburne, John Lachs, Henry Teloh, Richard Harrison, Bill Hook, the late Bob Williams, Ed Farley and my fellow graduate students in Philosophy, especially Don Boehm.

I thank those teachers over the years who encouraged my inquiry and supported my intellectual development, especially Paul Wassenich, George P. Fowler, Ken Lawrence and Ted Klein of Texas

Christian University, and Harry Oliver of Boston University School of Theology.

I am grateful to all my colleagues in the Department of Philosophy at Kent State University for their conversations and suggestions. I wish to especially thank James Dickoff, Departmental Chair, for his appreciation and support of my work. I am grateful to Gayle Orminston whose publishing experience is a valuable resource which he gladly shares with his colleagues. I thank Mary Snodgrass, department secretary, and the staff of Computer Services for their technical knowledge and assistance.

I am grateful for the support afforded me by Dean Eugene P. Wenninger of Research and Sponsored Programs and the Research Council of Kent State University for funding the final preparation of the manuscript.

I thank my former colleagues at Fisk University, especially Academic Dean Ormond Smythe, and Mike Awalt and Ronnie Littlejohn of the Philosophy Department of Belmont University, for discussion and criticisms of parts of this book in its earlier stages.

My gratitude goes to Jon Berquist, Phillips Graduate Theological Seminary, Tulsa Center, for his many helpful suggestions and criticisms of the work in progress. I am especially indebted to Jon for his careful reading and critical comments of Chapters 6 through 9 which greatly improved the final work.

I wish to thank Susan Brooks Thistlethwaite and Robert Hauck of the Academy Series of the American Academy of Religion, and Dennis Ford of Scholar's Press, for their support and helpful suggestions in getting this text to press. I also thank the anonymous readers of the series for their constructive criticisms.

My thanks to the editors of *Biblical Theology Bulletin*, David Bossman and Leland White, for permission to use the following articles in Chapter 8: "Let The Women Speak in Church: An Egalitarian Interpretation of 1 Corinthians 14:33b-36," *BTB* 13.3 (July, 1983):90-93, and "In Defense of an Egalitarian Interpretation of 1 Cor 14:34-36: A Reply to Murphy-O'Connor's Critique" *BTB* 17.3 (July, 1987):100-103. Their early support of my work is most appreciated.

I thank my parents, Bill and JoAnn Scott, for their unwavering encouragement and faithful support. This study is an expression of their expectation that their children think for themselves and to not take things at face value. I hope to pass on such a legacy to Megan and Paul.

It is difficult to acknowledge all the ways Lauren participates in the production of this work. Every page traces conversations, comments, marginalia, glances, glares, and laughs between us. To write that I am indebted to Lauren would violate--in a sense--the very intimacy and struggle of our life together. That we labor together is to say the least. That there are traces of our relationship--our intimate struggle--in this work goes without saying. I dedicate this labor to Lauren.

PART ONE

ENDINGS IN PHILOSOPHICAL THEOLOGY

The Christological De-Structuring of Orthodox Theology

1

ENDINGS

> Experienced in virtue of the dawning of the origin, metaphysics is, however, at the same time past in the sense that it has entered its ending. The ending lasts longer than the previous history of metaphysics.[1]

Heidegger did not defeat metaphysics. He did not slay the demon who distorted our thinking, leaving its carcass near the path to be devoured by varmints who follow his departure. He did not break metaphysics as one would a tool present-at-hand and then cast its pieces upon the rubbish heap. Heidegger did not establish a new doctrine whose logic and truth abolished and replaced the old doctrine. Metaphysics is too closely akin to "man"--and the idea and the power of "man" is so thoroughly metaphysical and self evident as a manner of being-in-the-world--to be slain, broken, or proven false according to logic and truth claims.

How are we to understand "the end of metaphysics" if metaphysics is not an adversary to be slain or defeated? What does it mean to assert the *end* of metaphysics if we do not mean the demise of metaphysics? And what sort of *ending* lasts longer than what it ends?

The term "end" has a rich etymological history derived from *ant* and *anti*, which mean "in front of, before; also opponents, opposed, against; the end."[2] The German prefix *un* indicates a reversal. End means the opposite of beginning, in opposition to the beginning. But the end of one thing marks the beginning of another. Thus, an "end" as *ant/anti* may run from one end to the other, marking both ends of something; the beginning and the end. As well, the end as *ant/anti* might run throughout metaphysics as the opposition which persists in opposition throughout, from beginning to end. In order to understand and appreciate such an "ending of metaphysics" which lasts longer than the previous history of metaphysics, a strange sort of "ending" which is not analogous to death, brokenness or falsity, we need to consider what Heidegger calls the "history of Being."

EPOCHS

The history of Being is not a study of the "development" or intellectual evolution of western philosophy. Heidegger does not seek to discover the single line which unfolds itself as the expanse of time. Rather, Heidegger's history of Being resembles the fractured lines between geological plates, or the lines of an atmospheric front which mark the places of interaction between different pressures. A history of Being is both a history of thoughtful relations and a history of the breaks, the limits, the gaps and endings in and between the various "epochs" of Being.[3] An epoch marks a cessation, a stoppage, a pause. The history of Being on Heidegger's terms traces the various pauses, stops, and limits within western thought. A study of the history of Being includes a study of discontinuity.

But this is only one of the ways Heidegger would have us understand the history of Being as epochal. Heidegger also suggests that "the history of Being means destiny of Being in whose sending both the sending and the It which sends forth *hold back* with their self-manifestation."[4] Being "withholds" itself, keeps itself back (*epechein*) from self-disclosure in order to make the gift which it has sent forth discernable. Heidegger names Being's "holding back" from self-disclosure in the unconcealment of beings, Being's epoch. Thus the history of Being may be discerned in the traces of the gifts of beings which conceal that which in its absence allows beings to-be. Such a history of Being's epoch, Being's "holding back," yields a convoluted and disruptive story which traces the various transformations of Being's epoch, the manners in which Being simultaneously discloses beings and conceals itself in the clashes of "epochs."

The epochs are not spans of time per se, but are rather the fundamentally different characteristics of sending which overlap and counter each other. "The epochs overlap each other in their sequences so that the original sending of Being as presence is more and more obscured in different ways."[5] In each subsequent overlaying, each self-concealment of Being is concealed in the sediment of layer upon layer. Each epoch simply covers another epoch. And each epoch, in its own way, conceals Being in the presentation of beings. In the history of Being's epoch, we discern that Being hides itself in various and sundry ways.

On Heidegger's terms the history of western thought is a complex conflict. The clash, the crisis which occurs in the event of beginnings and endings, marks the strife of different epochs. These differences are most evident in the crisis. However, in the resolution of the crisis, in the inauguration of a new epoch, previous epochs are overcome by the orders of intelligibility and authority which are established as the "rule" and "principles" of the new epoch.[6] What is intelligible in one is unintelligible in another. What counts as authority in one is powerless in another. What is not assimilated from the former epoch in the emerging orders of intelligibility and authority must submit or be forced into a subterranean existence. In other words, previous epochs move to the unseen, the unthought, the "underworld." What disrupts the dominant epoch is buried, repressed, concealed and entombed, and so dwells in opposition to that which is dominant and present.

What can be thought in one epoch may not be thought in another. What makes sense in one may be senseless in another. For Heidegger, that which ceases to be carried over in the overcoming of one epoch by another is said to be *aporetic*. Absurdities and mysteries often mark the limits of the epoch in which they occur, and may be the counter-memory of another epoch which in having been overcome, discloses itself *under* disguise so as to appear as if it belonged within the dominant epoch. Or in the domination of a particular epoch, other epochs persist as that which is unthought and unsaid in the self-evident presence and practices of an age.

THE ENDING AT THE BEGINNING

Heidegger's contention that metaphysics has entered its ending is inseparable from his work in the origins of western thought. First, he delimits metaphysics by showing the pre-conditions of metaphysics which make metaphysics possible but which are metaphysically aporetic. Thus Heidegger's characterization and critique of metaphysics, his delimitation/**term**ination of metaphysics, happens in **terms** of his study of early Greek thought which precedes and prepares for the possibility of metaphysics.

Heidegger is not claiming that if we could uncover all the epochal layers of ontology we could return to some *archē* where Being would disclose itself in full presence. Quite the contrary, it is not the full presence of Being that is expected. If the epochal layers of ontology could be uncovered, then the ontological difference which has been forgotten in metaphysics' epoch could be recalled. It is a difference which is intelligible as difference in the pre-metaphysical early Greek thought of Heraclitus and Parmenides. It is a difference which can not be thought of within or as a category of the metaphysical tradition.

Metaphysics is not capable of thinking its own end or closure. Metaphysics is a history of beings which must forget Being. Thus, metaphysical thought fails to conceive the abundance of epochal transmutations. Metaphysics discerns in the "historical" sequence of philosophy the appropriate belonging together of the various historical (and intellectual) periods of thought. But it does so at a high cost. In forgetting Being, and thus being unable to conceive of the epochal transmutations, metaphysics must strive to account for the various ruptures in the history of beings. It does so customarily by asserting that western philosophy is coherent. The coherence may be said to originate in the thought of some ancient thinker to which all of subsequent western thought is simply a footnote. Again, coherence may be discerned by way of identifying a set of perennial philosophical problems which provide a category for every conceivable idea. Or, coherence may be provided by an appeal to the intellectual evolution of western thought.

However, the demarcation of the borders of the different epochs in terms of intelligibility/ unintelligibility and authority/unauthorized, discloses more than a historical crisis or event. The retrieval of early Greek thought allows Heidegger to trace in the metaphysical texts themselves those orders of intelligibility and authority which, though they have been overcome, nevertheless rupture and violate metaphysics' *principium*.[7] The presence of the end of metaphysics, anti-metaphysics, within the very weave of metaphysics marks the end of metaphysics from its beginning. The end of metaphysics (like Dasein's own deathliness) is marked from the beginning to the ending of metaphysics.

The demarcation of the end of metaphysics is not simply the border which differentiates one epoch from another. The "end" crisscrosses the very terrain of metaphysics. What is assumed to be a solid whole, what appears to be stable and ordered, the terrain of metaphysics, is found to be fractured. These fractures, these lines, mark the instability of the terrain and recall the differing and conflicting forces at work. The heart of metaphysics, its foundations and ultimate presuppositions are non-metaphysical. Metaphysics violates itself. The essence of metaphysics is an infidelity or deception.[8]

Conflicting texts are brought into a unity and remain in a more or less stable coherence by the power of some authority. That authority dominates so long as the unity holds together, so long as the inter-textual coherence is maintained. Thus, the critique of authority is a critique of some existing structure which can be traced in the (inter-) textual coherence. The inter-textuality is not discernable so long as the authority which maintains the coherence is powerful. This inter-textuality is visible only in the creation of the system or when the unity is seriously challenged. In the beginnings and the endings the coherence is seen as coming to be or as coming to an end.[9] And in each instance, the text's seams reappear as seams. The coherence is called into question. The domination of the authority falters as the text's "texts" reassert their independence from the overriding structure. The hermeneutic's limits are disclosed, not by its horizons, but by gaps within itself.

THE ENDING WITHIN

Heidegger's play upon the double meaning of epoch, (1) as Being's withholding itself in the illumination of beings, and (2) the different ways where by Being's epoch happens in subsequent ages, frames a convoluted history of Being. Such a **history** of Being is a metaphysical conundrum. Being is not specific, it is not a being, it is a non-thing. And a history of no-thing is **no** "history" at all, at least in any common sense of the term. Heidegger's history of Being traces the gaps and spaces which fracture the attempts to present the metaphysical tradition as coherent.

Such a history of Being yields an overtly sensitive (maybe too sensitive?) reading of texts. It is a reading in which tracing exposes the varying layers which texture a text. It is the fractured text which gives witness to the inter-play and thus the incoherence of the inter-textuality of every text.

Derrida, working with this sense of "end" or, as he prefers, the "closure" of metaphysics, contends that the resources to critique any particular metaphysical system may be traced within the metaphysical text itself.[10] Inscribed within the text are the means for surpassing it. Such traces occur "under erasure" in the text. They are aporetic (unintelligible; illegal; deviating from the rule) and yet are traced in the text.

> In order to exceed metaphysics it is necessary that a trace be inscribed within the text of metaphysics, a trace that continues to signal not in the direction of another presence, or another form of presence, but in the direction of an entirely other text.[11]

The "endings" of a coherence occur like the New Madrid fault which cuts the heartland of North America. It is a cut recalling a geological memory which counters the identity and stability of a continent and a nation. At the heart of the homeland are fractures which mark the seams between geological plates. These plates reassert themselves in quakes and shifts. The limits of the continent are disclosed not only by its shorelines but also by the shakes and quakes along the internal seams/fractures. These seams, or fractures recall borders which have long since vanished from the memory of those living on the land. Yet, the fractures--covered over--covered by the leisure and commerce of the Mississippi, Ohio and Missouri rivers--lie at the heart of the homeland and its people.

Scott contends that the phrase "wholly different text" means that something wholly different is crushed out of sight and sound by the power of metaphysical texts. It is a power which when used to interpret texts, forgets that texts are inherently textual.[12] Only those markings which are "present" are real. The textuality of the text, how it folds and twists, what it conceals and discloses in its weave, how it incorporates fragments of other texts into itself and cuts loose that which is not the same, is overlooked and forgotten in the preoccupation with what is present. The borders which mark a difference in the text, which allow the textuality of a text to be seen in its reading, are lost.[13] What is erased, what is "crushed out of presence," nevertheless "bleeds" through as an erasure. (Why do we speak of what has been erased as nevertheless *bleeding* through? Can it be that we sense the violence of metaphysics' erasure?) The clarity of presence and absence is blurred in the evidence of metaphysics' manipulation and violent domination of the text by those marks which are *sous rature*.[14]

This "effacement" is inscribed *in* the metaphysical text. A text dominated by the power of metaphysics can not conceive of the possibility that metaphysical ways of thinking delimit themselves. Because of the power of the idea of presence, metaphysics does not admit (recognize to itself, or allow entry of) its own effacement or that it effaces another.

A metaphysical reading of a text picks out and gathers into itself that which is available to, that which is "the same" as, metaphysics. What is not metaphysically "intelligible" is nothing. And nothing (i.e., mere differing from presence) can not be incorporated into metaphysics' (inter-) textuality.

Deconstruction marks the "end" or "closure" of metaphysics by tracking those traces which metaphysics has sought to exclude through marginalization or which metaphysics has ceased to re-trace (thus ending the continued inter-textuality of a trace in the reproduction of texts).[15] Or, as we have seen, deconstruction also seeks to force outside whatever seems to stand within metaphysics.[16]

Metaphysics, for Derrida, is marked by a series of opposites in which one of the terms is privileged over the other. The first task of deconstruction is to render a metaphysical reading of the text which draws attention to the opposites and the priorities at work in the text. This reading is followed by a reversal of the priorities. What was primary becomes secondary and vice-versa. Finally (in that it ends the metaphysical preoccupation with hierarchy), the privileging of terms (evidenced in the first and second reading) gives way to a reading in which the terms are "at play" with one another. With the hierarchy deconstructed, the terms in opposition "play" on and off one another as difference.[17] Each is itself in opposition to its other in a play of difference which has a logic of its own, a logic which exceeds metaphysics.[18] It is a logic which we call Heraclitean.

As we will see, one of the ways Heidegger calls metaphysical texts into question is to trace the fragments of Heraclitus or the traces of his fragmented thinking within metaphysical texts. The fragments are preserved by and large only in metaphysical texts. And they are preserved--traced as **pieces** of something that has been dismantled, broken, brought to an end--in order to demonstrate the absurdity of pre-metaphysical thinking for philosophy and Christian theology. One of the strategies of Heidegger's study of the fragments of Heraclitus is to trace an epoch of western thinking that ruptures the dominance of metaphysics in metaphysical texts.

NOTES

1. Martin Heidegger, "Overcoming Metaphysics," *The End of Philosophy*, translated by Joan Stambaugh (New York: Harper & Row, Publishers; 1973), 85.

2. Joseph T. Shipley, *The Origins of English Words: A Discursive Dictionary of Indo-European Roots* (Baltimore: John Hopkins University Press; 1984), 14 & 15.

3. "Epoch" comes from the Middle Latin *epocha*, which is derived from the Greek *epochē*, and means "check, cessation, stoppage, pause." *Epochē* comes from *epechein* which means "to keep back, withhold, stop, pause" (see Klein, E. *A Comprehensive Etymological Dictionary of The English Language* (New York: Elsevier Publishing Co.: 1960), and may be traced to its Indo-European root *segh* which Shipley notes means "seize, hold; have, pause" (see Shipley, *Origins*).

Schürmann notes that Heidegger's "'phenomenological destruction of the history of ontology' first announced in *Being and Time* (H 39) centers upon the notion of *epochè*." (Reiner Schürmann, "Principles Precarious: On The Origin of the Political in Heidegger," 245, in *Heidegger: The Man And The Thinker*, ed. Thomas Sheehan (Chicago: Precedent Publishing, Inc., 1986)). Heidegger derived the term from the Stoics for whom *Epechein* meant to abstain, to cease seeking (Heidegger, *Early Greek Thought*, translated by David Farrell Krell and Frank A. Capuzzi (New York: Harper & Row, Publishers; 1975), 26).

4. Martin Heidegger, *On Time And Being*, trans by Joan Stambaugh (New York: Harper & Row, Publishers; 1972) 9. Emphasis mine.

5. Ibid., 9.

6. Each epoch emerges as an economy of presence and absence through theoretical "principles" (a hierarchical ordering of what is present and intelligible) and "princeps" (from "princes," a structure of authority which determines rewards and punishments in terms of compliance with the economy).

7. The Latin term *Principium* names both the theoretical "principles" of a time and its practical *princeps* (from "prince" or "authority"). Schürmann, 246.

8. Irene E. Harvey, "Derrida and the Concept of Metaphysics," *Research in Phenomenology* 13 (1983): 116.

9. "(T)he 'texts' that have guided and grounded previous generations often appear illegible in the modern and post-modern worlds. Instead of expressing a single story or coherent plot, human lives tend to be inscribed in multiple and often contradictory texts. What makes sense and is meaningful in one situation frequently seems senseless and meaningless in another setting. The resulting conflict creates confusion that extends far beyond the pages of the book." Mark Taylor, *Erring: A Postmodern A/theology* (Chicago: The University of Chicago; 1984) 3.

10. Derrida prefers to write of the "closure of metaphysics" as opposed to the "end of philosophy" or "the end of metaphysics." For Derrida, "end" and "closure" are not equivalent. To suggest that philosophy has an end is to say it has a termination (*Of Grammatology* (Baltimore, John Hopkins University Press, 1974, 1976)p. 4). As Bernasconi has pointed out, Derrida employs "closure" instead of "end" to state his concern that "it is impossible for us simply to transgress metaphysics, to leave it unambiguously behind us and stand unequivocally outside it." ("The Transformation of Language At Another Beginning," *Research in Phenomenology* 13 (1983): 1) Yet it also is being suggested, hinted at by Derrida, that Heidegger's use of "end" might mean "termination," which it does not.

11. Derrida, "Ousia And Gramme: Note on a Note from *Being and Time*," *Margins of Philosophy*, Translated, with Additional Notes, by Alan Bass (Chicago, The University of Chicago; 1982), 65.

12. "When the idea of presence is used to interpret texts, including the *texts* of presence, it loses--forgets--the textuality, the discursiveness. The text in its happening is other than what it said about it, and cannot properly be said to be either present or absent." Charles E. Scott, *The Language of Difference* (Atlantic Heights, N.J.: Humanities Press International, Inc., 1987, Contemporary Studies in Philosophy and the Human Sciences, series editor, John Sallis), fn 39, 163.

13. "...the inconceivability of traces may be thought of as a border phenomenon--not only the border that demarcates identity, but the borders that crisscross discourses and line out passing names and emerging differences. Borders differ. And at borders, as transmuting goes on, traces of the transmuted occur. At and in borders, through them, language traces both the passing and the emerging. In this language now, and in Derrida's, the dominance of identity and presence is overridden as "border" and "trace" come into play." Ibid., fn 39, 164.

14. "If the text is not *present*, but is something that witnesses against its interpretation as metaphysical presence, how are we to speak of it? The text speaks, produces, interplays. Effacement goes on, differencing goes on, the imperceptible goes on, and the metaphysical polarity of presence-absence fixes too quickly, rejects

too fixedly, gives status and station too routinely, and encompasses too thoroughly. Presence is, always, but never wholly. Absence is and is not, but never absolutely." Ibid., fn. 39, 164.

15. Derrida writes, "It is in this way that the difference between Being and beings--that which has been 'forgotten' in determining Being as presences and presences as the present--is so deeply concealed that *no trace of it remains. The trace of différence* is expunged.... It is the trace of the trace which has disappeared in forgetting the difference between Being and beings" ("Ousia And Gramma," 82). Scott notes that for Derrida all we have remaining for thinking is "the trace left by the removal of the trace." And if we 'name' the trace, then we 'give it determination,' and revert back to metaphysics. We make the trace left by the removal of the trace into a presence. But Scott argues that to so assess "naming" (of the trace that is left by the removal of the trace) as reinscribing metaphysics "...would appear to be so only if the naming were in a discourse totally dominated by 'presence' or if the discourse did not override or ride through the presencing specificity of names and determinations. The presencing of names is not final or total: discourses de-presence. Names can override determinations." Names can produce nonpresencing options. "They present, re-present, de-present, perhaps in the same movement. The 'thing itself' too is played through and out. As the emerging language of difference functions, there is as-such, none-such, de-such, no-such." (Scott, *The Language of Difference*, fn. 39, 163 & 164).

16. Bernasconi cautions, "For Derrida, to impose the closure on a text does not only mean to draw back within metaphysics what has pretensions to transgress it; it is at least just as much to force outside metaphysics whatever seems to stand within it. Of course, and this is crucial, the inside-outside opposition which is being used here to situate the closure is itself metaphysical. The two strategies of drawing within and forcing outside are inseparable. They belong together in an ambiguity for which Derrida prefers the title 'play'."(Bernasconi, 3) Derrida writes, "The presence-absence of the trace which one should not even call its ambiguity but rather its play (for the word 'ambiguity' requires the logic of presence...." Bernasconi notes that, "It is assumed that something is "ambiguous" because it is somehow lacking a clear and present identity. The term "play" conveys a sense of difference which fails to be one or the other, unless of course we oppose play with work or seriousness. Play is within the Derridian text playful work or the serious playfulness of deconstructed terms" (Bernasconi, 3).

17. "We pass from a reading which is referred to the author's intentions or an influential interpretation or even a standard translation and arrive at a reading which displays working through the text a logic which is not that of traditional metaphysics. And yet this passage is not arbitrarily enforced on the text, but it attained by and large through the use of fairly conventional hermeneutical techniques. The differences between Derrida and, for example, Gadamerian hermeneutics lies more in the greater resolution with which Derrida applies these techniques than is generally realized. The sense in which Derrida's readings are immanent is indicated by his claim that every metaphysical text carries within itself the resources that will be borrowed from the metaphysical system to criticize it (M70/60). The justification for reversing the hierarchy of terms is found inscribed within the text itself; the means for surpassing metaphysics are to be found within metaphysics itself. But this surpassing is not to be understood as a Hegalian *Aufhebung*" (Bernasconi, 2).

18. "Metaphysics is, according to Derrida, marked by a certain series of oppositions, the most fundamental of which is that of presence versus absence. In each of the metaphysical oppositions (inside/outside; speaking/writing; remedy/poison, etc.) one of the terms is privileged over the other and the privileging of presence governs all these others. So Derrida's first task is to render the metaphysical reading of the text in hand and this tends to be accomplished by drawing attention to these oppositions and priorities at work throughout the text. This prepares for a reversal of the priorities whereby what was primary becomes secondary and vice-versa. Finally this gives way to a reading in which neither term is privileged and we are introduced to a sense in which the terms (which at first--and second--reading were opposed) are "at play" one with the other; the play takes place according to a logic which we do not associate with metaphysics. This play which exceeds metaphysics is thus found inscribed in texts which we provisionally took to be metaphysical. The inscription of this excess is in Rousseau borne by the word *supplement* and in Plato by the word *pharmakon*" (Bernasconi, 1 & 2).

2

DE-STRUCTURING METAPHYSICS

Heidegger's way of calling metaphysics into question happens as a rereading of metaphysical texts. We have noted that the ending of metaphysics is no simple affair. Such endings mark more than a simple cessation. The endings of metaphysics will be, at least, as complex as the metaphysical enterprise. In the chapters to follow we will concern ourselves with the relation of philosophy and theology in Heidegger's deconstructive work (as metaphysics and as other than metaphysics, as pre- or anti- metaphysical, or as metaphysically indifferent) as we trace the play of ontology and theology in metaphysics.

THE QUESTION OF BEING

Heidegger traces one of the endings of metaphysics to Aristotle's question which is the question of Being.

ti to on ē on
What are beings as beings?

The ambivalent terminology of Aristotle's "metaphysical question" yields a grammatical ambiguity which Heidegger employs both to characterize and to deconstruct metaphysics. Put simply, the term *on* equivocates in the metaphysical question. There is a failure in the inquiry to remember the *difference* between **what beings are as beings** and **beings**. The ambiguous distinction between "beings" and "as beings" (*on ē on*) is *glossed* in the search for "**what are** beings as beings." This failure to remember the *difference* between **beings** and **what is not a being** (Being) yields metaphysical discourse.

Aristotle's question, however, does not begin metaphysics. Metaphysics par Heidegger finds part of its issue with Socrates' and Plato's distinction between sensible beings as a world of shadows and the Being of sensible beings as a world of Ideas.[1] In the Metaphor of the Cave, Socrates and Plato distinguish between "going over" (*met' ekeinē*) the shadows and "over to" (*eis tauta*) the Ideas.[2]

Richardson comments,

> Aristotle's question was, to be sure, a "metaphysical" question. Whatever the post-Aristotelian origin of this word in the libraries of Rhodes, clearly the question about beings as beings was a "passing beyond" beings to that which makes them be,.... Hence even if Aristotle called such an interrogation "first philosophy," we see with what justice may be attributed to the word "metaphysics" itself an interpretation that has become common currency since Simplicius in the fifth century: a "going beyond" (*meta*) the "physical" (*ta phusikē*). This "going beyond" the Latins would call *transcendere*, so that metaphysics always comports in one way or another the process of transcendence....[3]

That metaphysics comports in one way or another the process of transcendence, marks the different trajectories of Platonic and Aristotelian thought. In the Platonic "going beyond" the sensible beings the ideas transcend the world of shadows in that they are "above." For Aristotle, "going beyond" the *phusikē* means to interrogate the *ousia* of beings, the foundations, the sediment. In this way metaphysics is the transcendence of beings to their Being, i.e., *ousia*. In either case, the division of supra-sensible and sensible beings, and their hierarchical ranking and valuation is a pre-condition for all metaphysics.

It is the distinction between a supra-sensible and a sensible world (between what is and what transcends--above or below) that is the essence of metaphysics.[4] It is an essence which is disclosed in Aristotle's question and the tradition which sought to reply. The question was assumed to be an inquiry into "beings as being." In the preoccupation with investigating "beings as beings," only one manner in the ambivalence of *on* comes to be considered.[5] In this dominant preoccupation with "beings as beings" in the division and hierarchical ordering of "beings," the Being of beings is forgotten.

Metaphysics is that history of Being in which Being is abandoned in a search for a **highest being**. What is forgotten in western thought, what can not be comprehended metaphysically, is that which is not a being. Born of this forgetfulness in the preoccupation with what is, metaphysics maintains itself. And so, we might ask, "But what is forgotten?" "What is Being?" However, such a question solicits a metaphysical reply; for "*what-is* forgotten" is "**not-***what-is*," but "*what-is* ***not***."

This quandary of how to question Being concerned Heidegger his entire life. In *Being and Time*, he notes that Being (*Sein*) is not something-which-is (*ein seiender*), nor is it a category of metaphysical epistemology.[6] In order to prepare a way to raise the question of Being, he thematizes *dasein*, the clearing for beings, whose being is always in question. In **its** question *dasein* finds its inability to define or designate Being.

It is Heidegger's contention that what is forgotten in the metaphysical inquiry into the "Being of beings" is the ambivalence of the term *on* and the grammatical ambiguity which the double sense of *on* yields in the formula *on ē on*. The ambivalence of the terms *on* names a *difference* between beings and Being, between the things-which-are and that which is not a thing but which allows beings to be.

One of the subtle points being made by Heidegger (and often too quickly passed over) is that the ontological difference is not a being. Neither is it Being. The ontological difference is the difference between Being and beings.

THE DIFFERENCE

Commonly offered in translation of the German *unter-schied* in the Heideggerian texts, the English "difference" is built upon the term "differ".[7] The prefix "dif-" is derived from "dis-" whose Latin origin denotes separation, removal, negation and reversal.[8] The root "fer" comes from *fara* which is derived from the Middle English *faren*, meaning "to go, travel." Akin to the term *faren* is the Middle English *ferien*, meaning "to carry, transport." *Ferien* is from the Old English *ferian*, which is related to the Old Norse *ferja*, "to pass over, to ferry, to transport." The difference (*unter-schied*) is the traversal of the separation, to travel the negation, or "to convey the separation," to carry the negation.[9]

For Heidegger the *unter-schied*, by its negating, clears a region in the density of things. In so clearing a place, the difference discloses a dimension in which things are allowed "to be." Things which are allowed presence in the dimension do not occur as things which are determined by their reference to other things. Things which are illuminated in the "clearing" are present and free of the clutter of things which are merely lying about. "To be" so illuminated is to appear "strange," to occur in relation to *no-thing* else. This dimension is the difference, the intercision which bears the negation in which things emerge and are illuminated. Di-mension, as "to measure asunder," is not a measuring of the distance or distinction between mere objects which are lying-around.[10] The di-mension is the inter-cision of the object and Nothingness, not the relative relatedness of objects.

This dimension is not an a priori space in which things reside side by side. Distances and distinctions between mere objects lying around are not measurable. The dimension is the *unter-schied*, the negating which discloses a thing as it is named and called forth in the clearing, not the relative relatedness of things one to another.

In other words, things occur standing forth (*phusis*), illuminous (*phantasia*), and revealing (*alētheia*) in the tensive space, the gap which disrupts, the error which in being called into question, calls all into question.

Attending to the difference as the cut-between which discloses world and things, Heidegger writes;

> Of itself, it holds apart the middle in and through which world and things are at one with each other. The intimacy of the difference is the unifying element of the *diaphora*, the carrying out which carries through. The difference carries out world in its worldling, carries out things in their thinking.[11]

The difference occurs as that which simultaneously holds apart and unites world and things. In holding apart, the difference intimately unites world and things in their opposition. To overcome the tension, by abandoning either Being in the calculation of beings, or beings in the mystical flight of negation (i.e., Being) would be simultaneously to forget both Being and beings. Being is the Being of beings. And beings are the beings of Being. Neither enjoys aseity. Each is itself in the difference, in the intimate tension.

In traditional metaphysical discourse, this discussion regarding the relation of Being and beings sounds very much like the problem of the one and the many. An obvious distinction between Being and beings is that the former is singular and the latter are many. A common metaphysical concern is to discern which is fundamental and which is a derivative or an abstraction. Is Oneness, Being, an abstraction from the many (possibly an Idea) or, are the many beings dependent upon, grounded on the One (Being as *ousia*) for their existence?[12]

Heidegger avoids these common metaphysical moves. He does so not by denying that the issues of the one and the many are intricately connected with his quandary over Being and beings, but by calling into question the hierarchical ordering which grounds one in the other. As we have briefly seen, Being and beings differ. In their (ontological) difference, beings and Being play one another. Each is itself in difference with the other. The metaphysical preoccupation with establishing some hierarchy with respect to the one and the many is possible only if their difference has been forgotten.

AN ENDING OF METAPHYSICS FROM THE BEGINNING

Heidegger finds that the ambivalence of *on*, the ontological difference of beings and Being, corresponds to the intimate correlation of One (*en*) and Many (*panta*) in the Heraclitean fragments.[13] One and Many (*en* and *panta*) are "held apart" and "gathered together" in the *logos*. Heraclitus names this intimate correlation--*eon*, which is probably a primitive form of *on*. Thus, Heidegger finds in the Heraclitean fragments the subtle play of ontological difference.

When addressing the intimate correlation of One and Many, which is intrinsic to the Heraclitean *logos*, Heidegger commonly refers to those fragments which have been characterized by contemporary commentaries under such various headings as "identity of opposites," "unity of opposites," and "simultaneity of opposites" (to name a few).

Those fragments characterized as naming the identity of opposites may be divided into two major groups. The first is composed of those fragments whose opposites are connected by being different points or stages in a single invariable process. The pair of opposites succeed one another in an endless continuum and are thereby united as day is to night and night is to day (Fragment # 57). Patrick identifies this kind of connection as "the endless passing into one another."[14] Other fragments which express this kind of unity include fragment #88,

> And as the same thing there exists in us living and dead and the waking and the sleeping and young and old: for these things having changed round are those and those things having changed round are these ones,

and fragment #126,

> Cold things warm themselves, warm cools, moist dries, parched is made wet.[15]

In each fragment, one of the attributes or entities is overcome or concealed as the other is disclosed. Night follows day, day follows night, and so on unendingly. Thus, night and day do not simultaneously exist but come to be each in its own time and according to its measure. Such opposites are said to be "the same" because one follows the other **in a continuum**.

The second major group consists of those fragments in which the opposites are "united" because they co-inhere. Unlike the first major group wherein only one opposite exists at a time, in the second group the opposites exist simultaneously. Within this cluster, Kirk identifies three distinct types of connections between evident opposites. In the first (i) "the same thing produces opposite effects upon different classes of animate objects."[16] Fragment #9,

> Donkeys prefer rubbish to gold, men prefer gold to rubbish,

and fragment #37,

> Pigs wash in mud, chickens in dust and ashes while men do not,

serve to illustrate this sort of relationship. In the second type (ii) "different aspects of the same thing may justify opposite descriptions." This type is expressed in fragment #60,

> The path up and the path down is the same

and fragment #103,

> In the circle the beginning and the end are the same.

In the last group (iii) "good and desirable things... are seen to be possible only if we recognize their opposites." Fragment #111

> Disease makes health pleasant and good, hunger satiety, weariness rest,

and fragment #23,

> They would not know the name of justice if these (unjust) things had not occurred,

are clustered together under this type.

Of the three types of relations identified by Kirk in the second major grouping, the second type is the most difficult and perplexing for modern (and not so modern) western philosophers to interpret and comprehend. In his monumental work on Heraclitus, Kirk more carefully explicates this type of identity of opposites under the following description:

> The same observer may ascribe opposing attributes to the same object, in certain special cases, because different applications or aspects of the object are being considered. In a sense, the opposing characteristics of such objects, belonging to the objects at one and the same time, show themselves to be connected, to be "the same."[17]

Clustered under this description, Kirk gathers fragments #48, #58, #60 and #103. It is from this small group of fragments that

Heidegger most commonly draws in his elucidations of the "difference" of *en-panta* in Heraclitus and the ontological difference of Being and beings.

In keeping with the Milesians, Heraclitus proposed that the cosmos was a harmony of contrasting elements, a harmony of opposites. The tension is never resolved. Peace does not reign. Nor does strife break the harmony. Like the bow and the lyre, there is an equilibrium in the cosmos, "measure for measure." "In being drawn apart it is being drawn together" (Fragment #51). And if one or the other (peace or war) were to dominate, then the cosmos would disintegrate (i.e., fly apart by the force of the strife) and/or fall back lifeless with each aspect indifferent to its other.

Heidegger's work with the Heraclitean texts is detailed and plays upon subtle distinctions, fine nuances which are not always clearly presented and elucidated. One such instance that is significant in our study is the play of the sets of terms *En* and *Panta*, *logos* and *phusis*. Heidegger writes,

> The popular interpretation of Heraclitus tends to sum up his philosophy in the dictum *panta rhei*, "everything flows." *If* these words stem from Heraclitus to begin with, they do not mean that everything is mere continuous and evanescent change, pure impermanence; no, they mean that the essent as a whole, in its being, is hurled back and forth from one opposition to another; *being is the gathering of this conflict and unrest.*[18]

It is commonly noted, and I believe rightly so, that Heidegger identifies Being as *en* and beings as *panta*. However, what is not commonly understood is that the many or all, the *panta*, **do not name everything**. Instead, the *panta* is better understood as those beings which are said **to stand in opposition**, which are at odds. As such, as those who stand in opposition, the "many" are said to be "one." That is, *those beings in opposition are simultaneously, in their opposition, one.*

"*Being* is *the gathering...*," (i.e., it is the one) which stands in contrast to "...this conflict and unrest" (i.e., the many beings). Contra the tradition, it is not that the many are one. Rather, those (many) in opposition are one.

Several things are happening at once in Heidegger's study of *En* and *panta*, *logos* and *phusis* in the Heraclitean fragments. As we have just seen, the "flow" of "everything," is the oneness of those things which stand in opposition to one another. The many are one because each is itself in opposition to another. This oppositional-oneness is the play of difference.

Having elucidated the *en* of the *panta*, the oppositional-oneness of the many, Heidegger eloquently shifts the discussion. Now, it is the opposition--not of the many--but of **"the one and the many"** about which he inquires. This play of one and many subtlely marks the pre-metaphysical *dif-* (to stand apart, "dis-cord") *-ferance* (to ferry, "unite") of *logos* and *phusis*. It is the subtle marks of a pre-onto-theological difference.

The *En-Panta* happens as "the drawing apart which draws together." One does not occur without the other. The opposites occur as a polarity which simultaneously pulls apart and unites. The opposites emerge by virtue of their relation, their tension. They are the same in that they occur, they are derived from, this single harmony which is an equilibrium of peace and war. Without this dynamic flux nothing would occur.

This dynamic flux, "the drawing apart which draws together," of the *en-panta* occurs in the *Logos*. Heidegger writes,

> *Logos* characterizes being in a new and yet old respect: that which is, which stands straight and distinct in itself, is at the same time gathered together in itself and by itself, and maintains itself in such together. *Eon*, beingness, is essentially *xynon*, collected presence; *xynon* does not mean the "universal" but that which in itself collects all things and holds them together. According to Fragment 114, such a *xynon* is, for example, the *nomos* for the *polis*, the statute that constitutes or puts together, the inner structure of the *polis*, not a universal, not something that hovers over all and touches none; but the original unifying unity of what rends apart. The opinionatedness, *idia phronēsis*, for which the *logos* is sealed, attaches itself only to the one or the other side and supposes that it has captured the truth. Fragment 103 says: "Gathered together, the beginning and the end of the circle are the same."[19]

Logos is a unity. But it is not a metaphysical identity. The unity of logos is the unity of opposites. Opposition is not suppressed; it is not overcome. Those in opposition are not one by virtue of having discovered some common essence which they share. Logos is the unity of struggle, or a unity disclosed in struggle, or the struggle of togetherness. If the tension be overcome, logos is lost.

Then, *idia phronēsis*, opinionatedness--which attaches itself to one of the opposites--asserts the primacy of one over the other. This *idia phronēsis* is metaphysics. It is an opinionatedness which asserts the ontological primacy of one over its other in an hierarchical ruling. Tension is thus destroyed.

In the ensuing domination of one over its other, the sovereignty of metaphysical thinking flattens all differentiations and renders a sameness devoid of tension. All opposition is out-rightly nullified, or is suppressed/repressed by the threat of violence or the fear of violence.[20]

Metaphysics, in having forgotten the ambivalence of *on*, has forgotten the ontological difference. In the loss of the difference--opposition, tension, gathering and harmony have been silenced. Metaphysics, concerned with ordering and calculating this indifference, is nihilistic. For in having silenced the play of *en* and *panta*, those things which are metaphysical are distributed in a lifeless region. The question of the Being of beings is forgotten.

In *Identity and Difference*, Heidegger continues his thinking of the difference between Being and beings in terms of Heraclitus. In an obvious play upon Fragments 103,

> Gathered together, the beginning and the end of the circle are the same

and 8,

> Opposites move back and forth, the one to the other; from out of themselves they gather together,

Heidegger writes,

> Inasmuch as Being becomes present as the Being of beings, as the difference, as perduration, the separateness and mutual relatedness of grounding and of accounting for endures, Being grounds beings, and beings, as what *is* most of all, accounts for Being. One comes over the other, one arrives in the other. Overwhelming and arrival appear in each other in reciprocal reflection. Speaking in terms of the difference, this means: perdurance is a circling, the circling of Being and beings around each other. Grounding itself appears within the clearing of perdurance as something that *is*, thus itself as a being that

> requires the corresponding accounting for through a being, that is, causation, and indeed causation by the highest cause.[21]

This play of Being and beings--in which Being and beings circle around each other in an endless difference and in which Being and beings move back and forth in the ceaseless play of opposition--collect in their collectedness.

In Heidegger's earlier work he called this play "the ontological difference" and later simply "the difference." Heidegger's work on the ontological difference is not a metaphysical postulation which having once been formulated is simply applied again and again. The ontological difference is not Heidegger's final word on "difference," let alone his final comment on difference and ontology. The ontological difference (simple) offers insight into a central feature of metaphysical thinking. However, the ontological difference may be said to yield more differences.

In his later work the concern to keep the distinction between Being and beings diminished. With his continued critique of western metaphysics, ontology's discursive power diminished. In other words, its ending began. In this transformation in the beginning of the ending of metaphysics, the *difference* itself as opposed to the "*ontological* difference" became central. Thus, in his later works on metaphysical thinking and language, Heidegger's attention shifts away from the "difference between Being and beings" to other differences and eventually "difference per se."

This shift can be discerned as early as *An Introduction To Metaphysics*. Heidegger begins by inquiring into what he titles "The Fundamental Questions of Metaphysics." This is followed by a short examination of the grammar and etymology of the term "Being" which is followed by an equally brief discussion of "The Question of the Essence of Being." It is at this point that we can detect a subtle shift, a play upon difference which is yielded by the ontological difference but which is itself not the difference between beings and Being.[22] It is a shift for which the preceding chapters have been preparatory. It is a shift from the difference between Being and beings, to a consideration of the (other?) limitations of Being.

"The Limitation of Being" is carried out in the consideration of four sets of oppositional pairs: "Being and Becoming," "Being and Appearance," "Being and Thinking," "Being and the Ought."

Heidegger contends that when we say "Being" we are compelled to continue "being and ...."[23] Heidegger continues,

> This "and" does not mean only that we casually throw in something else; no, we are adding something from which "being" is distinguished: being *and not*... But in these formula-like titles we also mean something which, differentiated from being, somehow belongs intrinsically to being, if only as its Other.[24]

Thus, the ontological difference which marked the difference between beings and Being, marked as well the intrinsic togetherness of beings and Being. In other words, Heidegger traces the intimate separation of beings and Being.

THE MEANING OF *LOGOS*

Heidegger contends that the meaning of *logos* stands in no direct relationship to language.[25] He writes that "long after the noun *logos* had come to mean discourse and statement it retained its earlier meaning in the sense of 'relation of the one to the other'."[26] "Logos here signifies neither meaning nor word nor doctrine, and surely not 'meaning of a doctrine'; it means: the original collecting collectedness which is in itself permanently dominant."[27]

John Williams writes,

> The theological meaning which Christianity has given to terms such as LOGOS has completely obliterated their original (philosophical) meaning, and Heidegger feels that we must go back to the period before onto-theo-logy was developed--i.e., to the pre-Socratic thinkers--in order to encounter non-theological philosophy in its original purity.[28]

In his continued dialogue with Heraclitus in *An Introduction To Metaphysics*, Heidegger contends that, "In confronting the *logos*, men are uncomprehending (*axynetoi*)--they do not comprehend the *logos* (fragment 34). It is the negation of *syniēmi* which signifies 'being together'." In other words, "men are those who do not bring together...," who in not comprehending do not gather or collect. Heidegger translates fragment 34, "Those who do not bring together the permanent together hear but resemble the deaf," and in exegesis offers the proverb "they are present yet absent."[29]

On the other hand, the focus of metaphysics is not the presenc**ing** of beings, but the beings present**ed**, those-things-which-stand-before-and-against-man. Metaphysical presence is the simple presence of "things-lying-around" which are seen only in-relation to one another. Concerned with the presence of one being to another, metaphysical knowledge is the calculation of one presence to another presence. The locations of beings are noted and their relations, that is their distances, are recorded. Logistics are elevated as true logic. In this "indifferent-presence," preoccupied with what-is, knowledge is the correct calculation of what-is.[30]

Logos, as the collectedness of the conflicting, as the event of difference, the gathering-of-opposition, is unthinkable within metaphysics. The difference *logos* marks is neither an idea nor is it an originating source. Thus, metaphysically, the difference *logos* marks is an absurdity in that *logos* does not make (metaphysical) sense.

* * * *

In our study of Heidegger's work with the Heraclitean fragments, I suggest that "logos" might be understood as a (the) historical antecedent to what has come to be called "the difference" in his later works and which is further developed by the deconstructionists.

Heidegger's study of the Heraclitean texts marks an "ending" of onto-theo-logical thought at the beginning of western metaphysics ("it is an ending 'experienced' in virtue of the dawning of the origin...."). In our study of "ending" we discovered that while an "end" may convey the common meaning of "at the conclusion," an "end" may also mark that which is before or is the condition for something. Playing upon such meanings of "end," Heidegger interrogates the "end of metaphysics" in texts which precede (and may be the necessary condition for) metaphysical thought. So, Heidegger turns to the fragmented work of Heraclitus of Ephesus to mark an "end" of onto-theological thought.

Derrida judges Heidegger's deconstruction of metaphysics to be **mistaken** in the assessment that Heraclitus **prepares** Greek thought **for** metaphysics. Rather, for Derrida, Heraclitus **is already** metaphysical.

However, the "historical claim" by Heidegger (which assumes that an epoch is a cessation) is yielded by and dependent upon the difference the fragments trace in a set of onto-theological texts. The work of Heraclitus is no longer available *as a work*, if it ever were. The lines attributed to Heraclitus occur as fragmented traces which are woven into philosophical and theological texts only (by and large) to be lampooned, and on occasion, refuted. The fragmentedness of the Heraclitean texts bespeak their brokenness, their lack of structure and coherence from the perspective of post-Socratic philosophy. Does the assessment that they are fragmented have to do with their incoherence for metäphysics or are they fragmented because their coherence--running counter to the epistemology of metaphysics--was crushed out of sight? The Heraclitean fragments are traced as "other" in order to be shown as marginalized. The fragments are *sous erasures*. They are traced to be erased. Under erasure they trace that which metaphysics must overcome. However, as *sous erasures*, they trace the disruption of and the possiblity for the closure of the metaphysical texts.

If we understand that all texts are inter-textual, and that a historical study is always a historical study of texts, then the distinction between the double sense of epoch becomes blurred. Thus, as well, Derrida's critique of Heidegger, dependent upon the distinction between Heidegger's historical deconstruction of metaphysics and Derrida's closure of the text, also grows blurred.

Surprisingly, Derrida's bringing the metaphysical text to closure which discloses a play whose logic is not metaphysical, is not unlike Heidegger's marking the end of metaphysics in his reading of the Heraclitean fragments which disclose a logic of its own. In each case, the logic which is disclosed is a logic in which opposites are one in their opposition.

According to Heidegger, the Heraclitean fragments trace an effacement of onto-theological thought inscribed in the metaphysical texts themselves. The Heraclitean fragments trace a language of difference. The fragments were copied and paraphrased in the metaphysical texts in order to be overridden, undercut or offset by the dominant language of the metaphysical discourse. Many of the theological and/or philosophical texts suggest by their ridicule that the Heraclitean fragments trace something that is inconceivable. Metaphysics is absolute and that which stands in opposition to the sovereignty of onto-theological thought is traced as fragmented in order to be presented as broken and cast aside. In other words, that which differs with the dominant metaphysical language of the text is assessed to be unintelligible.

Heidegger thematizes logos as a means by which to mark the limits of metaphysics. In his study of the Heraclitean fragments, *logos* is absurd in the onto-theo-logical texts in which the fragments are traced. The absurdity of the Heraclitean *logos* in the onto-theological texts in which they occur, traces beginnings and endings of epochs. The gaps which differentiate these epochs, the textures of the texts in their folding and reversing, trace the aporetic of logos and metaphysics.

THE FOUR-FOLD

The privilege of metaphysics over anti-metaphysics has been traced and reversed, and has given way to a manner of thinking in which neither is privileged in the play of one with the other.[31] The ætiological and anti-ætiological longings stir in a play of difference which fails or defers to resolve. Metaphysics may be said to be ending in that its dominating drive to determine cause has lost its power though not to a new drive which has come to power.

In the indifference to metaphysical concerns other ways of thinking, speaking and writing happen. Charles Scott contends that, "The movement through *Being and Time* to *Time and Being* or 'Building, Dwelling, Thinking' is also one that moves from de-struction of metaphysics to a way of thinking that is neither anti-metaphysical nor metaphysical."[32] One of the ways Heidegger thinks that which is neither anti-metaphysical nor metaphysical is in terms of the four-fold (*welt-geviert*).

Heidegger writes,

> The things that were named, thus called, gather to themselves sky and earth, mortals and divinities. The four are united primally in being toward one another, a fourfold. The things let the fourfold of the four stay with them. This gathering, assembling, letting-stay is the thinging of things. The unitary

> fourfold of sky and earth, mortals and divinities, which is stayed in the thinging of things, we call--the world. In the naming, the things named are called into their thinging. Thinging, they unfold world, in which things abide and so are the abiding ones. By thinging, things carry out world.[33]

Richardson notes that while the term "*geviert*" is used for the first time by Heidegger in a published philosophical piece in *An Introduction To Metaphysics* (1953), the theme appeared earlier in a meditative piece, "The Pathway," made public in 1949.[34]

> The oak itself spoke: Only in such growth is grounded what lasts and frucifies. Growing means this: to open oneself up to the breadth of heaven and at the same time to sink roots into the darkness of earth. Whatever is genuine thrives only if man does justice to both--ready for the appeal of highest heaven, and cared for in the protection of sustaining earth.[35]

The duality of earth and sky explains the coming-to-presence, the growth, of the oak tree. Richardson contends that,

> "The Pathway" suggests the duality of earth and sky in the coming-to-presence of the oak-tree. The duality of gods and man might have been inferred from the Holderlin interpretation, where the poet was called a half-god, because he inhabited the domain in-between gods and men.[36]

But, continues Richardson, such an interpretation "does not help very much." Richardson notes that Heidegger employs the four-fold as a means of elucidating the richness of Being as the One which has been conceived as the gathering-process of *logos*. The four-fold seeks to disengage the aspects in the "mutual mirroring which constitutes the collectiveness of Being as such."[37]

It is worth noting at this point the use of a standard christological theme, i.e., the incarnation, to interpret the four-fold. As we will see later in this study, the suggestion is made time and again in the interpretative corpus, but is never carefully followed.

Let us not draw too hasty a conclusion as to the relationship of things and world. We might conclude that "things" are the origin of the world. But that is not the "position" being asserted by Heidegger (if a position is being asserted at all). The relationship is not causal. One is not the **cause** of the other. "Thinging, things are things. Thinging, they gesture--gestate--world."[38] The world is carried and "birthed" not **by** things, but in the e-vent of thinging which bears the world.[39] Heidegger goes on to suggest that, "This appropriating mirror-play of the simple onefold of earth and sky, divinities and mortals, we call the world."[40] But he warns that we not jump so hastily as to conclude that "world" names some precinct into which things come to "settle," some ground upon which things may rest and be grounded. Rather,

> ...the world's worlding cannot be explained by anything else nor can it be fathomed through anything else.... Rather, the inexplicable and unfathomable character of the world's worlding lies in this, that causes and grounds remain unsuitable for the world's worlding.

That "the world presences things by worlding" means that things happen in the **open** play of opposition. That "things bear the world" means that the world is disclosed in the oppositional play of the four-fold.

In the bidding, "things bear the world" and "world grants presence to things". "But neither are they merely coupled together," warns Heidegger. "For world and things do not subsist alongside one another. They penetrate each other. Thus the two traverse a middle. In it they are one."[41]

> The intimacy of world and thing is not a fusion. Intimacy obtains only where the intimate--world and thing--divides itself cleanly and remains separated. In the midst of the two, in the between of world and things, in their *inter*, division prevails: a *dif-ference*.
>
> The intimacy of world and thing is present in the separation of the between; it is present in the dif-ference. The world dif-ference is not removed from its usual and customary usage. What it now names is not a generic concept for various kinds of differences. It exists only as this single difference. It is unique. Of itself, it holds apart the middle in and through which world and things are at one with each other. The intimacy of the dif-ference is the unifying element of the *diaphora*, the carrying out that carries through. The dif-ference carries out world in its worlding, carries out things in their thinging. Thus carrying them out, it carries them toward one another. The difference does not mediate after the fact by connecting world and things through a middle added on to them. Being the middle, it first determines world and things in their

> presence, i.e., in their being toward one another, whose unity it carries out.[42]

Note that Heidegger is not asserting that the world is one, nor is he contending that things may be said to be one in the world (as if the world were a container into which things are placed). Rather, in Heidegger's work on the four-fold, Heraclitus' distinctions of the oneness of opposites, and the oneness of the *en* and the *panta*, are played out (in a different key and differently--the way jazz is played) in terms of world and thing. In Heraclitus, this intimate separation of *en* and *panta* is named *logos*.

CONCLUSION
LOGOS, FOUR-FOLD, DIF-FERENCE

The themes of difference--discerned in the *logos* in the Heraclitean fragments and developed as the ontological difference with respect to Aristotle, are traced in *An Introduction To Metaphysics* as the "*Geviert*" which is commonly translated as the quadrate or the four-fold. Richardson does not find these earlier uses of the theme helpful in explaining the fourfold. He writes,

> The essential seems to be that the author here is trying to discern the richness of Being, and since Being, as the One, has been conceived already as the gathering-process of Logos, the Quadrate seems to disengage those "features" in Being whose mutual mirroring constitutes the collectiveness of Being as such.[43]

Richardson, acknowledging his **puzzlement** over Heidegger's development of *logos* as a four-fold polyvalence, continues,

> When Heidegger speaks of the Being of things as essentially a gathering-process, we understand Being in the sense of *logos*, which, of course, is to be understood as the original One. The puzzling part of the essay, however, lies in the fact that Heidegger sees in this One a four-fold polyvalence. What does he mean by Being as the Quadrate?

Richardson is puzzled because the "original one" is neither *One* nor is it the first cause in a series of causal events. What is said to be "one" is the event of difference in which gods and mortals, sky and earth, simultaneously separate and gather. Such oneness is incapable of satisfying the ætiological desire for a *causa sui*. Identity is generated not by a causal line of sameness, but by the tensive gathering of difference.

Richardson contends that the four-fold polyvalence reminds him of the trilogy characteristic of classical metaphysics: namely God, man and world.[44] He continues,

> This is a hierarchy of beings... and we are dealing here clearly with Being. But is it possible that the sense of the Quadrate consists in suggesting that polyvalent plenitude of (the "simple") *En*, by reason of which it can come-to-presence in *Panta*, sc. *as* God, *as* man, *as* world?

Richardson's allusion to classical metaphysics is not helpful, at least, in that he hesitates to follow through. For in the metaphysics to which he refers, the polyvalent plentitude in which God, man and world happen is also named. Nevertheless, the hierarchy of beings in classical metaphysics is clearly lacking in the interplay of the four which mark a difference.

> The dif-ference is neither distinction nor relation. The dif-ference is, at most, dimension for world and thing. But in this case "dimension" also no longer means a precinct already present independently in which this or that comes to settle. The dif-ference is *the* dimension, insofar as it measures out, apportions, world and thing, each to its own. Its allotment of them first opens up the separateness and towardness of world and thing. Such an opening up is the way in which the dif-ference here spans the two. The dif-ference, as the middle for world and things, metes out the measure of their presence. In the bidding that calls thing and world, what is really called is: the dif-ference.[45]

If we are still compelled to inscribe metaphysics, if we must engage this issue in terms of ætiology, then each of the four might be said to be the cause of its opposite. But to so resolve causality is to leave the search for a final or ultimate cause unsatisfied. If each is the cause of its opposite, the ætiological search is left--finally--with nothing.

that the inter-relation of logos, difference and the four-fold is too complex to be adequately explained in this thesis. That they are interconnected and play upon one another in Heidegger's work is sufficient for our present purposes.

It is evident that the four-fold plays upon both philosophical and theological concerns (if we can still use the terms "philosophy" and "theology" to name what is happening). It has been argued that the theological implications of Heidegger's four-fold is pagan in terms of orthodox christian theology. Such themes are the concern of the chapter to follow, to which we will now turn.

NOTES

1. William J. Richardson, *Heidegger: Through Phenomenology to Thought* (The Hague: Martinus Nijhoff; 1974) 5.
2. *Politeia* VII. 514 A 2 to 517 A 7.
3. Richardson, 4 & 5.
4. Ibid., 11.
5. Ibid., 13.
6. Martin Heidegger, *Being and Time*, translated by John Macquarrie & Edward Robinson (New York: Harper & Row, Publishers; 1962), H 4.
7. Scott, *Language of Difference*, 140. "The German is *Unter-schied* and carries the sense of intimacy (*Unter*, viz. the Latin *inter*, re *intimacy*) and separation (*Schied*)." In other words, difference is intimate separation (or, as well, separate intimacy?).
8. *Oxford English Dictionary* (Oxford; Oxford University Press, 1971).
9. On rare occasions *unter-schied* is translated as "the inter-cision," and offers a slightly different nuance of meaning. The English term "inter-" is from the Vulgar Latin term *interrare*, which means "to place in the earth," formed from the term *in-*, "into, in," and *terra*, "earth" (Klein, 804). The common use of "inter-" as a preposition means "among, between." The root "incise" is from the Latin *incisus* which means "to cut into, cut through, carve, engrave" (Ibid., 782). The inter-cision is "the cutting-into-and-through--clearing-a-place-for-in-the-earth."
10. Ibid., 450.
11. Martin Heidegger,"Language," *Poetry, Language, Thought*. Translated and Introduction by Albert Hofstadter (New York: Harper & Row, Publishers; 1971), 202.
12. It has not been uncommon to transpose this problem into the discussion of the primacy of existence or essence.
13. Richardson writes, "The fact is that it characterizes the entire history of Greek thought. The primitive form of *on*, Heidegger claims, is most probably *eon*, as the word is found, for example in Homer (v.g. *Iliad*, I, 70), or even in Parmenides and Heraclitus. The *e-* would indicate the stem *es-* (hence *estia*, *est*, *ist*, *is*), in whose dynamic power the participle shares in double fashion. What is more, in Parmenides and Heraclitus, *eon* can mean, in addition to the ambivalence we have mentioned already, the ultimate and unique process that we know as one-in-many (*En-Panta*).

That is why the author, in a much later expose (1957) of the onto-theo-logical structure of metaphysics, feels free to mediate the ambivalence of *on* under the guise of Heraclitus' *En*, which in turn is identified with *logos*, conceived as the process of grounding beings. *En*, the grounding process, is correlative with *Panta*, the ensemble of beings that are grounded, and the correlation is so intimate that one correlate cannot "be" without the other: *En* can no more serve as ground unless *Panta* be grounded than *Panta* can be grounded without *En*. This intimate correlation between *En* and *Panta*, intrinsic to the Heraclitean *Logos*, corresponds precisely to the duality of Being and beings that we call the "ambivalence" of *on*." Richardson, 11.

14. G.T.W. Patrick, *The Fragments Of The Work Of Heraclitus Of Ephesus "On Nature"* (Baltimore: N. Murray; 1889), 63.

15. G. S. Kirk, *Heraclitus: The Cosmic Fragments* (Cambridge: At The University Press; 1954), Fragment # 88, 135; Fragment #126, 149.

16. Ibid., 190.

17. Ibid., 87.

18. Heidegger, *An Introduction Tō Metaphysics*. Translated by Ralph Manheim. (New Haven: Yale University Press; 1959), 133 & 134. Emphasis mine.

19. Ibid., 131.

20. "What has the highest rank is the strongest. Therefore being, the logos as gathering and harmony, is not easily accessible and not accessible to all in the same form; unlike the harmony that is mere compromise, destruction of tension, flatting, it is hidden: *harmoniē aphanēs phanēres kreittōn*, 'the harmony that does not (immediately and easily) show itself is mightier than that which is (at all times) manifest' (Fragment 54)." Ibid., 133.

21. Martin Heidegger, *Essays In Metaphysics: Identity And Difference*. Translated by Kurt F. Leidecker (New York: Philosophical Library, Inc.; 1960), 69 & 70.

22. The play of difference in *An Introduction To Metaphysics* is obscured in the English translation. Chapter Four is entitled "*Die Beschränkung des Seins*" and is fairly translated by Ralph Manheim as "The Limitation of Being." The four sections that follow trace the "limitation" of Being in oppositional terms ("Being and Becoming," "Being and Appearance," "Being and Thinking," and "Being and the Ought"). However, missing in the English translation are the subsection divisions and headings which lay emphasis upon the limitation of Being as "difference" or *unterscheidung*. It is this play with "difference" that is de-emphasized in the English translation--and thus re-inscribes the work in metaphysics--that ties *An Introduction To Metaphysics* more closely to Heidegger's later work, and which marks the lectures as pivotal in his continued development of a language of difference.

Subsection 34, the first section of Chapter Four, is entitled "*Die Formelhaft gewordenew Weisen des Sagens des Seins in Unterscheidungen (Sein und ...)*" Subsection 35 "*Die seiben Leitsätze Gezüglich der Unterscheidungen des Seins gegen Anderes*". Section 2. "Being And Appearance" begins with Subsection 37 "*Selbstverständlichkeit und Geläufigkeit diesen Underscheidungen Nichtverstehen ihres ursprünglichen Auseinandertretens und ihren Zusammengehörigkeit Drie Weisen des Scheins*."

23. Heidegger, *Introduction to Metaphysics*, 93.

24. Ibid., 93.

25. Ibid., 124. "*Legō, legein*, Latin *legere*, is the same as the German word *lesen* <to gather, collect, read>."

26. Ibid., 125.

27. Ibid., 128.

28. John R. Williams, *Martin Heidegger's Philosophy of Religion* (Wilfrid Laurier University Press, Wilfrid Laurier Univeristy, Waterloo, Ontario, Canada; 1977) Canadian Corporation For Studies In Religion Supplement #2. I will argue that Williams has failed to point out that Heidegger also suggests that we encounter the pre-Socratics as a means of encountering non-ontological thought.

29. Heidegger, *Introduction To Metaphysics*, 128-130.

30. In this regard, the "correspondence theory of truth," i.e., truth as the correspondence between belief and fact, and the "absolute idealist theory of truth," i.e., truth consists in the coherence of beliefs, are both calculative modes of thought which refer to the relations of things-which-are.

31. Bernasconi, 1 & 2.

32. Scott, *Language of Difference*, 6.

33. Heidegger, "Language," *PLT*, 199 & 200.

34. Composed in 1935 and published in 1953 (Richardson, *Heidegger*, 679 & 677), *An Introduction To Metaphysics* was actually written before "The Pathway."

35. "The Pathway," by Martin Heidegger. Edited and translated by Thomas F. O'Meare, O.P., *Listening*, 2 (1967) 89.

36. Richardson, 571.

37. Ibid., 571.

38. Heidegger, "Language," *PTL* 200.

39. Heidegger reminds us that the Old High German "*beran*," meaning to bear, is related to *gebaren* meaning "to carry," and *gestate*, "to give birth," and *gebarde* meaning bearing, gesture.

40. Heidegger, "The Thing," *PLT*, 179 & 180.

41. Heidegger, "Language," *PLT* 202.

42. Heidegger, *Identity And Difference*, 202.

43. Richardson, *Heidegger*, 570.

44. Ibid., 572.

45. Heidegger, *Identity And Difference*, 203.

3

DE-STRUCTURING METAPHYSICAL THEOLOGY

INTRODUCTION

In the preceding chapter we discerned the strategies employed by Heidegger to deconstruct the metaphysical domination of philosophy. First, we considered his study of the "ontological difference" in Aristotle. Next, we traced the various ways Heidegger sought to deconstruct metaphysical thought by a re-reading of the Heraclitean fragments. It was Heidegger's contention that such a re-reading of the fragments would mark the limits of metaphysics **within** onto-theo-logical texts and trace the metaphysical epoch at its beginning in western thought. Our study of *logos* in the Heraclitean fragments disclosed a (pre-ontological, or pre-onto-theo-logical?) difference in the play of the one and the many in the *logos*, and the play of difference which marked *logos* and *phusis*.

We will now consider the implications of Heidegger's characterization and critique of metaphysical thought for theology in general, and Christian theology in particular. Towards that aim we will examine what Heidegger has to say about the "union" of theology and philosophy in onto-theo-logical thought and his suggested strategies for the deconstruction of metaphysical theology. However, first we will briefly consider what has been written regarding the theological implications of his work.

HEIDEGGER AND THEOLOGY

Heidegger persistently claimed that he was not competent to deal with religious matters. Nevertheless, he offered Christian theological and scriptural critique of metaphysical theism. So, we might ask, is this issue of competence a cover for his lack of institutional orders, given his wide range of interest and intellectual competence in religious matters? While Heidegger's theological and scriptural critiques of philosophy are few and brief in length, they nevertheless supplemented his critique of metaphysics. Therefore, we will take such critiques into account in what is to follow.

Theologians, philosophers, philosophers of religion and biblical scholars have had a great deal to say both about Heidegger's implementation of theology and scriptural passages (as few and as brief as they are) in his critique of onto-theological thought, and, as well, the implications of his thought for theology, philosophy, philosophy of religion and biblical studies.[1]

Much has been made of Heidegger's early training in theology and its impact upon his subsequent work.[2] Far more has been written regarding whether Heidegger's thought is secretly or not so secretly theology (renegade theology, mind you, but theology nevertheless) or religious. Or, whether Heidegger's work is atheistic. Or, if there are theological/religious implications, whether such implications are Christian/anti-Semitic or Judeo-Christian, pagan, pan-theistic, or polytheistic.

I am convinced that much of the confusing and ofttimes contradictory critiques of the implications of Heidegger's work for "theology," are generated by the failure to keep many of the distinctions Heidegger makes in his work. Also, much confusion is generated when the interpretation assumes that all discussion of the relation of philosophy and theology happens as onto-theo-logy, whereas Heidegger often is concerned with the relation of theology and Christian faith, or orthodoxy and early Christian texts (both of which are exclusively religious concerns as opposed to issues which address the relation of philosophy and theology directly), or the relation of theology and pre/post-metaphysical philosophy, or the relation of philosophy as metaphysics and pre/post-metaphysical (or pre/post-theological?) Christian faith.

Theology And Philosophy

In the preceding chapter we made only passing comments regarding the theological issues which arise in the deconstruction of the onto-theo-logical. Nevertheless, it was Heidegger's contention that in metaphysics philosophy and theology were united in ways which violated the integrity of each field. Heidegger meant that given the duel composition of onto-theo-logical thought, philosophy at the end of metaphysics would rid itself of **theo**-logy. Theology on the other hand would rid itself of **onto**-logy. Thus, theology would have nothing to do with philosophy and philosophy would have nothing to do with theology. But such an understanding of metaphysics and the deconstruction of onto-theo-logical thought fails to take into account Heidegger's deconstruction of metaphysics. The relation of philosophy and theology, the endings of metaphysics and the implications of such endings for philosophy and theology are far too complex to be characterized as a return of each to its own field, i.e., philosophy to ontology and theology to God. Instead, as we saw in Chapter Two, Heidegger's deconstruction of the metaphysical domination of "philosophy" was first traced in terms of "ontological difference" and later in terms of "difference". Surely we would not wish to characterize the endings of metaphysics with regard to philosophy as a return of philosophy to its own field, i.e., foundational ontology. In Chapter Two we considered philosophy's self-overcoming of metaphysics. The ending of metaphysics takes place within philosophical/metaphysical texts.

But what of the endings of the metaphysical domination of theology? In which texts might the fractures be traced? What ideas, identities, structures will be destrued, destructured or deconstructed (respectively).[3] Before we consider the deconstruction of the metaphysical domination of "theology," we will first address the relation of philosophy and theology in onto-theo-logical thought as characterized by Heidegger.

> Will Christian theology make up its mind one day to take seriously the word of the apostle and thus also the conception of philosophy as foolishness?[4]

> Only epochs which no longer believe in the true greatness of the task of theology arrive at the disastrous notion that philosophy can help to provide a refurbished theology, if not a substitute for theology, which will satisfy the needs of the time. For the original christian faith philosophy is foolishness.[5]

It has been argued that with respect to the relation of philosophy and theology, Heidegger has been ambiguous if not inconsistent. We have noted that he has powerfully expressed his misgivings about Christian theology's appropriation of philosophy.[6] On the other hand, claims Portier, "In spite of his protestations of philosophy's incompetence in theological matters, Heidegger has encouraged theologians in the use of **his philosophy** even if that encouragement itself has not been without ambiguity."[7]

I emphasized the phrase "his philosophy" in the above quote by Portier to draw attention to Portier choice of terms. Heidegger used the term "philosophy" sparingly if at all to label his own thinking. That Heidegger encouraged theologians and biblical scholars to think through the implications of his work for their study is obvious. However, it is misleading to suggest, as Portier does, that Heidegger encouraged their use of his *philosophy* while at the same time asserting that for Christian theology the conception of philosophy is foolishness.

Heidegger's contention that *Christian* theology should take seriously Paul's word that philosophy is foolish is a more complex assertion than first meets the eyes. It has been pointed out in numerous studies that Paul's epistles are filled with fragments borrowed from various stoic philosophers which he employs to substantiate his own positions. And it has been pointed out just as often that much of Paul's "theology" is stoic in style and content. As we will see, the stoic characterization of Paul is as inadequate as the stoic characterization of Heidegger. Thus, Heidegger, who spent no little time with the epistles of Paul, might read the admonition that philosophy is foolish to mean that for Christian theology, philosophy **as** "metaphysics" is foolish. To the extent that Christian theology has not taken Paul's admonition seriously, and has sought to work within and thus accommodate onto-theological thought, the union of philosophy (as metaphysics) and Christian thought is an absurdity.

It is important that we note the complexity of Heidegger's thought regarding the appropriateness of the mutual appropriation of theology and philosophy. If we fail to appreciate the subtle points of his writing on this subject we will succumb to an overtly simple rendition which will merely serve to perpetuate the common categories (philosophy/theology) and the traditional resolutions of their relation. Heidegger writes,

> The popular understanding of the relationship between theology and philosophy is fond of opposing faith and knowledge, revelation and reason. Philosophy is the interpretation of the world and life which is removed from revelation and free from faith. Theology, on the other hand, is the expression of the *creedal* understanding of the world and life--in our case a Christian understanding. Taken as such, philosophy and theology give expression to a tension and a struggle between two world-views.[8]

Theology and philosophy are competing "world-views." Philosophy proposes and defends *rational* "propositions" which interpret the world and life while theology offers and defends *faithful* "creedal" understandings of the world and life. The tensions and struggles between theology and philosophy are generated by conflicting "positions" regarding the onto-theological constitution, and the primacy of "ontology" or "theology," "reason" or "faith/revelation" within the enterprise.

However, in his address entitled "Phenomenology and Theology" delivered in 1927, Heidegger asserts,

> Within the circle of actual or possibly sciences of whatever is--the positive sciences--there is between any two only a relative difference, based on the different relations which orient a science to a specific region of being. On the other hand, every positive science is *absolutely*, not relatively, different from philosophy. Our thesis, then, is that *theology is a positive science, and as such, therefore, is absolutely different from philosophy.*[9]

In other words, theology *as* a science--as a branch of metaphysical knowledge--is absolutely different from philosophy which is not a science. The difference is between one of the positive sciences and that which is not a science. Thus Heidegger contends that "...theology, as a positive science, is closer to chemistry and mathematics than to philosophy." But in the debate over the relationship of theology and philosophy in Heidegger's work, little if anything is said as to the context of the distinction. And further, mention of the relative difference between the positive sciences of the academy and their absolute difference with philosophy is absent. Thus, Heidegger's contention that theology and philosophy are absolutely different is not very different from saying that chemistry and philosophy are absolutely different.

It should be noted, however, that Heidegger deferred the question of whether theology *is* a positive science. "The central question is whether, indeed, theology is a science. This question is deferred here...."[10] Nevertheless he returned to the question in a number of later texts. In those texts, his conclusions only seem to complicate the issue. By his later work it is clear that for Heidegger *metaphysical* theology is indeed a science since God **AS** *causa sui* offers a causal explanation for what-is.

The Divine God-less Thinking

Heidegger suggests to the theologians that they engage in an extensive re-reading of the early Christian texts. Such a re-reading is necessary if Christian thought is to discern the endings of its domination by metaphysics.[11] The "closure" of metaphysics for Christian thought will happen within the onto-theo-logical texts of orthodox Christian theology.[12] Orthodox Christian theology (dominated as it is by metaphysics) is inadequate as an interpretation of Christian faith in much the same ways traditional western philosophy (dominated by metaphysics) is inadequate as thought.

God, Gods and The Divine

Heidegger writes, "the god-less thinking which must abandon the god of philosophy, god as *causa sui*, is thus perhaps closer to the divine god."[13] In other words, in abandoning god as *causa sui* (the study of which would be theology as science), such "*thinking*... is thus *perhaps* closer to the divine god" (emphasis mine). What are we to make of such a strange suggestion?

Heidegger reminds us that the metaphysical interrogation of what-is seeks for that which is responsible (causally and morally) for the beingness of beings in which "beingness" is understood as *ousia*. As that which is at bottom, at base, common to all and in general accounts for all, the metaphysical search for the being of beings is a search for that which grounds all.

> Metaphysics thinks of beings as such, that is, in general. Metaphysics thinks of beings as such, as a whole. Metaphysics thinks of the Being of beings both in the ground-giving unity of what is most general, what is indifferently valid everywhere, and also in the unity of the all that accounts for the ground, that is, of the All-Highest. The Being of beings is thus thought of in advance as the grounding-ground. Therefore all metaphysics is at bottom, and from the ground up, what grounds, what gives account of the ground, what is called to account by the ground, and finally what calls the ground to account.
>
> Why do we mention this? So that we may experience the shopworn terms ontology, theology, onto-theology in their true gravity.[14]

Heidegger bids us to experience the shopworn terms of onto-theo-logical thought in their true *gravity* in order to disclose the interconnection and interdependence of causality and foundationalism in metaphysics. In the ontological inquiry of the beingness of beings wherein beingness is understood as *ousia*, metaphysics is an investigation of causality. And *ousia* of beings, the grounding-ground, what-is at bottom of all that is (the true gravity--what is at base but which is not drawn down by another) is named the *causa sui*. It is the *summum ens* which grounds all beings. "This is the metaphysical concept of God."[15] But, writes Heidegger,

> This explanation, though it supposedly touches upon something that is correct, is quite inadequate for the interpretation of the essential nature of metaphysics, because metaphysics is not only theo-logic but also onto-logic. Metaphysics, first of all, is neither only the one nor the other *also*. Rather, metaphysics is theo-logic because it is onto-logic. It is onto-logic because it is theo-logic. The onto-theological essential constitution of metaphysics cannot be explained in terms of either theologic or ontologic....

As we will see, under the power of metaphysics' sovereignty, the cultic creator God of Hebrew tradition and scripture is identified with the metaphysical first cause of Aristotle in a strange hermeneutic which has dominated Jewish and Christian though for over a millennium and a half. And in the very next paragraph, Heidegger raises the issue which has yet to be thought.

> For it still remains unthought by what unity ontologic and theologic belong together, what the origin of this unity is, and what the difference of the differentiated which this unity unifies.[16]

Metaphysical thought is preoccupied with causality, with the inquiry of the beingness, the *ousia*, of beings because it assumes that there is a foundation, a first cause which is *summum ens*.

Metaphysics is onto-logic
because it is theo-logic.

On the other hand, the *summum ens* who/which is *causa sui*, the "god" of metaphysics is itself disclosed only as a result of the ontological inquiry. In other words,

Metaphysics is theo-logic
because it is onto-logic.

The *causa sui* is dependent upon metaphysics' ætiological preoccupations.

Heidegger moves to a marginal concern of metaphysical theology, but central to Christian faith when he contends that the God of philosophy as *causa sui* is not much of a God in terms of worship and celebration. "Man can neither pray nor sacrifice to this god. Before the *causa sui*, man can neither fall to his knees in awe nor can he play music and dance before this god."[17] Worship and celebration have been of little or no concern in onto-theological discourse for such a God does not satisfy the ætiological strivings of metaphysical inquiry.[18]

* * * *

"Metaphysical-theology" and "ontology" are mutually dependent upon one another. Each generates the other within the onto-theological matrix. "The essential constitution of metaphysics is based on the unity of beings as such in the universal and that which is highest."[19] That theology and ontology are mutually dependent and originating in the onto-theo-logical matrix does not address how metaphysical thinking came to dominate western philosophical and religious texts and thought. For that matter, it doesn't address the appropriateness to philosophy or to the religions of such an accommodation.

Take for example a passage we considered earlier. "The god-less thinking which must abandon the god of philosophy, god as *causa sui*, is thus perhaps closer to the divine god."[20] If we assume that the choice is between the God of philosophy and the God of theology, we are merely continuing the onto-theo-logical debate over the primacy of ontology or theology in the onto-theo-logical tradition. But such a reading of the passage fails to take seriously Heidegger's characterization of the onto-theological union.

Might Heidegger be suggesting something far more disruptive to the onto-theo-logical enterprise? If abandoning the God of philosophy entails abandoning the God of theology as well, what is Heidegger suggesting when he writes that perhaps such thinking is closer to the *divine* God? Are we to understand by these vague suggestions, that in the deconstruction of the onto-theo-logical matrix, Christian faith discloses itself as itself?

What is missed in most readings of the Heideggerian texts is not that Heidegger is or is not a theist, or that he rejects one God and adheres to belief in (an)other God(s). Heidegger is *suggesting to Christian thinkers the* ***possibility*** that in the God-less thinking of the ending, that such "...*thinking* is thus *perhaps* closer to the divine god." Not that such thinking *is* closer, but that it **might** come closer. But in what sense can we say that "thinking" is *closer* to the "divine god"?

In terms of the modern theistic/atheistic debates, Heidegger is neither.[21] One might conclude that for Heidegger--Gods abound. On the other hand it has been "charged" that Heidegger is a pantheist. Because Heidegger's work might be polytheistic and/or pantheistic, one might say that his thinking is not within the perimeters of Christian or Judeo-Christian *theo*-logy. Of course, such an assessment is correct, but in uncommon ways. As we will see, the issue is over the meaning and status of *theos*.

Heidegger suggests that the marginalization of Heraclitus in western thought, while it had begun in the work of Plato and Aristotle, was accomplished by the church fathers. Was it feared by the "old church fathers" that the doctrine of logos presented in Heraclitus' thought might come to dominate the early church's understanding of logos (and thus of Christ and salvation)?[22] And if this connection were to be made, what was at stake--intellectually and institutionally--for the church fathers that they would so strongly react and attack the work of Heraclitus? And finally, how did *(onto-)theos* enter into and come to establish its power and domination of Christian thought in the emergence of *theo*-logy?

> The onto-theological constitution of metaphysics stems from the prevalence of that difference which keeps Being as the ground, and beings as what is grounded and what gives account, apart from and related to each other; and by this keeping, perdurance is achieved.[23]

Heidegger's reading of the Heraclitean *logos* recalls the difference of Being/being and unsettles the perdurance that is achieved in the lifeless categoricalization of *meta ta phusis*. The difference of Being/being can no longer be thought within the scope of metaphysics for in the metaphysical search for an origin, the differentiation of Being/being can not yield a cause. Instead, the difference differentiates but it does not provide an answer to the ætiological search of metaphysics. Logos traces the non-originating origin of the ontological difference as difference in the play of opposition. And as such, logos marks the "end" of (not satisfaction of) metaphysics and its ætiological desire. Logos undoes, unsettles, the perdurance achieved in the metaphysical stratification which keeps Being as the ground and beings as what is grounded.

Heidegger contends that "deity" entered philosophy as the satisfaction of ætiological desire.[24] *Theos*, God, of the onto-theological enterprise, is *theos* by virtue of its ability to satisfy the essential desire of metaphysical thought.

Logos, by unsettling the onto-theo-logical arrangement and calling into question the foundational enterprise, unsettles as well the privileging of *theos* in the onto-theo-logical arrangement as ground, as *causa sui*, as the Being of beings.

What then are we to make of Heidegger's use of "theological language," or better put, how are we to understand Heidegger's use of differing theological languages (plural). His use of "God," "Gods," "divinity," "divinities," and "the holy" complicate and frustrate our attempts to offer a simple assessment. He protests against the charge that he is an atheist, suggests godless thinking for Christian thinkers, traces Holderlin's poetic anticipation of the return of the gods, and speaks of the four-fold as holy. Is he a polytheist, a pantheist, or a crazy mystic? Or do Heidegger's "theological" comments cross and contradict one another and thus defy coherence?

We will not address the virtual sea of charges and counter-charges regarding the above assessment. The battering, for the most part, perpetuates metaphysical categories and fails to elucidate the subtle deconstructive themes pertinent to the uses of (can we call it) *theo*-logical languages by Heidegger.

And, of course, present in the debate is the issue of whether or not Heidegger's thinking and uses of theological languages are within or beyond the limits of Christian thought. It might be concluded that there are significant theological implications in Heidegger's work but the implications are clearly beyond the limits of Christian theology and faith, i.e., the implications conclude in polytheism, pantheism or mysticism. In other words, Heidegger's philosophy of religion can not serve as philosophical theology (at least for Christianity).

For now, the issue before us is whether the various **theo**-logical characterizations (polytheism, pantheism or mysticism) are valid interpretations for some aspects of Heidegger's work, rather than what such characterizations insinuate.

The contention that Heidegger's thought is--in terms of theology--pantheistic appears to be supported by what he has written regarding the four-fold. If the world's worlding is the four-fold play of divinity-mortals, sky-earth, and the two-fold play of mortals-divinities is called "the holy," then it would seem that the world's worlding is "the holy." In other words, the world is the holy and the holy is the world. Or, if you prefer the adverbial rendition, worlding is the holy, and the holy is worlding: worlding-holy/holy-worlding.

Hans Jonas, in ways he did not expect, has identified what is a stake.

> My theological friends, my christian friends, don't you see what you are dealing with? Don't you sense, if not see, the profoundly pagan character of Heidegger's thought? ... in order to show that I have not overstated the essential immanentism of Heidegger's thought let us have one brief look at his own exposition of the ground work for a natural theology. It occurs in his "Letter On Humanism" and belongs to those loci from which the friends of religion can prove that he is not an atheist. Surely he is not--we have heard of the return of the gods in his world-view. But then the *real opposite* to the christian and jewish view is not atheism which contemplates a neutral world and thus does not preempt divinity for what is not divine, but paganism which deifies the world.[25]

Jonas addresses his remarks to his "theological friends" and warns them of the "essential immanentism of Heidegger's thought" which he claims marks Heidegger not as an atheist but as a pagan. Asserts Jonas, being a pagan is "the real opposite to the christian and jewish view" (note the singularity of "view") for being a pagan "deifies the world." In other words, being a Christian and/or Jewish entails belief in a divinity transcendent to the world, a world which is in opposition to the divine, and is thus, a world which is not-holy.

Jonas, assuming a metaphysical standpoint, contends that those Gods (note the plurality) which fail to meet metaphysical criteria are not true or real to the world-view of the faith (assuming that there is **a single** world-view implied in the faith, or that there is such a thing as **a common faith** shared by Christians and Jewish communities, or even **a common** faith within either Christian or Jewish communities). Metaphysics thus provides Jonas the possiblity for such a union given the privilege of such a God in relation to the theological differences between various groups and sub-groups.

It is Jonas' assumption that those who counter **theo-**logy, that is, counter the transcendence of God (singular) to the world and the essentialistic difference between God and the world, are counter to the Christian/Jewish faith.

What is forgotten by Jonas is the historical occurrence of the assimilation of various pagan divinities and beliefs into Christian and Jewish theology. To forget or to rule as non-essential to the notion of God the various Gods which were integrated into monotheism, is historically and philosophically, let alone theologically, naive.[26]

What is interesting in Jonas' comment is his failure to address the issue which divides Christian and Jewish believers, an issue which he dare not bring up in polite company for it might fracture the union upon which his argument rests. Jonas' bidding is addressed first to his **theo**-logical friends, and then his **Christian** friends. What difference is marked by this double bidding? Does it not mark a first and a second, a fundamental and a derivative? The double bidding and the attempt to present as singular views which have been intellectually and historically in opposition attempts to manipulate not his "theological friends" but "my christian friends," for the double-bidding is an attempt to present as one that which is two. It is his assumption that pagans worship (a) false God(s). But, assuming the monotheism of the Hebrew tradition, Christian faith--belief in a crucified god named Jesus--is pagan. However, the force of Jonas condemnation is directed not at Heidegger's polytheism but his explicit pantheism or at least the pantheistic implications of his work.[27]

The assessment that Heidegger's work is atheistic because it does not allow for divine transcendence or that his work is polytheistic because it speaks of the gods, or that there is a sense of immanence about Heidegger's thinking about the divine are not--as we have seen--novel assessments.[28] What is lacking in the critiques listed above are many of the "standard theological distinctions" which Heidegger (a philosopher) gives voice to, distinctions which Fabro, Barth and Jonas (theologians) gloss over. Heidegger distinguishes between theology *in general*, which is metaphysical, and **Christian** theology, which is not *in general*: not to mention the complex relations of philosophy and theology which he explicates.

While it is the case that traditional metaphysical theism is monotheistic, Christian theology has been confounded by the multiplicity of its divinities. While it is the case that traditional metaphysical theism holds that the divine is transcendent to the world, Christian theology has traditionally been in a quandary over this point as well. One of the gods in Christian thought is transcendent or at least begins as transcendent, while the other, depending on the christology, is either sent into the world by the transcendent god or is the union of god and the world. In either case, transcendence in Christian theology is not equivalent to the transcendence of metaphysical theism.

Williams writes, "The major problem in any Christian interpretation of Heidegger is the location of the concept of God in relation to his thought."[29] Despite the rather questionable use of "concept" in this regard, Williams has identified a major problem in ways that I suspect he never expected. That problem is the location of God in Heidegger's thought and whether or not such a locating is of use to Christian interpretation. It is assumed that the major focus of Christian thought is God. Throughout the extended discussion of Heidegger and theology, the bias has gone unnoticed. For with the identification of the issue as the relation of Heidegger and **theo**-logy, the obvious has passed unnoticed. Is Heidegger a ***theist***? Or is Heidegger an *A-theist*? or some hybrid *A/Theist*? Or, ala Jonas, is Heidegger a ***pan***-*theist*, or God forbid, a ***poly***-*theist*? What is forgotten in this discussion is that Heidegger himself qualifies his discussion as a "philosopher" with "**theo**-logy" by asserting that when he speaks of theology he means, Christian Theology. Now, this of course is a qualification that is passed over very quickly. The reasons for such a speedy passage over such a qualification are multifaceted. Why is it that in the academic discussion of the theological import of Heidegger's philosophy, so little is made of Christian theology? Is there a fear that by recognizing his limitation, charges of anti-semitism might reoccur, that Heidegger is addressing **CHRISTIAN** theology, and not **JEWISH** theology, or not Judeo-Christian theology?

Might a reason for the erasure of the qualification be that those who engage the issue are still bound by metaphysical theology. Substantive theology must be metaphysical theology, and of course a Christian theology must concern itself with other non-metaphysical issues such as salvation, worship, prayer and the like. Thus, the erasure of Heidegger's qualification provides the space in which metaphysical theism may be re-inscribed. It is a theology which is essentially monotheistic. And as we have seen, for monotheism, the idea of a Christian theology is a problem.

Historically, it has been a problem. For the tradition, that is, for the dominant forces within the institutions of Christian faith, the problem has been, how is it possible to be monotheistic and at the same time, confess a belief in another divinity, Christ?

Throughout Williams work, the issue of "christology" is never addressed. Such is the case as well in the virtual flood of material which followed Jonas's condemnation. All of the talk was God-talk. The issues were formed about the constellation of issues of whether Heidegger's "theological implications" were "true" to the Judeo-Christian tradition (as if they were singular), or whether Heidegger's thinking offers theological implications at all. In all of this theology held the upper hand. Even in showing that "christology" is missing in the (theological?) discussion, we have employed a language which was coined in the enlightenment and which carries within it the subordination of *Christos* to *Theos*, christology as a subspecies of theology, which is itself a branch of knowledge. It is this forgetting what passes unsaid in the discussion of Heidegger and "*theology*."[30]

In recent years (and not so recent), philosophers of religion and philosophical theologians have begun to consider whether there is any possible relationship between christology (concerned as it is with the other divinity in Christian thought who is not "god") and Heidegger's later work which makes much of "gods," and the like, especially in regards to the "four-fold." That the four-fold appears to be "christological" is not a novel assessment. But few have taken the time to fully think through the deconstructive themes of the four-fold, in relation to a thorough reading of the christological sources.

THE FOUR-FOLD AND THE INCARNATION

> Since neither men nor the gods can bring about a direct relation to the holy by themselves, men need the gods and the heavenly beings need the mortals....[31]

In opposition to *both* "theism" and "humanism," Heidegger plays the gods and mortals one off the other. Neither the gods nor the mortals are privileged in the four-fold. Causality does not happen. To contend that "Causality does not happen" suggests that causality does not have a cause. The ætiological search for origins is not an issue and cannot be satisfied in the four-fold play. The most that can be said in answer to causal inquiry is that mortals and gods are mutually dependent upon each other. And, there is no *summa ens* which is the *causa sui*, for in fact there is no *causa sui*. The gods are no more the causal agents in the four-fold than the other participants. As such, the four-fold is *causally god-less*.

And yet, Heidegger speaks of "the holy" in much the way he spoke of "the divine god" in the passage "the god-less thinking which must abandon the god of philosophy, god as *causa sui*, is then perhaps closer to the divine god." What are we to make of such a suggestive verse that neither the gods nor the mortals *by themselves* can bring about a direct relation to the *holy*? Are we to summarize that the "holy" is other than the gods themselves (or the mortals themselves for that matter)? Therefore, are we to conclude that the gods are not *per se* holy? Of course! Then we might ask, what is "the holy" for Heidegger?

ORR'S INCARNATIONALISM

Robert Orr, in *The Meaning of Transcendence: A Heideggerian Reflection*, writes,

> In contrast to the claims which ordinary beings impose upon us, the claims which are encountered as divinities do not occur in the context of relative purpose and thus are not in principles circumventable.[32]

He continues,

> The holy is that meaning-domain (i.e., Orr defines each of the four-folds as a "meaning-domain") within the fourfold which allows the unsurpassable overwhel-mingness of claim as such to prevail.... Only as divine is meaning encountered as transcendent.... In the transcendence of meaning as encountered in the divinities, man receives his fundamental and essential measure.[33]

Thus Orr, while claiming to elucidate a Heideggerian meaning of transcendence, dismisses the contention that mortals and gods are mutually dependent. For, while "man receives his fundamental and essential measure... in the transcendence of meaning as encountered in the divinities" it is not clear on Orr's terms how or if the divinities receive their fundamental and essential measure in their encounter with mortals.

Orr goes on to suggest that "the meaning of transcendence" as a meaning-domain of the four-fold is that it leads one "towards a post-theistic theology." And while Orr suggests that this "trajectory" runs parallel to "incarnationism," the most he seems able to say about this "trajectory" is that such a *theo*-logy does not present the meaning of transcendence as "essentially separate from human being."[34] While he is at a loss as to the meaning of the claim that transcendence is essentially not separate from human being, he goes on to assert that "Transcendence is thus incarnate." It is a rich claim. Orr takes it to mean that transcendence is therefore not reducible to "an ontic component of the world." In other words, each aspect of the four-fold is a meaning domain that is not reducible to an ontic component of the world, and so the divinities which "represent" a transcendence can not be identified in the world as this or that.

There is some confusion at this point as to what Orr means by simultaneously contending that the divinities of the four fold "are" *the presence* of transcendence in the four-fold (that "transcendence is incarnational"), and that the divinities "are not" *an ontic component of the world.* But he fails to elucidate the meaning of such a claim and suggests instead that transcendence occurs in the four-fold, but not as one of the "meaning-domains."

Orr's interpretation of Heidegger's four-fold reasserts the privilege of the gods in relation to the mortals. In this economy of privilege mortals receive their fundamental and essential measure in the transcendence of meaning as encountered in the divinities. Relative to mortals, the gods hold a reserve of meaning, a reserve mortals can bank on. However, Orr does not suggest that mortals have a privilege relative to the gods. The hierarchy of privilege is static and non-relative.

In answer to the question, What is "the holy" in the Heideggerian four-fold, Orr the *theo*-logian might answer that *the holy is* ***one*** *of the four*-fold, but it can not be identified as such in the world. Orr suggests that the holy participates in the world, i.e., is incarnate, but can not be said to be anything particular in the world. As such, given the holy's lack of particularity, Orr concludes that such a thinking is "Towards A Post-Theistic Theology." If you contend that some**thing** is not "the holy" but assert, nevertheless, that there is "the holy," then on Orr's terms you are not a theist. Instead, "transcendence is incarnational." Orr goes on to suggest that such a meaning of incarnation is not restricted to any single-individual or period of history. To do so would entail particularizing "the holy." To so reduce transcendence to "an ontic component in the world" would be to reassert a form of theism which Orr contends is overcome in the four-fold. While one might conclude that such a post-theistic theology in which transcendence is incarnate is also post-Christian, Orr does not advance such a claim.

Despite comments to the contrary, Orr's work is dominated by *theos*. It is a strange domination in that it is deceptive. We are led to believe that "theism" is coming to an end as transcendence is presented as incarnate. We are told that transcendence is "present" to/with mortals but that it can not be identified with any-**thing** in the world. Transcendence is **present** but it is **no-thing.** But then we are told that such a manner of thinking is towards a post-theistic *theo*logy. It is a *post-theology*, but a *theo*-logy nevertheless.

For Orr to suggest that the issue is over the difference between theistic theology and a post-theistic theology fails to take into account the subtle play of the four-fold and the distinctions Heidegger kept between "the divinities" or "the gods," and "the holy." In Heidegger's meditation on the four-fold the holy is not anyone of the four. Instead, the holy is the four-fold play. Transcendence is not incarnate, i.e., "in-flesh". Rather, the incarnation--the four-fold play--is the domain of transcendence.

Orr, in asserting that the gods and the holy are the same in the four-fold has failed to see the difference the holy traces, or the holy different trace, in the four-fold play. As such, despite itself or himself, Orr reinscribes several themes characteristic of metaphysical theology. First, he perpetuates the bifurcation of the sensible/supersensible in terms of the orthodox mortal/divinity division. Second, Orr's post-theistic theology assumes that "transcendental meaning" has an *origin* (possibly it is its own origin (*causa sui*)) and that such meaning issues forth to the mortals from the original.

Nevertheless, the power of Orr's elucidation of Heidegger's later thought is striking and suggestive. His work falters in that he hesitates and then fails to follow through with one of his most striking suggestions. And that suggestion was that we consider the four-fold as running parallel (tracing possibly?) to "incarnationalism."

Clearly the extent to which Orr failed to follow through is evident in his casual use of the term "incarnation" (which means, etymological, "to cover with flesh"). To suggest that "transcendence is incarnate" would mean, in such terms, that transcendence is covered with flesh. Such a reading of the phrase would contradict Orr's contention that transcendence is not an ontic occurrence in the world. Orr never engages the historically significant texts and meanings having to do with the "incarnation." Nor does he even offer a stipulate definition. Orr simply offers a suggestive course of study. "Transcendence is incarnate." He takes the claim to mean that transcendence is not "essentially separate from human being."[35] But apart from its suggestiveness, Orr never enters into a detailed discussion of the suggestion.

As we shall see later in this study, Orr's suggestion that the four-fold play might run parallel to "incarnationalism," and his quandary over the meaning of his claim that "transcendence is incarnate" (which he elucidates with confusing and often self-contradicting claims) in terms of the four-fold is the outcome of attempting to think an incarnational theme (that transcendence is not essentially separate from human being) which is unthinkable so long as *theos* is sovereign and onto-theo-logical thought is the norm. The incarnational theology Orr is attempting to think is incomprehensible, as it has been throughout orthodox Christian theology.

THE WORD ~~OF THE LORD~~ NOW IN ~~FLESH~~ TEXT APPEARING: TAYLOR'S *ERRING*

> Radical Christology is *thoroughly* incarnational--the divine "is" the incarnate word.[36]

The incarnate word--what "the divine is"--"is not only itself but is at the same time other...."[37] "With the appearance of the divine that is not only itself but is at the same time other, the God who alone is God disappears. The death of God is the sacrifice of the transcendent Author/Creator/Master who governs from afar."[38] The incarnation, the "embodiment of the divine is the death of God." A little later Taylor writes, "it is important to realize that in radical christology the divine is *forever* embodied."[39]

> To insist that God "is" eternally embodied in *word* or that the divine "is" incarnate *word* is to imply that "there is a sense in which the word 'God' refers to the word 'word' and the word 'word' refers to the word 'God.'" God is what word means, and word is what "God" means. To interpret God as word is to understand the divine as scripture or writing.[40]

For Taylor, embodiment strings together God, word and writing in significant (through certainly not in altogether novel) ways as incarnation. In other words, scripture is divine. Scripture is the incarnate word. But in the inscribing of the incarnate word, in the embodiment of the divine, the transcendent Author/Creator/Master is sacrificed. God dies in and for the writing.[41]

In all of this Taylor employs the standard (among theological and biblical scholars) or common (what is commonly meant by Christians when they use the term) meaning of "incarnation" as the descent of God from above. The descent structure is conspicuous in the "Prologue" of the Gospel of John, and is often refereed to as the Johannine incarnation because of its poetic presentation. "And the Word became flesh and dwelt among us, full of grace and truth" (John 1:14).

The Christian Apologist of the second century and following, playing upon Platonic philosophy and the incarnational themes in the Gospel of John, asserted that Jesus was the *logos* of *theos* which was sent from above by *theos*, took on flesh and dwelt in the world until, following the crucifixion, the *logos* was called to ascended back to the *theos*. Christ is the Son who is God the Father's *Logos*. As such, Christ is the mediator between the Father and the world. Christ is a being who stands between God and the world, a being who unites the two, but who is utterly dependent upon the father for presence. Holiness is the "presence" of God which descends to earth and dwells in earthly things, such as mortals.

Taylor notes that "Without his father, he (the incarnate word) would be nothing but, in fact, writing."[42] So, Taylor's radical christology reveals itself in the death of God which issues in the divine trace which has no present (note the temporal cessation of the) transcendent author. The father who sent forth the word is now dead, disseminated in the seed/word, and that which has been sent forth is present in the absence of the sender. Thus, without the transcendent father, Taylor's deconstructed radical christology is nothing but writing.[43]

Taylor attempts to mark the closure of metaphysics by ceasing the ætiological trace which explains "holy" writing. Cessation is marked in the death of God as author of the trace (as well as Creator of the world, and Master of believers). It also issues in the death of the self as author. In other words, for Taylor, the scriptures--the incarnate word, Christ--do not originate. In contrast to traditional theism, God is not the author. In contrast to modern biblical scholarship Taylor contends that the scriptures are re-productions which do not have an origin and thus lack both an author and authority (in so far as authority issues from the signifier). Writing--scripturing--reproduces itself in an endless/beginningless play of signification. This writing--scripturing--is the incarnate word. Christ is the endless/beginningless scripting.

That Taylor seeks to de-construct this network by means of a radical christology, I find insightful. However, it does not seem to me that the radical christology that Taylor alludes to is all that radical in relation to the onto-theo-logical network given that it follows the standard Johannine incarnational motifs though with a twist, i.e., the death of God. Taylor contends that the *causa sui* becomes embodied in the series of writing in a way which then denies the existence of the *causa sui* in the re-production of signification. As such, Taylor surely adds to the death of God theological tradition, even if--as he claims--a/theology is at the limits of both **theo**-logy and the death of God.[44] But the limit that is marked in his radical christology is one which must of necessity assume the structures of causal sequence in order to deconstruct causality. The chain of signification, the re-production of writing, appears to have a beginning that ends in the embodiment, in the writing. For "...writing inscribes the disappearance of the transcendental signified. In this way, scripture embodies and enacts the death of God, even as the death of God opens and releases writing."[45]

> The incarnate word inscribed in writing spells the closure of all presence that is not at the same time absence and the end of all identity that is not also difference. Writing is an unending play of differences that establishes the thoroughgoing relativity of all "things." This complex web of interrelations is the divine milieu. Within this nontotalizable totality, nothing is itself by itself, for all things emerge and fade through the interplay of forces.... In

> the eternal play of the divine milieu, nothing is fully autonomous or solely sovereign. Thus there is no *cause sui*, antecedent to and the ultimate origin of everything else. The absolute relativity of the divine milieu renders all other things completely co-relative. As a consequence of the eternal cross(ing) of scripture, nothing stands alone and everything "originates" co-dependently. "Codependent origination" is nothing other than the nonoriginal origin that erases absolute originality.[46]

For Taylor there is a "necessary interrelation between the death of God and radical christology." But in the withholding of the father in the letting be of the trace--has Taylor re-inscribed metaphysics into the text? Has difference been brought to resolution in the death of God the father? In this case Taylor does not seek to "save difference," as he so nicely described the atoning which his incarnate word allows to happen.[47] Instead, his is an atoning which saves differences except for the difference generated in tension with "the one God who alone is God" and the incarnate word, the absolute origin and the nonoriginal origin. What is missing in Taylor's theological deconstruction is the differential tension between God and Christ which he traces but in the end, resolves.

That Taylor has identified his deconstructive work of the western theological network as a radical christology is more than telling. It bespeaks to a great extent the internal conflict which has pulled at the seams of Christian theology since its emergence as theology. Within Christian theology there are de-constructive themes. However, I find in Taylor's deconstructive work in *Erring* a lack of concern for the *closure* of theological texts, except for brief insightful renderings of a few stories from the gospels which are scattered in the latter half of the book.[48] In *Erring*, he does not so much offer a deconstructive reading of theological texts as he offers a more or less post-modern death of God a/theology. Ironically, it is an a/theology which is not unlike systematic theology, albeit a twisted systematic theology mind you. Clearly, the course of *Erring* is to work its way though the systematic theological network of western thought. Thus, in the working with and through, *Erring* traces the systematic theological network in its deconstructive reading/rendering of the system, which brings *theos* to conclusion/cessation. Instead of attempting to mark the gaps **internal** to the western theological network within the texts of the tradition, Taylor is preoccupied with ending the ætiological beginnings.

Such a reading, to a great extent, does not play the difference so much as it makes of the "difference" a historical move that overcomes (ceases) the epoch of metaphysics. Such is evident in that the reading--the new reading--deconstructs the text rather than the less active middle voiced occurrence in which deconstructing happens within the text.

I believe that Taylor's/*Erring*'s writing is limited in that it engages too clearly and employs to quickly the language of the *death* of God, a language which I believe runs counter to many of the deconstructive themes Taylor attempts to play.[49] Further, it seems to me that Taylor's "radical" christology might have been better served if he had followed a different "incarnational" trajectory than the one he follows. It is a trajectory he traced at various points in the text, but which he never differentiated from the Johannine "incarnation." As it is, his christology is "**radical**" to the extent that it follows through the logical implications of a deconstructive literary criticism of Christian scripture. But in order for Taylor's deconstructive move to work one must accept a non-scriptural assessment of the Christian scriptures as the "*logos*/word of God." That the "*logos*/word of God" is identified as Christ in the texts is obvious. That the texts are the "*logos*/word of God," and therefore are identified as Christ, is a connection which is developed very late in Christian thought and one which is not commonly held outside of biblical literalism. The position is that since the *logos* was with god, and is god, and became flesh (a Johannine incarnational theme), then the Bible, which is called the word of God, must also be with God and is god. But therein lies the problem for one must assume that the biblical text, Christ and God are strung together in some sort of **causal** series. Taylor assumes this **causal** connection, but then "deconstructs" the causal series by asserting the death of the transcendental signifier, God--the father/author--of the word which became flesh/text.

INCARNATIONAL DIFFERENCE

The other incarnational trajectory which Taylor does not fully develop is nevertheless evident in *Erring*. It is most evident in what he has to say about *coincidentia oppositorum*[50] and the "Divine

Milieu." Taylor writes that "insofar as writing is hiero-glyphic,.... scripture appears to be the Divine Milieu."[51] It is a milieu in which "everything arises and passes away but which does not itself arise or pass away,...."[52] As "the forceful play of difference that forms the nonoriginal origin of everything,.... The creative/destructive negativity of writing stages an *eternal recurring* drama through which the differences constitutive of identity are engendered." Taylor contends that scripture is such an eternal recurrence, and nothing other. What recurs is not a being. One thing does not repeat itself endlessly in the script(ure). As the divine milieu, the script is a perpetual play of the passage of diversity which in its recurrence neither begins nor ends. In other words, script(ure) does not trace a causal series. The divine milieu is--with respect to causality--a *coincidence.*

> This milieu marks a middle way that is thoroughly liminal. At this threshold, opposites cross. The margin itself... is not reducible to the extremes whose mean it forms. The medium, in other words, can never be contained, captured, or caught by any fixed pair of terms. Consequently, the milieu is always paradoxical.[53]

The divine milieu is not so much a center as it is the milieu, the place of opposition, which inverts and subverts the contrasts.[54] As such, the divine milieu is a non-identity. Or, if one must speak of the identity of the milieu, then it is the *coincidentia* (co-incidental, non-causal) *oppositorum* (opposition).

As we will see later, the "christological" trajectory which the "divine milieu" and *coincidentia oppositorum* trace is one of the themes of "incarnation" which Taylor develops, but which he fails to differentiate from the Johannine "incarnation". I will contend that his failure to differentiate these differing christological themes is partially responsible for Taylor confusing--if not self-contradicting--joining of deconstructive methods with the death of god theology. The "death of God" is a logical outcome of the dominant presence of the Johannine incarnational christology in Taylor's work. However, as we shall soon see, the divine milieu, "the god of nonidentity" or the god whose identity "would be ... *coincidentia oppositorum*," are themes not unlike the Chalcedonian "doctrine of the mysterious incarnation" and "in Christ" in the Pauline epistles.

* * * *

As we have seen in the works of Orr and Taylor, "incarnational themes" have been suggested, elucidated (more or less depending upon the text) but rarely differentiated.[55] Neither writer engaged in a detailed, let alone casual reading of the significant historical theological texts which work with the incarnational themes.

In the various texts in which Heidegger works with the four-fold, I do not find a descent/ascent structure in which the gods come to mortals or the sky descends to the earth. Such is clearly lacking in the texts and bespeak the theistic bias of those who inscribe such into their interpretation.

The confusing and ofttimes self-contradicting manner in which Orr elucidates the claim that "transcendence is incarnational," is, I shall argue, expressive of the double meaning of "incarnation" in Christian thought. Orr's suggestive interpretation and the ensuing confusion in his work on transcendence is the outcome of attempting to think as singular two mutually exclusive incarnational themes.

Taylor also fails to differentiate the mutually exclusive incarnational themes which are developed in *Erring*'s radical christology. His or its' failure to so differentiate yields both a Christian atheism in which Christ is the written word, and a "divine milieu" or "coincidental opposition."

In both texts, *theos* exercises presence and power. In Orr's work the sovereignty of *theos* renders the incarnational *theo*-logy he is attempting to think--incomprehensible. In Taylor's work, the authority of the originator and the power of the author must first be called into question and subverted/overthrown and brought to an end before the subsequently incomprehensible incarnational theme can be traced.

SUMMATION

Within the onto-theo-logical enterprise, philosophy and theology are competing "world-views." The privileging of one over the other is a matter of contention between competing categories which stand in opposition.

In the course of our study we discovered that Heidegger seeks to de-construct the onto-theo-logical coherence by identifying and pulling at its various seams. As to whether the division of philosophy and theology is his last word on the subject, or one of the strategies in ending or bringing to closure the metaphysical text will be addressed later. Heidegger applies his critique of onto-theological thought "in equal measure to traditional western philosophy and traditional christian theology...."[56] Heidegger's use of the Christian scriptures (dominated as it were by the epistles of Paul) and his call for theology to return to such texts can be taken as an attempt to re-assert those texts which have been crushed out of sight by the power of onto-theology. We might regard his critique as an attempt to allow what has been erased in orthodox theology--a metaphysical theology--to bleed back through.[57]

Orthodox Christian theology is inadequate as an expression of Christian faith. Heidegger's assumption is that a theology developed out of a re-reading of the early Christian texts would, perhaps, be closer to ancient Christian faith or the divine god than the onto-theological union within Christian theology.

We must keep several things in mind here. First, Heidegger did not contend that philosophy as metaphysics was incapable of elucidating *dogmatic theology*. That is Portier's point. Heidegger differentiates between "philosophy" and "theology," "theology" and "*Christian* theology" as well as between "Christian *theology*" and "Christian *faith*." These distinctions are commonly held by theologians but are commonly glossed by philosophers. (Apparently they are glossed by Portier as well.) Heidegger stands with those theologians who contend that traditional western philosophy is inadequate to elucidate Christian faith, just as orthodox Christian theology is inadequate to elucidate Christian faith or interpret early Christian texts. The incompatibility--the inability to exchange or translate or interpret--lies in the difference between what is and what is not metaphysics.

It is important that we see the parallels between Heidegger's critique of metaphysical philosophy and metaphysical theology. Heidegger did contend that philosophy *as metaphysics* was incompetent in elucidating original Christian faith. But, as we saw above in Chapter Two, he also held that philosophy *as metaphysics* was incompetent in elucidating early Greek thought. To demonstrate the difference between metaphysics and early Greek thought, Heidegger engaged in an extensive re-reading of the fragments of Heraclitus.

Towards the end of the chapter we considered the suggestion by Orr and Taylor that the inter-related themes of *logos*, dif-ference and the four-fold play upon incarnational themes.

CONCLUSIONS

In drawing metaphysical thought to a close, the onto-theological coalitions (one of which is the union of *causa sui* and the god of Christian orthodoxy) which have dominated both religious and philosophical thought, are broken. Metaphysics' domination of western thought and institutions begins to end. It is believed that in the wake of metaphysics's demise early Christian thought reasserts itself.[58] Christian thought happens much the way thinking happens in the ending of metaphysics.

If we understand the *ending* of metaphysics in the sense of historical cessation, then we will seek to delineate the closing of the onto-theological matrix in terms of the cessation of the ætiological desire for a *causa sui*. In this cessation, the ætiological drive and the desire for its satisfaction will cease. Metaphysically--this cessation spells the death of god and yields metaphysical and epistemological chaos. In the death of *causa sui*, in the failure of the ground, causal order is lost. Without foundations, metaphysical epistemology--driven by a desire for certain knowledge--counts for neither certainty nor knowledge. The end of metaphysics is the end of an epoch. The desires and powers of the metaphysical age grow indifferent and impotent.

We might ask, In the cessation of metaphysics, as the onto-theological enterprise draws to a close, will other non-metaphysical manners of Christian thinking show themselves? What of the disciplines of philosophy? Theology? Will they draw to an end? With the cessation of the ætiological drive for *causa sui*, will theology also pass?

These questions, of course, give voice to a whole genre of thought, not the least powerful have been the "death of god theologies" which elucidate the death of god the father, and the end of theology as a science.

However, so to read the *end* of metaphysics as the cessation of the onto-theological enterprise is only one of the meanings of metaphysical ending or anti-metaphysics. The "end" of metaphysics is not simply marked at the edges or joints which divide and unite one age with another in a temporal series. As we have seen, the "end" or "closure" of metaphysics crisscrosses the very terrain of metaphysics. Inscribed within onto-theological texts are fragments of texts which efface the text and mark the limits of metaphysics' coherence and sovereignty.

Will we find inscribed in the authoritative texts of orthodox Christian theology (an onto-theological enterprise) marks which efface the text and mark the limits of metaphysics' coherence and sovereignty? Will the surreptitious power of Christian orthodox theology be disclosed in the deconstruction of the metaphysical domination of Christian thought?

We have considered Heidegger's work on the four-fold. Now, we will follow the suggestion of Orr and Taylor that such a manner of thinking is "incarnational." After we have studied the orthodox Christian doctrine of the incarnation, we will return to reconsider the various charges that the real opposite of Christian thought is one that defies the world, and that Heidegger's thought yields a polytheism and/or pantheism which mark him as "outside" Christian thought.

NOTES

1. Among the Christian theologians who directly treat Heidegger's philosophy, Williams offers a tripartite division: (1) Catholic theologians, (2) Karl Barth and his followers, and (3) Rudolf Bultmann and his associates. The first two divisions, Catholic theologians and the Barthians, have offered a negative evaluation of Heidegger's philosophy for theology. They conclude that Heidegger's philosophy is either atheistic or pagan.

Williams writes,

> Despite Heidegger's protest against being called an atheist, Barth holds that his philosophy contains implicitly the same atheism which Sartre makes explicit, in that his trinity of beings, *Dasein* and Nothing leaves no room for God. Heidegger does not go so far as to say explicitly that Nothing is God, but Barth has no doubt that his philosophy must be so interpreted. Even

> though Heidegger, in his 1946 *Letter On Humanism*, shows that Nothing is no different than Being itself, but just another name for Being, Barth holds that this concept is antipathetic to the Christian understanding of God. In fact, its use is equivalent to "proclaiming the devil as the source of all beings and all *Daseins*" (Williams, 14).

Interestingly, I find it surprising that Barth, noted among 20th century theologians for asserting the radical transcendence of God, would be adverse to an interpretation of God as nothing. The traditions of "negative theology," which seek to assert and protect the transcendence of God, God's otherness, against the various forms of "natural" theology, are best served by asserting that God is no-thing. The traditional rendering of negative theology has usually to do with the negation of all predicates of the One God, a God who is being predicated in negation is always and in every way *transcendent*. Constitutive predication of the divine, in which all that is decent and best in the world is assumed to be an expression of the ideal which is predicated of the deity, is abstracted and negated, thus the one God is presented in iconoclastic splendor. That Barth would be adverse to such a theology I find surprising.

Barth asserts the absolute division of theology and philosophy, and asserts God's aseity with respect to the world by a play upon 1 Corinthians 1:20 ("has God not made foolish the wisdom of the world?"). Williams writes, "The relation of God to man depends entirely on God: he gives himself to man in the way he chooses (pre-eminently in the person of Jesus Christ), and man is absolutely incapable of evoking this relationship by his own means (such as philosophy)" (Ibid.). Barth's point is that all causality is from God and proceeds outward under God's direction. Nothing outside of God can invoke God's action. Anything less is pagan.

One of the things I find interesting about Williams' characterization of Barth is his use of the parenthesis. In fact, one issue which Williams fails to address in his study of Heidegger's philosophy of religion, an issue which is silent--unapproachable--in his discussion of Heidegger is not the issue of God, but the issue of the other God in Christian theology. Williams addresses the issue in the parenthesis. Barth adheres to A doctrine of the incarnation. In particular, he asserts that God reveals himself into the world pre-eminently in the person of Jesus Christ.

On the other hand, Bultmann and his associates believe Heidegger's philosophy can be interpreted theistically or at least it can serve theological inquiry in the application of its anthropology. Bultmann assumes that Heidegger's Dasein analysis will provide the means by which to disclose the existential "realities" behind the biblical texts. John Macquarrie on the other hand has asserted that "Heidegger's philosophy is positively theistic in import and can serve as the basis of a valid contemporary natural theology" albeit a Scottish natural theology (Ibid., 7).

Williams contends that relatively few academic theologians oppose Heidegger's critique of traditional Christian theology as metaphysics. Notable exceptions include Maurice Lorvez and Hans Meyer who assert that there is no other God than the one described by previous theologians, and Hans Jonas, who held that metaphysical thinking is part of the human condition. However, Williams does not provide a follow up analysis to determine whether those academic theologians who agree with Heidegger's critique of traditional Christian theology as metaphysics merely oppose *traditional* Christian theology in favor of biblical theology. Much if not most of previous theology has concerned itself with the onto-theological tradition to the exclusion of biblical thought. Thus, theologians as different as Karl Rahner, Rudolf Bultmann, Erest Fuchs, and Gerhart Ebeling have sought to overcome the limitations of traditional metaphysical theology by employing aspects of Heidegger's thought in the development of biblical hermeneutics (Ibid., 32). They assume more or less that Heidegger's critique of metaphysics provides a means by which they might overcome the burdens of onto-theological thought in the search for the truth and/or reality to which the biblical texts seek to speak. Most of the theologians listed work with the texts of *Being And Time* and thus fail to pick up on the more radical de-constructive themes in Heidegger's later work.

Williams notes that while most interpretations of the religious import of Heidegger's philosophy have come from theologians rather than from philosophers or historians of religion, he claims that "when non-theologians have offered evaluations of Heidegger's religious significance, they have generally done so from a theological, rather than a philosophical, perspective" (Ibid., 7). In many such cases, the theological perspective is naive. It is a naivety which shows itself in statements like "...the theses of Heidegger's philosophy are, in fact, the mere transposition of a strictly personal experience of existence, experience which is, without a doubt, the exact contrary of Christian experience...." which assumes that there is such a thing as **a** Christian experience. Williams points out that A. de Waelhens fails to offer an analysis of the Christian experience of existence, and that his judgment of the total incompatibility of the one with the other is evidently based on some unexpressed preconceptions of Christian theology. In other words, **the** Christian experience is as simple as its theologically dogmatic counter-part.

Another such example of a philosopher evaluating the religious import of Heidegger's philosophy from a naive theological standpoint is Helmut Danner's *Das Gottliche und der Gott bei Heidegger, Meisenheim am Glan: Verlag Anton Hain,* 1971). Danner writes,

> ...with regard to the *God* and the divine in Heidegger's thought, it must be stated unequivocally that, except for the word itself, they have *nothing in common* with the Jewish-Christian *God*....the God of the Old and New Testaments does not in the least enter into his horizon--which is consistent insofar as the God of Revelation cannot be experienced by thinking (Danner, 175, as found in Williams, 8).

As Williams is correct to point out, Danner is more than naive about the conceptions of God presented in the scriptural texts.

> To speak of the "God of the Old and New Testaments" without any further description implies that there is general agreement as to the meaning of this expression. One need only think of the differences between Judaism and Christianity, not to mention the variety of concepts of God within these two religions, to realize that this assumption is mistaken. For Danner to argue convincingly that Heidegger's concept of God is incompatible with that of the Bible, he would have to be much more precise about his understanding of this latter term. (Ibid., 8 & 9)

Despite Williams persistent critique of those theological naive philosophers who attack Heidegger, Williams is sufficiently theologically naive himself. He writes of "the Bible" as if Jews and Christians shared the same book, which they do not. And, further, his assumption that "each scripture" (Hebrew or Christian) is a "bible," (literally *a single book*) fails to see how the seams which separate the collected texts are obliterated by the technologies of re-production and binding. The technological production--a one volume book that re-produces each text in a uniform fashion--obscures the differences between the various texts gathered.

Other problems with Danner's comment include his insensitive use of Christian titles and concepts (such as the Christian division between the biblical texts and the titling of the Hebrew scriptures as **Old** Testament) while contending that he is defending both Christianity and Judaism. Danner is also wrongly under the impression that throughout the Jewish and Christian scriptures "God" is antithetical to thought and is event only as revelation.

In summation, it would seem that many of the philosophers who are critical of the theological implications of Heidegger's work are theologically naive and assume more or less a non-historical, dogmatic conception of theology.

2. See Thomas Sheehan's "Heidegger's Early Years: Fragments for a Philosophical Biography," in *Heidegger: The Man and the Thinker* (Chicago: Precedent Publishing, Inc.; 1981).

3. The play of the term deconstruction as destrued, destructured or deconstructed is given by Robert P. Scharlemann in "The Being of God When God Is Not Being God: Deconstructing the History of Theism." in *De-Construction and Theology*, Thomas J. J. Altizer, Max A. Myers, Carl A. Raschke, Robert P. Scharlemann, Mark C. Taylor, Charles E. Winquist (New York: Crossroad; 1982).

4. "The Way Back Into The Ground Of Metaphysics" in *Existentialism from Dostoevsky to Sartre*. Walter Kaufmann (rev. ed: New York: Meridian Books, New American Library, 975) 276.

5. Heidegger, *An Introduction To Metaphysics*, 6

6. William L. Portier. "*Ancilla invita*: Heidegger, the Theologians, and God." *Sciences Religieuses/Studies In Religion* 14/2, 161. Of course both Heidegger and Portier assume the common interpretation of the Pauline text. The verse referred to, but never quoted directly in the discussion is 1 Corinthians 1:20b which reads, "has God not made foolish the wisdom of the world?" (R.S.V.) The meaning of the phrase "wisdom of the world" is a matter of interpretation. We do not have time here to engage in an extensive study of the passage. In the texts from which the verse is extracted, foolishness and wisdom are played off and on one another in such a manner than in the end the reader is no longer clear as to what counts for wisdom or foolishness. As will become clearer in chapters 7 through 12, the use of oppositional language is a common strategy employed by Paul. Traditionally the passage is assumed to differentiate theology and philosophy, faith and reason. That Heidegger employs this traditional interpretation is clear. The purpose of his using the traditional interpretation is another matter.

7. Ibid., 163. Emphasis mine.

8. Martin Heidegger, "Phenomenology and Theology," translated by James Hart and John Maraldo in *The Piety of Thinking* (Bloomington: Indiana University Press; 1976), 5. Emphasis mine.

9. Ibid., 6.

10. Ibid., 7. It is Bultmann's assumption that theology is a positive science (Heidegger's 1927 address). Heidegger investigated the possibility that theology is a positive science, but he deferred assessment in "Phenomenology and Theology." Thus, Bultmann employs Heidegger's analysis as the means of elucidating the ontological pre-Christian structure which calls Dasein into question and for which Christian faith is an answer, an ontic answer. Tillich follows a similar trajectory in his Christology (Volume Two of *Systematic Theology*) and in *The Courage To Be*.

11. The distinction between tradition and text, is, of course, a dominant theme in Christian thought since the reformation. The distinction held since the protestant reformation between tradition and scripture, played upon by Luther, is played out in a sense by Heidegger in his manner of reading ancient Greek philosophical texts. Heidegger is forever calling into question the dominant (metaphysical) interpretations of the originating texts of western thought. Radical protestantism has always been suspicious of tradition. Tradition as the means of interpretation conceals in the moment of its disclosure. Traditionally, interpretations are yielded by and maintained in a political play of manipulation and domination.

Portier alludes to this distinction himself with regards to the difference between *christlichkeit* and *christentum* which Heidegger employs. He writes, "For Heidegger, then, the given of theology appears only through faith. Theology becomes a kind of practical science which enhances Christianness (*christlichkeit*) as a concrete way of being in the world" (Portier, 165, see fn. #15). However, Portier fails to keep the distinction in his critique of Heidegger above.

12. Heidegger is careful to distinguish between Christian *faith* (*Christlichkeit*) and institutional Christianity (*Christentum*). Writes Williams, "(T)he condemnation of Christianity (*Christentum*) is in no way an unqualified criticism of Christians, just as a critique of theology is not necessarily a critique of faith, of which theology is supposed to be an interpretation" (Williams, 99, regarding Heidegger's "*Nietzsche's Wort 'Gott ist tot'*", *Holzwege*). Williams goes on to note that Heidegger is justified in his critique because "Christianity" (theology? christendom?) is largely responsible for the domination of Greek metaphysics during the past 2000 years. Yet, the adoption of the metaphysical hermeneutic is radically incompatible with the primitive interpretative texts of Christian faith (Williams, 99 & 100).

13. Heidegger, *Identity And Difference*, 72.

14. Ibid., 58.

15. "The original matter of thinking presents itself as the first cause, the *causa prima* that corresponds to the reason-giving path back to the *ultimate ratio*, the final accounting" (Ibid., 60).

16. Ibid.

17. Ibid., 72.

18. Thus, Heidegger divides--in a rather standard protestant fashion--the God of faith from the God of philosophy. This division calls into question the coalition of Plato's "good," Aristotle's "first cause" and Hebraic "monotheism."

19. Ibid., 61.

20. Ibid., 72.

21. Much of the modern theistic/atheistic debate happens in-house (in terms of metaphysics). The issue is often expressed as a debate over whether "God" is or is not the *causa sui*. Atheists often assert that God is not the ground or origin or structure of the world. But, in asserting that some "thing" else is the cause, one *causa*

sui (God) has merely been replaced by another *causa sui* (God). Players have changed but the play or game is the same. The onto-*theo*-logical network is not called into question.

22. Heidegger, *Introduction To Metaphysics*, 126.

23. Heidegger, *Identity And Difference*, 71.

24. Ibid.

25. Hans Jonas, "Heidegger And Theology," in *The Phenomenon of Life* (New York: Harpers; 1966), 248-249. Emphasis mine.

26. Jonas appears to assume that Heidegger is both poly- and pan- theistic, a position that is commonly mutually exclusive. That the characteristics are commonly mutually exclusive is rarely addressed. How can you have more than one god if god is the world? Of course, one could assert that there are many worlds and thus many gods. Such a position has not been proposed to my knowledge in the discussion.

27. The assessment that Heidegger is pantheistic is not novel. Williams notes that Cornelio Fabro, in his extensive history of modern atheism, *God In Exile*, judges the theistic potential of a philosophy according to its allowance for divine transcendence (immanence equals atheism) (Williams, 13).

28. Others have noted that the theological immanence of Heidegger's suggests that Heidegger is a neo-stoic (including Regis Jolivet). Karl Barth's critique of Heidegger plays upon this same theme in a different key.

29. Williams, 33.

30. "Theology" is now a dubious term which recalls that it is itself in question and which in being traced bespeaks the reinscribing of the onto-theological into our discussion.

31. Heidegger.

32. Robert P. Orr, *The Meaning of Transcendence: A Heideggerian Reflection*. AAR Dissertation Series 35, Edited by Wendall Dietrich (Chico, California: Scholars Press, 1981), 117.

33. Ibid., 117 & 118

34. Ibid., 142.

35. Ibid., 142.

36. Taylor, *Erring*, 103. Taylor repeats the claim that "Radical christology is thoroughly incarnational" at page 168.

37. What the divine truly is? Is Taylor suggesting here that the divine really *is* the incarnate word rather than...?

38. Taylor, *Erring*, 103.

39. Ibid., 104.

40. Ibid. The quote with the text is from Robert Scharlemann, "The Being of God When God Is Not Being God: Deconstructing the History of Theism," in Altizer et al., *Deconstruction and Theology* (New York: Crossroad, 1982), 101.

41. "We have already discovered the close relationship between the death of God and radical christology in which the incarnate word is interpreted in terms of writing. Scripture stages an unending play of differences that constitutes the universal medium or divine milieu in which all "things" arise and pass away. The eternal cross(ing) of forces brings the death of transcendent originality and marks the end of any solitary *causa sui*. Since the absolutely relative divine milieu negates any thing-in-itself or self-in-itself, everything is emptied of self-subsistence and self-existence. Scripture is radically, and thus "originally," kenotic. ....just as the death of God does

not result in a simple absence but involves a self-emptying that issues in a complex divine milieu, so the death of the self does not entail mere destruction but points to the inscription of erratic markings or traces" (Taylor, *Erring*, 141).

42. Taylor, *Erring*, 106. Parenthetical comment my own.

43. Taylor's radical christology plays upon the double meaning of epoch which we considered in Chapter One. The father who sent forth the word is "held back" in the disclosure of the son. However, this sending also accompanies, accomplishes or accommodates the death of the God who did the sending.

44. If such is the location of *Erring*, that a limit of the western theological network is the death of God and Taylor's work is at the edge of both the death of God theology and the western theological network, then he sees the interconnection of the two, their co-origination, and thus seeks to mark what is marginal to both. This is no simple task, if it is a task at all. But as such, as the taking to the limit of both, *Erring* as a post-death of God a/theology is preoccupied with ending in a rather common sense of the term end. As the end of an epoch, it marks a temporal cessation, despite Taylor's rejection of such an interpretation.

45. Taylor, *Erring*, 105 & 106. Taylor writes, "The hieroglyphic is thus sacred inscription, holy writ. The hierophantic character of scripture must not be allowed to obscure the 'materiality' of the word. Writing, which is necessarily bound to the death of the father, is bodily or **incarnate** (emphasis mine). In script, word is made flesh and flesh is made word. Freed from the domination of a disembodied logos, hieroglyphics form 'a system of signs (which) is no longer controlled by the institution of voice'" (Ibid., 106, referring to Jacques Derrida's *Writing and Difference* [Chicago, The University of Chicago, 1978] 191).

46. Taylor, *Erring*, 118.

47. "This unending interchange of forces fissures all closed economic systems by creating an opening that saves difference" (Ibid., 112).

48. Mark 4:3-8 at 119, and road to Emmaus at 103.

49. "Implications: Interview With Henri Rouse," in Jacques Derrida, *Positions* (Translated and Annotated by Alan Bass. (Chicago, The University of Chicago Press; 1981), 6. "Derrida: I try to keep myself at the *limit* of philosophical discourse. I say limit and not death, for I do not at all believe in what today (Dec. 1967) is so easily called the death of philosophy (nor, moreover, in the simple death of whatever -- the book, man or god, especially since, as we all know, what is dead wields a very specific power). Thus, the limit of the basis of which philosophy became possible, defined itself as the *episteme*, functioning within a system of fundamental constraints, conceptual oppositions outside of which philosophy becomes unpracticable."

50. Derrida writes, "Thoth extends or opposes by repeating or replacing. By the same token, the figure of Thoth takes shape and takes its shape from the very thing it resists and substitutes for. But it thereby opposes *itself*, passes into its other, and this messenger-god is truly a god of the absolute passage between opposites. If he had any identity--but he is precisely the god of nonidentity--he would be that *coincidentia oppositorum* to which we shall soon have recourse again. In distinguishing himself from his opposites, Thoth also imitates it, becomes its sign and representative, obeys it and *conforms* to it, replaces it, by violence if need be. He is thus the father's other, the father, and the subversive movement of replacement. The god of writing is thus at once his father, his son, and himself. He cannot be assigned a fixed spot in the play of difference." *Disseminations*, Translated, with an Introduction and

Additional Notes, by Barbara Johnson (Chicago: The University of Chicago Press; 1981), 92 & 93. Taylor quotes the full verse in *Erring* at 116 & 117.

51. Taylor, *Erring*, 112.

52. Ibid., 113.

53. Ibid., 115. "*Mitte* designates not only center but also middle, midst, mean, and medium.... Closely related to *Mitte*, *Mittel* refers to measure, mean, and medium.... *Mittle* can also "mean" remedy or medicine. The French *milieu* captures various nuances of the German *Mitte*. *Le milieu* is the middle, midst, heart, center, medium, and mean. In addition to this cluster of meanings, *milieu* refers to one's environment, habitat, or surroundings. Through a curious twist of meaning, *le milieu* is sometimes used to designate the criminal underworld, the world of gangsters. Two English words closely related to *Mitte* and *milieu* are mean (including "mean" as cruel) and medium....By drawing on this fund of associations, it is possible to suggest that *Mitte*, or *milieu*, is 'medium in the sense of middle, neither/nor, what is between extremes, and (a) medium in the sense of element, ether, matrix, means.'" Parenthetical is my entry. And the quotation at the end is from Derrida, *Disseminations*, 211.

54. "...the eternally recurring *coincidentia oppositorum* inverts and subverts the traditional contrast...." Taylor, *Erring*, 113.

55. In his comments on "Building, Working, Thinking," Perotti unsuspectingly (?) gives voice to both meanings of the term incarnation in Christian theology. He writes, "Holiness is the wedding of the sky and the earth; holiness is the presence of the gods in earthly things" (Perotti, *Heidegger On The Divine* [Columbus: Ohio University Press; 1974], 118).

In the second verse, "holiness is the presence of the gods in earthly things," Perotti gives voice to what is commonly designated the Johannine incarnation. It is a christology which is concerned with the "presence" of the gods in non-divine things. It is a metaphysical incarnation.

Perotti's first verse is strikingly different from the second. "Holiness is the wedding of the sky and the earth." Here there is no suggestion that holiness is the *presenting* of one thing in/to another. Neither sky nor earth appears to enjoy holiness in themselves. Rather, "holiness is the *wedding*...," the union/the intimacy of the separation/the difference of earth and sky. It is a union of opposition, the wedding of difference. The holy is a "divine milieu."

56. Williams, 31.

57. Elsewhere, Heidegger writes, "Theology is seeking a more primordial interpretation of man's Being towards God, prescribed by the meaning of the faith itself and remaining within it. It is slowly beginning to understand once more Luther's insight that the "foundation" on which its system of dogma rests has not arisen from an inquiry in which faith is primary, and that conceptually this "foundation" not only is inadequate for the problematic of theology, but conceals and distorts it." *Being And Time*, H.10.

58. The wake is the occasion in which the gathering of those once dominated by the dead one who has yet to be committed to the earth, who in this time between death and burial (overcoming) remember things long forgotten in the dominating presence of the one who is no longer present.

4

THE DOCTRINE OF THE INCARNATION

THE INTRODUCTION

In the double endings of metaphysics, in the cessation of its drive and the limits of its sovereignty, the coherence of the interpretative canon unravels. The inter-textuality of the text, the differences which have been forced into submission and identity, happen in and as the endings. A particular tradition, and the hermeneutical practices which it fosters and protects, loses some of its power of persuasion. In this loss of power other hermeneutical practices, readings which differ with the tradition, happen. In the free play (free in the sense that the former power no longer exercises sovereignty) texts and interpretations play on and off one another.

In the study to follow, we will concern ourselves with two significant texts within orthodox Christian theology. Both texts are within the canon of the tradition. I have selected the texts because both are concerned with the issue(s) of "incarnation." The first is regarded as **the** authoritative text on the subject of orthodox christology. The second is the biblical text which is believed to substantiate (in terms of scripture) the authority of the first.

The first (first in our selection, second of the texts selected in terms of historical sequence) is the Creed of Chalcedon issued by the Ecumenical Council which meet in Chalcedon in 451 C.E.. In the

Chalcedonian document the "doctrine of the incarnation" is presented. The Ecumenical Council which issued the Creed asserted that the doctrine of the incarnation presented is the orthodox christology of the Christian faith. All other christological positions are heresy, and any who fail to ascribe to the orthodox position will be punished.

As we will see with regards to the doctrine of the incarnation presented in the Ecumenical Creed of Chalcedon (Chapters Four and Five), the adoption of metaphysics as the dominant hermeneutic of Christian theology was yielded by the manipulation by the powers-that-be in the union of the Roman state and christianity. Metaphysical theology both dominated institutionalized Christian thought (i.e., orthodoxy) and made its rule possible, as an institution of standardization, assessment, and punishment.

The second text is believed to be one of the oldest texts included in the New Testament canon. It is divided in the New Testament into the First and Second Epistles to the Corinthians, but few biblical scholars put much stock in the division.[1]

The doctrine of the incarnation has been the subject of philosophical/theo-political controversy for centuries. The controversy was inevitable. It was inevitable because as a central tenet of orthodox faith by which persons were included or excluded, saved or damned, "the doctrine of the incarnation" was at the same time also consistently characterized as "the mystery of the incarnation." Thus, it was regarded as "incomprehensible" even for the ecumenical council which was compelled to frame and canonize it.

In the sections and chapters to follow, I will attempt a re-reading of the doctrine of the incarnation which will show the surreptitious appropriation or accommodation of metaphysical theism into Christian thought, an appropriation or accommodation which attempts to substitute one semantic world for another. The doctrine of the incarnation is a mystery in the chalcedonian document because a pre-metaphysical Christian conviction cannot be appropriated or substituted by metaphysics. Something has failed to be translated. Something has been held back or barred from entry. The doctrine of the incarnation is a mystery in the metaphysical doctrine because there is a failure in the play of signification as one constellation of thought/ conviction/ discourse is surreptitiously displaced by another.

As we will see, these gaps or spaces in the text will reveal that the fault which is traceable in the incarnation is only the most obvious trace of a lapse which runs the entire length of the Chalcedonian document. For throughout the text, we shall find other gaps which result from manipulative attempts to disguise, displace, substitute and reverse concepts, convictions and the like.

I will argue that the doctrine is an absurdity, a self-contradicting assertion, a gap in the conceptual terrain, a fault which runs the breadth and length of Christian theology. Thus, as a central tenet of orthodox theology, as one of the foundations of christendom, the doctrine of the incarnation fails to support that which is built upon it.

UNORTHODOX CHRISTOLOGIES

Just preceding the doctrine of the incarnation in the Chalcedonian document is a short conceptual summation of those christological formulations which fail to fulfill the "mystery of the Incarnation" and were condemned. We'll not rehearse or re-present the vast material which links the various positions rejected with some historical groups. Our concern is to discern in the summation what is assessed as untrue concerning the "mystery of the Incarnation."[2]

> For the Synod opposes those who presume to rend the mystery of the Incarnation into a Duality of Sons;
>
> and it expels from the company of the priests those who dare to say that the God-head of the Only begotten is passable,
>
> and it withstands those who imagine a mixture or confusion of the Two Natures of Christ,
>
> and it drives away those who fancy that the form of a servant, taken by Him of us, is of a heavenly or different nature;
>
> and it anathematizes those who imagine Two Natures of the Lord before the Union, but fashion anew One Nature after the Union.

> The Synod rejects those who hold that in Christ there is no union of God and man.[3]

> It rejects as well those who hold a "union" of God and man in Christ made of Christ a second order divinity.[4]

The Synod rejects any "union" of the two natures which breaks down the natures in Christ, thus mixing and/or confusing the individual natures. The Synod also rejects any "union" which results in the two natures being replaced by a new nature.

The Synod "opposes," "expels," "withstands," "drives away," and "anathematizes" those who hold the various positions rejected in the Creed. The Synod "excludes" and "damns to hell" those who corrupt "the mystery of the incarnation." Though we have yet to consider the acceptable, orthodox incarnational christology presented in the Chalcedonian document, it is nevertheless clear that for the Synod, "the mystery of the incarnation" is a central doctrine of the Christian faith. It is a conviction which traces the very limits of Christian belief and community, salvation and damnation.

THE DOCTRINE OF THE MYSTERIOUS INCARNATION

The following text has been spaced and ordered below in such a way as to emphasis the problematic relation of the singularity of (left) and the dual nature of (right) Christ.[5]

> Following, then, the holy Fathers, we all unanimously teach that our Lord Jesus Christ is to us -
>
> One and the same Son,
> the Self-same Perfect in Godhead,
> the Self-same Perfect in Manhood
> truly God and truly man;
>
> the Self-same
> of a rational soul and body;
> consubstantial with the Father according to the Godhead,
>
> the Self-same
> consubstantial with us according to the Manhood;
> like us in all things, sin apart; before the ages begotten of the Father as to the Godhead, but in the last days,

the Self-same,

for us and for our salvation (born) of Mary the Virgin *theotokos* as to the Manhood.

One and the Same Christ, Son, Lord, Only-begotten acknowledged in Two Natures, unconfusedly, unchangeable, indivisibly, inseparably.

The difference of the Natures being in no way removed because of the Union, but rather the property of each Nature being preserved, and (both) concurring into

One Prosopon and One Hypostasis

not as though He were parted or divided into Two Prosopa, but

One and the Self-same Son and Only-begotten God, Word, Lord, Jesus Christ.

T. Herbert Bindley's outline/analysis of the Chalcedonian Definition of Faith will aid our seeing the structural characteristics of the Definition.[6]

The Holy Synod ... confesses One and the Self-same Son our Lord Jesus Christ--

Perfect in Godhead;
Perfect in Manhood:

Truly God;
Truly Man:

Co-essential with the Father as to Godhead;
Co-essential with us as to Manhood:

Begotten of the Father eternally as to Divinity;
Born of the Virgin, Theotokos, temporally as to Humanity:

One Christ IN TWO NATURES,

unconfusedly, unchangeable, indivisibly, inseparably, according to Holy Scripture, the teaching of Christ, and tradition.

The positive statement of the doctrine of the incarnation begins by asserting that "Our Lord Jesus Christ is to us *One* and the *same* Son."[7] This is followed by the assertion that this "One" is "two";

"the Self-same Perfect in Godhead, the Self-same Perfect in Manhood; truly God and truly man." That is, Christ is "One" not "Two," and yet, Christ is **both** "truly God" and "truly man". The two things, the two natures which are one in Christ are not just any two natures. That would be enough of a problem given the concept of nature in the Creed. But, these two natures are natures which "stand in opposition to one another;" i.e., God and humanity.

This binary opposition, in which the opposing terms "God" and "man" are presented as being "truly" and "perfectly" in opposition (i.e., themselves), but are nevertheless one in Christ, is repeated and elaborated throughout the remainder of the Definition.

> Our Lord Jesus Christ is to us-
> One and the same Son...
>
> the Self-same
> of a rational soul and body...
> consubstantial with the Father
> according to the Godhead,
> the Self-same
> consubstantial with us according to the Manhood....[8]

The opposition is then repeated in temporal terms.

> ...One and the same Son...
> before the ages begotten of the Father as
> to the Godhead, but in the last days,
> the Self-same,
> for us and for our salvation (born) of Mary the Virgin
> *theotokos* as to the Manhood.

Christ is both "unborn" (i.e., begotten of the Father) and "born" (born of Mary).

TWO *PHUSEŌN*, ONE *HYPOSTASIS*

A subtle shift is discernable at this point in the text. Having elaborated the various ways in which Christ is both "truly God and truly man," "co-essential with the Father" and "co-essential with manhood," both "unborn" and "born," the text proceeds by an analysis of the "natures" of the natures, and the "economy" of the union.

> One and the Same Christ, Son, Lord, Only-begotten
> acknowledged in Two Natures, unconfusedly, unchangeable, indivisibly, inseparably.
> The *differences* of the Natures being in no way removed because of the Union, but rather the property of each Nature being preserved, and (both) concurring into
> One Prosopon and One Hypostasis
> not as though He were parted or divided into Two Prosopa, but
> One and the Self-same Son and Only-begotten God, Word, Lord, Jesus Christ.[9]

The natures are preserved as they are, *asugchutos* (unconfusedly, not mingled together),[10] *atrētos* (unchangeable, unmovable, inflexible)[11] and *adiairetos* (indivisible, undividable).[12] Each *phusis* is static. Each *phusis* is preserved in and as itself, undivided and unchanged: complete. The *phusis* of "God" and the *phusis* of "man" persist in their differentiation, in their opposition. And each, "God" and "man", by virtue of being a static *phusis*, is individually "intelligible" and "present."

And yet, in some way, by some means, these two static *phuseōn* are *achōristos*, "inseparable," in Christ. The individual *phusis*, present in their individualization, (unconfused and unchanged in relation to one another) are now said to be *hypostasis*, "inseparable" in Christ.

The two *phuseōn* are one *hypostasis*. A *hypostasis* is "that which settles at the bottom," as in the "sediment" which settles at the bottom of a bottle of wine. In metaphysical discourse, a *hypostasis* is that which having been settled, is the support, groundwork, or the foundation; the substance, nature, or essence upon which something stands or appears. The root *-stasis*, from *-histēmi* and *histēmai* (which lengthens the older term *stao*, means "a standing, the posture of standing."

Histēmi carries either a causal or an intransitive sense. Causally, *histēmi* conveys the active sense of "to make to stand, set, place," or "to make to stand still, stop, check, to make fast, fix," or "to set up, set upright, to rise up" or "to place in the balance."

Intransitively, the terms suggest "to stand, be set or placed," as in "to lie, be situated," or "to stand still, take one's stand, to stand firm, remain fast, be fixed, to cause," or "to stand upright, rise up, be set up."

The two *phuseōn*, the two natures, are *stasis*, are "at bottom" (*upo-*) one *histēmi*. The two are "made to stand" (causal) or the two "stand" (intransitive) as one. Christ is one and two.

What sense does it make to say that two individual *phuseōn* are acknowledged to be individually unmixed, unmoved, inflexible, unchangeable **and** undivided, and that the two are inseparably one *hypostasis* in Christ?

THE MYSTERY

In three of the four instances in which the term "incarnation" occurs in the text, the union is qualified by the adjective "mystery," as in "some dare to corrupt the mystery of the Lord's incarnation for us...," "those who attempt to corrupt the mystery of the incarnation...," and "those who presume to rend the mystery of the incarnation...." In each instance, the "mystery" of the incarnation which some are said to corrupt or rend designates the "union" of the two natures in Christ. Able to name the perversions of the union, the synod concedes that the orthodox "definition of faith" is a mystery. The union of God and man in Christ is "beyond them."

The doctrine of the incarnation states that the one who is two, the one who is the mysterious union of two natures, the physis of God and the physis of man, is Christ. And this mystery, this gap in logical meaning, this thought which cannot be rationally conceived in the creedal formulation, this conundrum, names "the incarnation." That is, within the incarnational formulation, at the very center of Christian orthodox theology, that which is crucial, that which saves, is not thinkable.

Dominated by a metaphysical epistemology, the *phuseōn* are assumed to be perfectly conceivable. The identities of God and man are "natural." Yet what is crucial, what lies at the very center of Christian orthodox theology, the incarnation, the "union" of the *phuseōn* is not conceivable at all. For the "union" of the *phuseōn* is not a *phusis*.

The union of God and man names the "mystery" of that which while heralded by the *phuseōn* (metaphysically conceived realities) is absent (inconceivable) to metaphysical thought.

The *nature* of "God" and the *nature* of "humanity" are in a union, a union which is not the overcoming or domination of one nature by another, is not the changing of the natures into a new nature, or some combination in which some aspects of the nature are discarded and others kept to create a new compound.

The doctrine of the incarnation, the central tenet of orthodox Christian faith by which persons are included or excluded, saved or damned, was, even for the Synod which was compelled to frame and define it, incomprehensible. For given the metaphysics of the Creed, the doctrine of the incarnation was metaphysically absurd and logically incoherent. This is not a novel assessment on my part. It has been reiterated time and again by those critical scholars who have taken the logic of the doctrine seriously.

At the center of orthodox Christian belief, at the heart of Christian convictions, is an absurdity, a self-contradicting assertion, a gap in the conceptual terrain, a fault which runs the breadth and length of Christian theology, a hole or cut or lapse upon which christendom is built.

Violation And Violence

Manipulated Traces

If the Doctrine of the Incarnation cannot be thought of in the conceptual terrain of the creed, then what is being invoked by this lapse that cannot be thought metaphysically? Or, put another way, given the dominance of metaphysical thinking in the creedal formulation, how are we or what are we to make of the mystery? What does the term "mystery" invoke? What does the doctrine of the incarnation displace? What is to be remembered that cannot be thought metaphysically? Who or what is being manipulated, and by whom or what and for which purposes?

I will argue that the doctrine of the incarnation is a play of signification that invokes and displaces a non-metaphysical thought/ conviction/ belief of the Christian faith. And that the invocation and exchange (substitution) are the result of political manipulation within the synod that issued the doctrine.

The irony is that in order for the political manipulation to succeed those seeking domination had to invoke that which they sought to erase. In order for the doctrine of the incarnation to be authoritative in the hands of those who would (be) execute (divine) authority, the "mystery" of the incarnation had to be invoked. In other words, a logical fault had to be traced in order that orthodoxy could cohere. But in so invoking that which they sought to conceal, the manipulative manner--the slight of hand--which had passed unseen (as manipulation and slight of hand) in the text is disclosed as such. And in the disclosure, orthodoxy is revealed to be the means of and the product of manipulation. As such, in our manipulation of the text to reveal its manipulation, that which has been concealed and dominated will be allowed to show itself anew.

I am arguing that the displacement of a non-metaphysical thought/ conviction/ belief in Christian faith by the doctrine of the incarnation invokes that which is absent, a trace which is erased, but which is nevertheless necessary for the coherence of the doctrine (and, as well, the political-theological union). This lapse, the doctrine of the incarnation, written in the gaps, traced and erased by the imperial commands, in its lapse of meaning, coherence, and thought, invokes the necessity of something which cannot be recalled. There is something to remember, but "nothing" comes to mind. For the incarnation is itself no *phusis*. The doctrine of the incarnation preserves what is metaphysically unthinkable and logically incoherent as a lapse in Christian thought, a memory that something is to be remembered but... nothing comes to mind.

I contend that the "*mystery* of the incarnation" bespeaks a *lapse* in the religious memory of the Christian faith.[13] This "lapse" of memory is a forgetting about how to think or say or write a central conviction/ thought/ belief of christianity. This lapse of memory lapses precisely because it asserts that there is something to remember, but in that "nothing" comes to mind, the doctrine of the incarnation is affirmed by the synod to be a mystery. In so being affirmed, the doctrine of the incarnation will be perpetuated within orthodox Christian faith ***as** a mystery, **as** an illogical conviction.* And further, I argue that this lapse of meaning which has been preserved as a lapse in Christian thought, is lapsing precisely because it is about no-thing.

But why has this lapse been preserved as a lapse within the document? And who is responsible for its being traced and canonized?

And, as we will see, the perpetuation of such mystery as legitimate, the legitimization of something illegible, is expressive of both the inherent disruption with orthodoxy--ortho/doxy is inherently para/doxical--and the "power" of orthodox institutions to demand compliance without offering any good reasons for doing so. Having faith that the doctrine is expressive of a logic that is "beyond" but which one day will be disclosed (in the kingdom which is beyond) entails accepting the authority of orthodoxy on its own authority.

Peace, Peace, But There Is No Peace

From the beginning of the text we can discern a surreptitious hand in the weave of the document. For the weave of the text reveals a struggle for domination, a struggle which we will see as we re-read the document, mindful that ideas, convictions and other texts are presented in order to be "used" in the contentious struggle. Thus, we shall proceed--sensitive to how the text is **textured**, mindful that the texturing of a text in the twisting and turning of words and phrases is a manipulation in service to some purpose.

The purpose of the Chalcedonian document is clearly presented in the second paragraph of the Definition.

> Our Lord and Savior Jesus Christ, confirming the knowledge of the faith to his disciples, said, "My peace I leave with you, my peace I give to you," to the end that no one should differ from his neighbor in the doctrines of orthodoxy, but that the proclamation of the truth should be shown forth equally by all.[14]

The overcoming of the differences, ("no one should differ from his neighbor in the doctrines of orthodoxy") and the repetition of the same by all ("the proclamation of the truth... shown forth equally by all") eradicate discontent and struggle, and brings "peace". Differences give way and are overcome, and the struggle between opponents is brought to rest in the all-encompassing proclamation of the same doctrines of orthodoxy.

But there is a disruption, a lapse in the very fabric of the piece we have just read, a lapse which is traced in the introductory remarks immediately preceding the stated purpose, erased in the discussion of the "peaceful" purposes of orthodoxy, and forgotten by the final decree. First, the erasure.

PEACES IN CONTENTION

The erasure occurs in the stated purpose of the assembly. It occurs as a gap or hesitation between two texts which are (inter-) woven. The Chalcedonian document has woven into itself a verse from The Gospel of John, a verse whose purpose is to warrant the purpose for which the Synod was assembled and for which the Chalcedonian document was written.

The text reads (again),

> Our Lord and Savior Jesus Christ ... said,
>
> "My peace I leave with you, my peace I give to you..."
>
> to the end that no one should differ from his neighbor....[15]

The verse from the Gospel of John is begun only to be cut short, abruptly ended. The text whose support is being invoked is re-traced incompletely. "My peace I leave with you, my peace I give to you..." is incomplete, calling to mind the remainder of the verse which in not being traced has been erased.

> Peace I leave with you; my peace I give to you;
> *not* as ~~the world gives do I give to you~~.

The creedal passage both recalls to mind and cancels its own scriptural support "to the end that no one should differ...." The peace of the Lord (which is in opposition to the peace of the world) will now serve the ends of this world, and in particular, the kingdom of the Emperors (the *Pax Augusta*). And those who differ with orthodoxy, those who disrupt "the peace" of the empire, who differ with that which has been "commanded" by the Emperors, will be "anathematized." For those who differ are said to have entered into the world of "the evil one" who seeks to supplant the seeds of orthodoxy by means of sowing tares. Therefore, "evil" is that which is unorthodox. Put another way, "to differ is to err" (fall, lapse). Those who differ with the doctrines of orthodoxy and disrupt the peace, who disobey the Imperial "command", who lapse or falter, are anathematized, i.e., consigned to Satan, cursed, damned to hell to be tormented and tortured again and again without end. What is erased from the stated purpose of the document are the traces of the Christian "peace" which differ from the *Pax Augusta*.

THE POLYTHEISM OF THE CREED

However, I stated that this lapse, which is erased in the discussion of peace and orthodoxy, is traced in the introduction. Returning to the beginning of the text,

> The holy, great and ecumenical Synod, by the grace of God and the command of our most orthodox and Christ-loving Emperors, Marcian and Valentinian Augusti ... hath decreed as follows....[16]

The Synod was assembled at the "command" of the Emperors. But we have failed to note the disjunction, the conflict, which is traced at the beginning. "The holy, great and ecumenical Synod" is assembled "by the *grace* of *God* and//the *command* of our ... *Emperors*, Marcian and Valentinian Augusti...."

The "command" of the Emperors is no simple order. It is *thespisma*. Built upon *theos* (divine, god) and *epos* ("a word, that which is spoken"), *thespisma* means "to declare by oracle, prophesy, divine."[17] The *thespisma* of the Emperors is a "divine declaration" or "a holy word". Thus, the verse might better read "By the grace of God and the *divine declaration* of the Emperors...."

The document suggests by its tone that the Emperors and God are in accord and that church and state are united, and that the Imperial *thespisma* is at least, an extension of, and expressive of, God's grace and word in the world.[18] And yet, there is a rift in the text in these opening lines. For despite the all too easy coherence between God and the Emperors, there are nevertheless traces of a fault. The synod is assembled by the authority of "God's grace" and the authority of the "Emperors' *divine word*". We are reminded in the opening lines that this synod and the document which is here issued is authorized by different (differing) divinities who rule different (differing) kingdoms.

Historically it is argued that the beginnings of the theo-political union between Rome and Christianity are evident in the Apologists who reflected on the coincidence of the advent of Christ and the *Pax Augusta*. Origen later called the coincidence deliberate, claiming that Augustus, by unifying the Empire and excluding particularism, presented Christianity with the chance to introduce (though not completely) a reversal of the state of affairs which began with the tower of Babel and the confusion of tongues.[19] It is a reversal which having begun will be completed at the Last Judgement.[20]

THE HOLY *PAX AUGUSTA*

In our rereading of that passage in which the establishment of orthodoxy is supported by an appeal to scripture, we discover that the "text" of the creed and the union it supposedly stitched together, was gaping (glaringly?) in the presentation of "peace." For the Chalcedonian text traced and attempted to erase the breach of the unity between the *Pax Augusta* and the peace of the Lord and in effect erased the peace of the Lord which stood in opposition to the peace of orthodoxy and the peace of the world.

Thus the text splits its seams. The cloth which appeared to be of one piece shows its divisions. The attempts to present the peace of Jesus and the *Pax Augusta* as being of one text fails. What was presented in the Creed as in accord is disclosed as being in opposition. The opposition of the

Peace of the Lord--*Pax Augusta*

is revealed in their difference.

This opposition, this difference is leaped over and forgotten in the subsequent document and its hermeneutical history, and for good reason. The inter-textuality of the Creed evident in the use of the passage from the Gospel of John (and in fact--the creed is little more than a collection of texts) marks the powerful presence of the divine word of the Emperors. So powerful is their presence in the text that even canonized scripture is made to reverse itself. The most holy of Christian texts are now surreptitiously twisted to reverse themselves and to serve the very powers the verse critiques. In the reversal, the peace of the Lord is invoked and displaced by the *Pax Augustus*. Thus, the peace of the world, in this instance the *Pax Augusta*, becomes the *Holy Pax Augusta*.

It was not that the *Pax Augusta* was not holy before the union which produced the Imperial Church. The emperors were "divinities" in their own right. And, they are presented as such, as we saw in our returning to the greek text above. The emperors do not draw their authority from the gods of the Christian faith. Nevertheless, in order to exercise authority within Christian communities the emperors must form a coalition with the Christian gods. In the invocation and displacement of the Christian gods, the emperors assimilate the legitimate power of christianity to themselves. Thus, the emperors seek to rule two kingdoms, to exercise sovereignty in both.

Grace And Decree

In the last paragraph of the document, we read that the Creed concludes with a "decree." A "decree" which is "decreed" in the creed in the name of the Holy and Ecumenical Synod, but is authorized by the grace of God and the divine decree of the Emperors. "...(I)t is **unlawful** for any one to present, write, compose, devise, or teach to others any other Creed...."[21] Thus, the church will be governed, just as the Empire is governed, by "laws" despite the prominence of the condemnation of legalism in Christian thought/faith since the earliest days. The creed sets the legal limits of theological activity. The "*legality*" of the Doctrine of the Incarnation, and the "*illegality*" of that which is outside the Doctrine of the Incarnation, is by action of the *divine command* of the Emperors, a *command* which though it appears to compliment the grace of God, stands in opposition to *grace* in the "Introduction," and later in the text, dominates unopposed in the erasure of grace.

And "those who dare either to compose another Creed, or to bring forward, or teach or deliver another symbol..." will be deposed from their positions and anathematized. Those who disobey the "Creed," those who are outside the "law," will be **outside** the "church," **outside** the kingdom of God, beyond God's grace--though under the reign, jurisdiction and punishment of the Emperors. In other words, those who disobey will be thrown down from their positions in this world and damned to hell in the next.

Conceptual conformity and the acceptance of Imperial sovereignty are offered in exchange for membership and its privileges.[22] Until conformity is universal and sovereignty is world-wide, world-order and human well-being will be vulnerable to conflicts, divisions and competition. Those who willingly refuse to conform, who differ, who will not submit to the exchange, who will not take part in the deal, will be cut off and cut out for their nonconformity threatens the safety of the world and the well-being of humanity.

What was traced in the "Introduction" and erased in the discussion of "peace," has been forgotten in the "conclusion." "Imperial divine commands," "*Pax Augusta*," "legal jurisdiction" and the "penalties for illegal activity" have come to dominate and to erase "the grace of God."

The Incarnation As Accommodation

The Imperial divine command opposes those who differ, disposes those who stand in opposition, and anathematizes all who disobey. The "grace" and "peace" which differ with the "Imperial divine commands" and "*Pax Augusti*," the God and the Lord who stand in opposition to the Emperors, are invoked--only to then be dis-posed, marginalized and erased in a surreptitious substitution and reversal.

In the "gap" yielded by the invocation and erasure of the grace of God and the peace of the Lord, the Emperors insisted that a single doctrine be traced which would **unite** heaven and earth, God and man. Such a doctrine would provide uniformity (one form, one structure) in the holy Imperial kingdom, a oneness which would bring order to the many and peace to differences.[23]

That doctrine, the doctrine of the incarnation (the ecumenical document itself for that matter), would not have been drawn up except for the insistence of the Emperors and the manipulation of their imperial commissioners in the Synod. It was the Emperors' pleasure that Leo's *ek duo phuseōn* be the formula of orthodox christology, and that all be required to accept the uniform formulation.[24]

However, this christological formula which the Emperors' desired would become orthodox, which is to bring "peace" (to the faithful? the Imperial Church? Rome?), can not be traced *in the creed*. The creed declares that the "arrangement" they have made works because of that which cannot be arranged. The *mysterious incarnation* is invoked to relate the two natures. That which cannot be arranged, which is absent to the text, will mysteriously complete the text and fill in the holes. To what extent does the incoherent union of the *ek duo phuseon* formula mirror the incoherent union of the Christian divinities and the Roman Emperors, the grace of God and the Imperial commands, the peace of Jesus and the *Pax Augusta*? In each instance the *ek duo phuseon* and the dissimilarities of the four divinities, those things or persons of attributes which are at odds, are said to be held together in unexplainable unions. But what purposes are served in such accommodations? What do the accommodations bespeak? or belie?

The Chalcedonian text may be said to lapse precisely because it is, in the rhetorical sense, an "economy". For, as we have seen, the stated purpose of the document is not the purpose it serves. It is claimed in the text that the purpose is to bring the peace of the Lord to christendom. But what is proposed by the definition and the condemnation of those who differ, is not the peace of the Lord. It is the peace of Rome. The unstated purpose of the text is to bring--not the peace of the Lord to Christendom, but the peace of Rome to Christendom. And in this substitution which displaces one peace for another, the structures of authority are also displaced. The grace of God and the peace of Jesus are invoked and their authority summoned. But, the Christian divinities and their powers are summoned in order to be taken over and used in service of the divine Roman Emperors. In this process, the structures of authority are assimilated. The differences and the tensions are disintegrated. The difference between the peace of Jesus and the peace of the world is erased by the assimilation and the domination of the peace of the Lord by the *Pax Augusta* "in order that no one should differ". The grace of God, as strange as it may appear, is dominated by the divine command of the Emperors. And with this collapse of the difference in the assimilation and domination, the authority of God and Christ pass to the Imperial Church and to its rulers. The Imperial divine command has issued in the collapse of all differentiations which might call into question the rule of Marcian and Valentinian Augusti. The emperors, having invoked and assumed the authority of the Christian divinities (God and Christ), now dominate and rule not only their kingdom on earth, but in this text and the synod that issued it, **they** rule christendom as if it were a non-regional providence of the Roman Empire. And the rulers/divinities of that providence (God and Christ) become **their** servants.

And yet, in order for the Imperial Church to assume the authority from above, it must in the end appeal to a doctrine which recalls the very **structure** which the Imperial Church is attempting to erase, and appeal to the authority which it seeks to assimilate and displace. Thus, in a sense, the doctrine of the incarnation is a fault in the document's purpose because the doctrine recalls the system of convictions which are everywhere being displaced in the text. For the incarnation is itself the union of differences in which those who differ nevertheless persist in their differentiation in the union. Thus, in a sense, the document traces the erasure and displacing of differentiation in the Imperial striving for power in a text which of necessity must nevertheless recall the differentiation in order for the re-conciliation to happen.

The paradox of this orthodox is that in striving to dominate, the Imperial Church must invoke that which it seeks to displace. And in the invocation, the differentiations (grace of God--Imperial Divine Commands, Peace of Jesus--*Pax Augusta*) reassert themselves. The success of the Imperial Church and the power of its orthodoxy depends upon, draws its power and authority--its life--from that which it must **always seek** to overcome.

However, it is an overcoming which must never be final, a seeking which must never be satisfied, a consumption which must never completely consume that which is its host. For the Imperial Church is parasitic. It feeds upon its living host. The success of the Imperial Church--the power and the authority of orthodoxy --depends upon the continued existence of its host which is must **always seek** to overcome, as opposed to simply overcoming. In other words, the

Imperial Church feeds upon its host which is the Host. As parasite, the church feeds upon that which it claims to serve.

The power of the Imperial Church and the Roman Empire is nourished by a process of assimilation. What is "other," "outside," and "different" becomes the means by which *salvation* and *civilization* exercise their all consuming desire. Christian orthodoxy and Roman civilization feed upon the unsaved and uncivilized for the fulfillment of their desire.

The Imperial Church and the orthodoxy it instituted is a parasite which must feed upon its unorthodox host. And yet, the unorthodox movements themselves feed upon the orthodoxy of the Imperial Church to gain power as "outsiders," or as the truly faithful.

The Creed is able to trace so clearly those christological positions it deems unorthodox precisely because the unorthodox christologies are the sustenance which sustains the orthodox desire to control. The unorthodox christologies are the substance of the creed--they are the nourishment which the creed consumes and uses and wastes. The process of identifying those christologies which are outside, of marking the inside/outside--is the means, the energy of orthodoxy. The creed is fueled by that which it seeks to overcome--it is energized by the desire to overcome, to dominate all, to rule all and make all the same by consumption or annihilation. The Creed is dominated by the unorthodox christologies it seeks to overcome. It is dependent upon that which it must forever seek to consume.

As the protector of orthodoxy and the instrument of salvation, the Imperial Church must assess a limit. Those who are outside the limit are improper and must be brought across the line and saved, or be annihilated. If those who are different are assimilated then the consuming desire of the church is satisfied--for a time. If the consuming desire can not be satisfied, if those who differ cannot be assimilated, then the Imperial Church--rejected bride--reacts in violent and brutal ways to appease its unfulfilled desire and to justify its existence.

CONCLUSION

The doctrine of the Incarnation, in that it disrupts both the stated and the unstated intent of the Creed, accommodates--hosts--those which everywhere in the text seek to overcome it. The success of the Imperial Church depends upon that which it must always seek to overcome but which it must always invoke in order to be legitimated.

But the legitimization of the grace of God and the peace of the Lord in the Imperial Church would have issued in the displacement of the Emperors and their "peace," "commands" and "decrees." For the grace of God would by virtue of being gracious, displace and overcome the "commands" and "decrees" of the Emperors. And the peace of the Lord, by virtue of being redemptive and "a peace not of the world," would have displaced and dominated the "peace of the world." And such domination by God's grace and the Lord's peace would have been the ruin of the Imperial Church. And, such domination, if it were legitimized in the Empire, would have been the ruin of Imperial authority, Imperial peace and the Imperial kingdom.

We wondered at the conclusion of Chapter Three whether the surreptitious power of Christian orthodox theology would be disclosed in the deconstruction of the metaphysical domination of Christian thought. Clearly in the Chalcedonian Creed, powers compete openly and subversively to establish their rule and dominance. The powers *accommodate* one another and in so *accommodating*, establish an economy which yields the doctrine of the mysterious incarnation/economy.

NOTES

1. It is believed that the division is the work of a later editor.
2. T. Herbert Bindley, *The Oecumenical Documents Of The Faith*, Edited with Introduction and Notes (London; Methuen & Co. LTD.; 1950) 234-235.
3. E.g., "those who...rend the mystery of the Incarnation into a duality of Sons," and "those who... fancy that the form of a servant, taken by him of us, is of a heavenly or different nature."
4. E.g., "those who dare to say that the God-head of the Only begotten is passible."
5. Bindley, 234-235.

6. Bindley, 188.
7. Emphasis mine.
8. Bindley, 235.
9. Bindley, 235. Emphasis mine.
10. Liddell-Scott, 264.
11. Liddell-Scott, 272.
12. Liddell-Scott, 22.
13. I do not say "theological" memory for as we shall see, "*theo*-logy" is part and parcel to the metaphysics which displaces.
14. Bindley, 232.
15. Bindley, 232.
16. Bindley, 232.
17. Liddell-Scott.
18. "Even before the time of Constantine, Christian Apologists had already been made aware of the coincidence of the advent of Christ, the founder of the Christian religion, and the Pax Augusta, the unification and pacification of the Roman empire and the *oikoumenē*." Aloys Grillimieu, *Christ In Christian Tradition: Volume One; From the Apostolic Age to Chalcedon (451)*, translated by John Bowden (Atlanta: John Knox Press; 1975), 250.
19. Grillimieu, 251, fn 9; see Origen *C.Cels.* II,30; *Koetschau* 157-8.
20. The political theology which asserted that the "divine declarations" of the Emperors implemented "the grace of God," assumes the UNITY of God and the Emperors, the kingdom of God and the Empire of Rome, the authority of God and the authority of the Emperors, the laws of God and the laws of Rome, the peace of Jesus and the *Pax Augusta*.

A. Grillimieu contends that Eusebius of Caesarea earlier proposed a historico-political theology in which "...the appearance of the Messiah and imperial peace, Christianity and the empire, are bound together in a indissoluble unity by the idea of providence. In the first book of the *Praeparatio Evangelica* (I,4,1-6) he sees two movements running alongside each other: polytheism, a diabolical pluralism, is overcome by Christianity; the polyarchy which separates the peoples is overcome by the Augustinian monarchy. Unity is now fortified against multiplicity in two ways: in Christianity, which is founded on the incarnation, and in the *Imperium Romanum*, which is based on the monarchy. Moreover, the Roman monarchy becomes the representation of the heavenly monarchy: the political union is matched by the spiritual victory over polytheism. For Christ has overcome the demons who were the real disrupters of both the religious and the political order.... For the divine Logos--embodied in Constantine's *monarchia*--sees to a universal and immutable order" (Grillimieu, 251-252).
21. Emphasis mine.
22. Scott, *The Language of Difference*, 151.
23. "Thus the Council was ready to fulfill the wishes of the Emperor.... (T)he majority of the bishops who assembled at Chalcedon considered it enough to uphold the faith as it had been drawn up at Nicaea.... But the imperial commissioners, aware of Marcian's desire for uniformity of belief, had so controlled the proceedings of the Council that at length they gained their end, and the second draft of the *Definitio Fidei* was set up as a doctrinal formula which all would be called upon to accept." R. V. Sellers, *The Council of Chalcedon* (London: S.P.C.K.; 1954), 207.

We will not go into all the political maneuvers between church and state in this study. It is unmistakably clear in recent studies that the Emperor Constantine had considerable influence upon the Council of Nicaea; upon its proceedings and its dogma. We'll not press the issue of whether or not as seems to be commonly held nowadays, Constantine manipulated the Fathers of Nicaea and forced the doctrine of the *homoousios* on them.

24. Grillimieu writes "It was only under constant pressure from the emperor Marcian that the Fathers of Chalcedon agreed to draw up a new formula of belief. Even at the fourth session of the council, on 17 October 451, the delegates of the emperor heard the synod once again endorse its purpose to create no new formula over and above the creeds of Nicaea and Constantinople. Ephesus had adopted the same attitude. But if, it was argued, a new account of the faith was already necessary, then it was to hand in the letter which Leo sent in condemnation of Nestorius and Eutyches (ACO II, 1,2,93, no.6). Nevertheless, the *Acts* do testify to some striving towards a new formula of belief. All the more important is the work of a special commission which had assembled on 21 October under the patriarch Anatolius. This commission had prepared a creed, the text of which is unfortunately no longer extant (cf. ACO II, 1,2 123, no.3). But we see from the subsequent discussion that it had a predominantly Cyrillian tendency. For it evidently avoided the emphatic diphysitism of Leo's letter and used instead the disputed formula *ek duo phuseon* (ACO II, 1, 2, 123f., esp. no. 13). Anatolius himself was the driving force behind it. But the imperial commissioners -- together with the Roman delegates -- brought about the turning point. The letter of Leo, they held, must be used in the new formula, for the council had already accepted it and subscribed to it, whereas Dioscorus of Alexandria had been condemned. Why, then, still the *ek duo phuseon*?

Leo or Dioscorus? Faced with this dilemma, the bishops gave way and expressed themselves agreeable that a committee, to be formed at the Emperor's pleasure, should work out a new formula in accordance with Leo's formula of the two natures (ACO II, 1, 2, 124f., nos. 22-8). Thereupon twenty-three bishops assembled with the imperial commissioners in the oratory of St Euphemia. When they returned to the full assembly, they were able to put before the synod a long declaration of faith, which was finally greeted with shouts of approval on 25 October. The Acts cite first of all quite a lengthy preamble, which is followed by the creeds of Nicaea (325) and Constantinople (381). After a long transition we then read the text which may be described as the 'Chalcedonian creed'" (Grillimieu, 543).

5

THE MYSTERY OF THE *OIKONOMIA*

INTRODUCTION

Adapted from the Latin *incarnare* (5th Century) meaning "to make flesh" (from *in-* and *caro*, *carn*--flesh), to incarnate means to cover with flesh, cause flesh to grow upon or in (a wound or sore), or to heal.[1] In the Latin translations, as with its many English descendants, the single term "incarnation" or "incarnare" stands for/translates/interprets/exchanges/displaces two separate Greek terms in the text, *enanthrōpēsin* and *oikonomias*.

The practice of translating the Greek terms *enanthrōpēsin* and *oikonomias* with the Latin *incarnare* began as early as *Collectio Vaticana*, A.D. 520.[2] *Enanthrōpēsin*, meaning "to live among" (*en*-) "men" (*anthrōpēsin*), or "to have the appearance of men," was rendered *incarnatio*. In the exchange, *carnatio* (flesh) was offered for *anthrōpēsin* (men) and *in-* for *en-* ("to live among" or "have the appearance of"). Such an arrangement appears to work very well. Both *enanthrōpēsin* and *incarnare* aptly present a common christological theme in the Johannine literature whose prominence continues today: as in "And the Word became flesh..." (*kai o logos sarx egeneto*) John 1:14. In most ecclesiastical circles and commonly in theological texts, this is the meaning commonly associated with the

Latin term *incarnare* and its English descendent. However, the term *enanthrōpēsin* occurs only once in the Chalcedonian text.[3]

Oikonomias, the other Greek term for which the Anglicized Latin term incarnation is exchanged, named the mysterious union of God and human which is put forth by the Chalcedonian Council as the symbol of true faith.[4] I have yet to find an English translation of the Chalcedonian text which offers the Anglicized phonetic equivalent "economy" in exchange for *oikonomia*. Instead, *oikonomia* is commonly translated in English as "incarnation" or "dispensation." In each instance above, the English translation follows earlier Latin practices. Latin has the trans-phonetic term *oeconomia*, but it does not appear in the Latin translations of the Creed.[5]

The use of "dispensation" began rather soon after the Council concluded in C.E. 451, while the use of "incarnation" began (as we have seen) no later than C.E. 520.[6] Meaning "to weigh out, pay out, disperse; manage, regulate, control, impart", **dispensation** plays heavily upon the "economic" character of *oikonomia*.[7]

OIKONOMÍA

Oikonomía is a compound composed of the terms *oîkos* (commonly translated "house," meaning both a "dwelling" and a tribe of people, as in the house of David) and *nómos* (commonly translated "manage" or "distribute"). Generally *oikonomía* is translated "household management" or "house order" in the sense of the ordering, administrating, and care of domestic affairs within a household. John H. Reumann concludes from his extensive study of the uses of *oikonomía* and its family of related terms through the hellenistic age that this general sense of the terms as "household management" enjoyed an extensive application extending from "the management of a larger household" (e.g., an army, a city or other grouping (political, religious, etc.), to "arrangement in general" (e.g., legal, the ordering of materials in the arts, to one's life plan) and, by ultimate extension, to "the management of the universe."[8]

This history of the use of *oikonomía* plays heavily upon the *nómos* character of the compound, with *oîkos* being adapted to cover any identifiable entity, be it a home, a city, an army, a life or the universe.

THEOLOGICAL *OIKONOMÍA*

There are two theological meanings of *oikonomía* which have survived. Both have a restricted technical, theological meaning. Neither has enjoyed popular coinage as has, say, the term "incarnation". In one sense, *oikonomía* is "the *method* of the divine government of the world," or "a *dispensation* or *method* or *system* of the divine government...."[9] In a related sense, it is "the judicious *handling* of doctrine," meaning that an *economy* is a *manner* or *method* of meeting the needs or conciliating the prejudices of persons addressed.

As such, the doctrine of the *oikonomía* is the means by which, the system by which, theological assessment is determined. It is a determination, a rule by which one may be assessed. The doctrine of the *oikonomía* sets the limit of Christian orthodoxy. Thus, the creed is a legal arrangement of divine government. We have already raised the issue as to which divinities it arranges, and we will return to the issue again below. But at this point, we may conclude that the creed is itself an *oikonomía* in that it is both a legal arrangement in service to the divine government of the world, and it is the document, the authoritative presentation, of that arrangement.

As such, the ecumenical council of Chalcedon is a *kosmic* economy. Meaning "open to the world," the *oikomenía* council is authoritative in the "inhabited" world. It exercises universal control by maintaining the "peace" and "order" of christendom by setting the divine limits of Christian thought.

The Council is the authority which conciliates those in doctrinal conflict in the church. And the means by which the ecumenical council brings "peace" and "order" is by **law**. That is, the Chalcedonian council manages the household of faith with law. The creed presents orthodoxy; the "correct," the "straight, right, true" "beliefs" of the household of faith.

NÓMOS/NOMÓS

As I suggested above, the uses of *oikonomía* are dominated by the *nómos* stem. And while we have noted that with respect to the term *oikonomía*, *nómos* is generally taken to signify "manage" or "distribute," *nomós*, means "roaming for pasture," and "grazing." Nomadic peoples must roam with their herds in search of pasture. In a sense, a nomadic *oikonomía* might be the "managing" which *orders* the "home" or "tribe" in the "roaming for pasture." Thus we see the association of wandering in search of pasturage and the general meaning of "manage."

Nomís and its close relative *nomás* both mean division and distribution (as in the distribution of an inheritance). *Nomàs* also could mean possession or regular usage, and so meant as well district, province, or sphere of command. *Nomîkós* meant "relating to laws," "resting on laws," or "conventional".[10] *Ta nomîkós* meant "law matters," while the adverb *nomîkís* "by legal process," suggesting "legitimate," "customary," and "prescriptive."

Thus, we come to see the association of *nomós* (pasturage) and *nómos* (law). Charles Scott notes,

> In both words habitual practice--the primary meaning for *nómos*, which means both law and melody--struggles with nomadic, uncivilized separation. This is a fateful struggle. In it the limiting principles of order and random movement without limiting principles each unsettle the other. To overcome randomness, principles of order must be applied beyond the locale to give order to the distances and differences of locales. And to maintain the distance and difference involved in the many ways of belonging and being well placed, one must resist the use of principles of order to overcome the randomness and to order differences in a dominant way.[11]

Given the assumed universality of the creed by the ecumenical council, it is easy to see how in the wandering from locale to locale, Christian thought would come to accommodate the cultural influences of a particular region. It is in response to and over against this randomness that the council prescribes an orthodoxy.

The doctrine of the *oikonomós* is a *nómos*. Or, to put it another way, the **rules legitimated** by the council by the **command** of the Emperors, are the **rules for all in the house or tribe of christendom**. The wandering people (*oiko-nomós*) will no longer wander in thought, but will be limited, bound, dominated by *nómos*. And this *nómos* will define the *oîkos* of God.

METAPHYSICAL GAP
DE-CREEDAL LIMITATIONS

VIOLATION AND VIOLENCE

Despite the various attempts to systematize--with the aid of this or that philosophical system or method--by Christian thinkers/writers spanning the better part of the past two millennia (almost since christianity's inception)--there has persisted a fault, a lapse which the various attempts at systematization or philosophical theology have sought to correct, heal, or at least, to fill in. The fractures which cut the body of systematic theology, and with which theological systemization attempts to work in overcoming, has to do with the incomprehensibility, the in-coherences of the doctrine of the *oikonomia*.

Time and again this riddle of the faith, enshrined in its mystery, has been the occasion for great violence (symbolic, physical, verbal). With the divine commandments of the Emperors there was an insistence that "the doctrine of the mysterious *oikonomia*" be accepted without deviation. And those who dare to deviate from the symbol, those who dare reject the divine command of the Emperors would be dis-placed from their positions, re-placed by another, and cast into eternal torment and torture.

DE-CREEING THE LEGAL LIMITS IN THE CREED

The limits of orthodoxy, the **theo**-logical positions of Christendom, are a settled affair. The Emperors have de-*creeded* that the *creed* is legitimate. That is, the Synod set the legitimate limits of theological opinion in the creed at the pleasure and by the authority of the Emperors. Thus, the Emperors have legitimized the church (with respect to Rome), at the same time that the church legitimized the Imperial Rule (with respect to the faith).

What was not possible to include in this process of legitimization was the grace of God and the peace of the Lord. For as we saw earlier, the grace of God, by virtue of being gracious, stands in opposition to the "commands" and "decrees" of the Emperors. And the peace of the Lord would by virtue of its difference with the peace of the world have stood in opposition to the *Pax Augusta*. Thus, the legitimization of the "creed" by the decree of the Emperors legitimated the forgetting of the other ("Lord" and "God" who stand in opposition as other with respect to the Emperors) in the infinite repetition of the same. The reproduction of the same is produced without concern for difference. As such, the legitimization of the creed entails a two-fold violation. As we saw in the preceeding chapter, the legitimization of the creed entails a violation of the sovereignty of the "Lord" and "God" for the faithful. But it also entails a violation of the anti-legalistic traditions of the faith.

What is legitimized in the creed is that which is illegitimate given the anti-legalistic traditions of the church. Within the "legal" perimeters of orthodoxy as decreed by the emperors and legislated by the Synod, the grace of God and the peace of the Lord are marginalized and deferred. We have already considered marginalization. They are deferred by the infinite repetition of the symbol of Chalcedon which perpetuates itself without concern for the various differences which it vacates, displaces, dominates. The creed is thus an "economy of death." For it spells the "death" of the divinities and their characteristics which are displaced and deferred in the exchange. And the creed sets the "legal" limits of salvation, life eternal, and the infraction, damnation (death) for illegal activity and opinion. These legal limits thus seek to legislate the limits of life and death.[12]

I think an argument could be made in significant detail and supported by the historical documents, that the doctrine of the *mysterious economy* of God and world in Christ parallels and is mirrored by the mysterious union of God and the Emperors in the theo-political configuration of the time. The economy/ dispensation/ incarnation may be so important for the Emperors because the Imperial Church rests upon an assumed *oikonomia* between the heavenly peace and the worldly order.

Thus, the ecumenical synod of Chalcedon was an economy. By its decrees and creeds, the synod was the "dispensation," the "method and the "system" of "governing the divine." The synod "judiciously handed doctrine." And it proceeded by means of decree and law at the command and pleasure of the Emperors.

As such, the synod was an ecumenical (i.e., literally, a "world order") *economy*. The ecumenical synod economized (administered, controlled the exchange of, cut the cost of) the "plan" and/or "order" of salvation **world** wide. World order and human well-being (salvation as opposed to damnation) depend on metaphysical identities, laws and principles.[13]

The Illegible Economy

The central tenet of orthodox Christian theology is illegible. The doctrine of the mysterious economy can not (or no longer) be deciphered. It is unreadable. The synod declares that that which is il-legible in the creed is legal, legitimate. For the union of the *phusis* of God and the *phusis* of man (are one) in Christ is declared a mystery. What is legitimate in the Creed is the gathering which is illegible in the document.

But to suggest that what is "legal" is "illegible" is like saying that what is legal is illegal, or what is illegible is legible. Both "legal" and "legible" are derived from the Indo-European root *leg* (meaning to pick together, gather, collect). The Greek *legein* suggested "to pick out, choose; to say, tell, speak." The Latin *legere* carried these meanings as well as preserved or added the sense of "to read or recite." Thus, the Latin *lectus*, later became (ML) lectura, or lecture (F,MF, ME). The sense of "to read" persists in "legible" meaning "to read, decipher." Legal, from the Latin *legalis* ("pertaining to the law") is also derived from the root *leg-*. What is "legal" is that which has been picked out, chosen, gathered, collected, and which can be read or recited. Something of the memory of this connection must persist in the now uncommon phrase, "S/he is reading law." That which is legal can be recited for it is legible. What is legal is legible.[14]

It is the *leg* character(s) (on the page) which confuses the reading. For, ironically, it is the *il-legible oikonomia*, **the** central tenet of orthodox faith, which *legitimated*. That is, what is illegible in the text (the mystery of the incarnation) legitimizes.

What is illegible, i.e., the doctrine which can not be traced in the creed and which can not be read in the document, is the means by which all shall be judged. To reject what is illegible (unreadable) in the document (the doctrine of the mystery of the incarnation) is to be illegitimate (illegal). The illegible union of the natures is the standard by which all shall be gathered or cut out, saved or damned.

In the creed, God, by virtue of being a *phusis*, is knowable and legible. In the Jewish tradition it is God whose presence is invoked in the text with illegible markings. Given God's reserve, God can not be traced in the text. And yet, we might ask, what brings about this change that in the creeds of christendom, (the *phusis* of) God is legible and assumed to be knowable and present--while Christ is the divine identity which can no longer be traced, a mysterious metaphysical absence which is nevertheless present.

But what is illegible also legitimizes the Synod's authority which in turn accommodates (*oikonomia*) the authority of the Emperors. And, as we have seen, the doctrine of the incarnation, as the mysterious union of the *phuseon* of God and humanity, that which is illegible in the metaphysical document, is assumed in the creed to be the means of legitimization. And yet, the doctrine of the incarnation is the last trace, illegible as it may be, of a comprehensive reversal wrought by surreptitious manipulation in the substitution, or the displacement or the disguising of one manner of thinking, one convictional system, one world of discourse, by another.

Christ is the "union" (gathering, *legein*, *logos*), the trace (legible) which is legitimate in the ecclesia. Nevertheless, in the ecumenical creed--a world wide creed--only traces of the erasure persist. What is legitimate in the ecclesia is not legible in the creed.

The metaphysics of the creed is the means by which the Emperors manipulated God and the world, and thus legitimated their divinity, their kingdom and reign, and the peace they sought to keep (with respect to Christian faith). In this manipulation the tension between God and the Emperors, heaven and earth, Jesus' peace and *Pax Augustus*, are collapsed. Christendom accommodates the powers-that-be, and so its authority passes from God and Christ who are displaced by the creed through the Imperial Church to the Emperors.

But there is a gap, a space that is illegable in the process of legitimation. In order for the accommodation to occur, in order for the exchange to be made, in order for the manipulation to succed, the incarnation, the economy, must occur. But if the economy is traced in the text, then a difference is reinscribed in a text which has sought to end differentiation.

The paradox is that in striving to dominate, the Imperial Church must invoke that which it seeks to displace. And in the invocation, the surreptitious collapse of differences is disclosed as difference is once again yielded in the doctrine of the economy. Thus, the success of the Imperial Church rests upon that which it must always seek to erase, but which it must always trace in order to be legitimated.

A Gap In The Metaphysics Of The Creed.

Is the *mystery* of the doctrine of the Incarnation traced in the text as a *mystery* because the "doctrine of the *oikonomia*" (i.e., an orthodox metaphysical doctrine) could not in the end--nor completely, substitute, displace or disguise that which it sought to dominate? Or is the doctrine of the *oikonomia* merely an anomaly in the metaphysical (con-)text?

The illegibility of the *oikonomia* is itself, in its being illegible, a trace of that which yet persists in the creed despite the manipulations to conceal and dominate. For the manipulations to conceal and dominate, in being disclosed as manipulations of concealment and domination, reveal "not what they have concealed" but trace something that has been concealed, displaced, substituted.

The "doctrine of the economy" substitutes far more than just another doctrine (orthodox or otherwise) in its concealment and displacement. For what is displaced in the surreptitious appropriation of metaphysics by the Synod under the domination of the Emperors is absurd.[15] Literally, metaphysics is deaf to it. It is senseless and unreasonable. And yet, this absurdity is traced as an absurdity, traced as something which is not clear, but yet persists in the text as unintelligible.

The *oikonomia* is in the strictest sense *un-natural.* It is unnatural in that the incarnate one, Christ, has no *phusis*. The contention that Christ is the mysterious incarnation is to hold that the *phusis* of God and the *phusis* of man are one in Christ. However, the absurdity of this claim bespeaks the unnaturalness, the non-**physis** of the union per se. Christ is the union which is no-*phusis*.[16]

* * * *

The "doctrine of the *oikonomia*" (i.e., an orthodox doctrine) is offered in substitution, a substitution or displacement which is not complete. For the "doctrine of the *oikonomia*" attempts to cover over, to disguise, that which can not be traced in the creed but which is necessary for the creed to cohere and for the de-cree to be authoritative.

In the metaphysics of the creedal document, that which is not metaphysical is illegible. That is, the gathering of the opposites (God and man) in their differentiation is not legible given the dominance of metaphysics and the sovereignty of the emperors. Despite the dominance of metaphysical thought in the document (at the pleasure of the Emperors), what is illegible is nevertheless traced in the text as that which has been displaced by the play of signs. Markings are traced in the text which are not metaphysical. Yet, given the metaphysical preoccupations of the document, those non-metaphysical marks which are nevertheless traced, can not be read. In the *textus* of the document, the "logos", the "gathering," the union of God and Humanity in Christ persists as a conundrum, a fault, unthought, unreadable; a mystery which riddles the document as the "logos" which is not "legible."

The metaphysics of the creed, despite its surreptitious substitution and displacement which conceals, nevertheless serves to disclose its own metaphysical and de-creed limits.

USES OF *OIKONOMIA* IN EARLY CHRISTIAN THOUGHT

Prestige points out that Tertullian and Hippolytus attempted "to produce a theological statement which would reconcile monotheism with the acceptance of the divine triad."[17] The "economy," the unity of the Triad, is constituted out of its own inherent nature,[18] the nature of the divine unity in its own interior organization. Prestige remarks:

> the divine economy is not an economy of redemption, nor an economy of revelation, but an economy of divine being.[19]

Prestige points out that in Hippoclytus' significant trinitarian writings, "the primary sense of economy is obviously that of coordination distinction in the **being** of the godhead."[20] In other words, economy is "the internal relationships and systematized co-ordination of the whole godhead."[21]

"Economy" served as a term to bespeak the unity of things which fail to unite forthrightly. For by its discretion an economy is able to establish a unity which goes so far as to reconcile two conflicting theological convictions: that there is *only one divinity* **AND** that there are *three divinities*.

To explain this "slight of hand" or poor addition, Reumann details the use of *oikonomia* by the Stoic rhetoricians. He contends that *oikonomia* was employed by Stoic rhetoricians prior to the emergence of christianity, but it was with the second century A.D. revival of interest in oratory, and following, that its usage is most clearly evident, particulary with the connotation of "arrangement" which is purposeful and at times deceitful.

As we have noted, *oikonomia* was commonly employed in Stoic ethics to denote an "arrangement of one's actions in accordance with inner intentions and purposes, involving a degree of feigning and dissimulation at times."[22] Thus, an "economic action" was an "accommodation," a means by which to accomplish something else.[23]

It is obvious to say at this point that the synod was an "economy". In one sense, the synod by its creed "dispensated," it was the "means" and the "system" of "governing the divine." The synod "judiciously handed doctrine." And, second, the synod did so as a means of accommodating the command and pleasure of the Emperors.

We have suggested that within the creedal document the *oikonomia* bespeaks the unity of God and humanity, but also the supposed unity of God and the Emperors. Both are complex unities which do not resolve into a sameness. The former is complicated in the text by the failure of "the doctrine of the *oikonomia*" to *present* itself in the creed. The latter is complicated by the questionable accommodation by the church to the powers that be. But might not the text be even more "complicated" than it appears?

By the time of the Synod, *oikonomia* was often employed in theological works as being in opposition to *theologia*. An *oikonomia* was regarded as "the structure, arrangement, or proportion of parts, of any product of human design," or in a wider sense, "the organization, internal constitution, apportionment of functions, of any complex unity." *Oikonomia* bespoke the complex unity of God and man in Christ, while *theologia* refered to the relationship of God and Christ in the Godhead.[24]

THE *OIKONOMIA* OF THE DOCTRINE OF THE *OIKONOMIA*

Might the accommodation of the Emperors by the council be understood **as** "an accommodation" by the council? as an accommodating of the powers-that-be (in the double sense of "the political powers that be" and (metaphysically) "the-powers-that-**be**"? That is, accommodation may be a contrivance, an act of diplomacy which in its accommodation conceals its purpose? In its ecumenical extension, by means of invocation and displacement, the surreptitious substitution, might not this accommodation, this *oikonomia*, serve another *oikonomia*? A hidden purpose which is nevertheless **secreted** in "the doctrine of the mysterious economy?" An economy which is hidden but nonetheless is disclosed in the text **as** concealed? An economy covered over by the domination of the Emperors and the surreptitious appropriation of metaphysics but evidenced by gaps and oppositions which disrupt the document and falter the exchange? Does the accommodation accommodate?

The "mysterious economy" is disclosed as a mystery, as a hidden agenda or purpose, by the evident economy of the text. The doctrine of the mysterious economy is that which can **not** be managed, dispensed or systematized in the Creed. It is a legal limit which must not be transgressed but a law which can not be traced.

G. W. H. Lampe points out that the two theological meanings of *oikonomia* (as "the method of the divine government of the world," and "the judicious handling of doctrine") had to do with God's providence as far as the church fathers were concerned.[25] As such, God governed the world "economically," accommodating human circumstances and conditions. For the church fathers, the "divine economy" was the transcendent God condescending to the world's limits. As such, the "divine economy" was a scheme, a strategy to accomplish divine purposes through the only means possible, i.e., the world. It was a means which always compromised the divine purpose. It was an economy which always sought to "conceal."[26]

Oikonomia As Concealment

Reumann calls this meaning of *oikonomia* its "shady meaning." And he argued that this "shady meaning" was acquired in the literary and rhetorical use of *oikonomia*. Reumann writes:

> Here as an arrangement in play or a speech, *oikonomia* could suggest a device which emphasizes expediency, or which makes the worse case appear the better, or which artfully conceals real intents, or which skillfully arranges dramatic details in a plot. Thus in rhetoric the word comes in the course of time to take on the meaning of expedient arrangement or material for stating and winning a case. Dionysius of Halicarnassus in the late first century B.C. called *oikonomia*, or the arrangement of subject matter, the most artful part of rhetoric, because it conceals and implies and generally makes one's case as strong as the facts allow--stronger, sometimes, if the practitioner is capable enough!--and he himself allowed all sorts of tricks as part of the process.[27]

In popular speech, when applied to "household management," *oikonomia* suggested shrewd, sharp actions. In rhetoric, it was a type of arrangement which reshuffled the facts and would by means of a host of tricks and devices, gloss over difficulties with the intent of persuading hearers to one's cause. In ethical application *oikonomia* suggested a clever, calculating ordering of one's actions in order to achieve an interior or ulterior, often unexpected purpose.[28]

In each instance, *oikonomia* bespeaks some manner of "concealment." In each context, *oikonomia* names an activity which **conceals one's purpose**, the value of some item, the weakness of one's cause or position.

We have noted that the common meaning of *oikonomia* as method, system, dispensation and management, rests upon the interplay of *nómos* and *nomós*. As such, I have suggested that "the doctrine of the mysterious *oikonomia*" is an "illegible law," a law which, in not being traceable in the creed, is concealed by the metaphysical theology of orthodoxy. However, the domination of *nómos* in the compound *oiko-nomia*, given its interplay with *nomós*, does not account for the sense of "concealment" prevalent in a host of applications of *oikonomia* which we have identified as its "shady meaning". I suggest that this "shady meaning" of *oikonomia* implies a subtle movement within the compound, a subtle movement which subverts the domination of *nomós*.

We have noted that *nomós* meant "hold, possess, inhabit, and even, dwell." These meanings might present a problem. For it might be suggested that a compound of *oîkos* and *nomós* is little more than a redundancy, playing upon the similarity of "house," "dwell," "inhabit," and the like.

But there is a difference.

Nomós, *nomadic*, pasture bespeak an "open" domain in which one lingers but for a time. The dominant spatial metaphor is of "openness" or even "randomness."

Oîkos on the other hand meant a "house," "shelter," "an abode;" or it designated a part of a house, "a room," or "chamber." An *oîkos* was a dwelling, a concealment in which things and people were gathered and sheltered against the wider world, against all that was not concealed. As such, *oîkos* and *nomós* are an opposition.

Oîkos--Nomós
Concealing--Opening
Selective--Random
Gathered--Dispersed

Heidegger has reminded us of the interplay of "dwelling" in *oîkos*, "house," and "tabernacle," suggesting that this interplay can not be limited to an active or passive voice.[29] "Dwelling" is not the abode per se, that is the "container" (passive) in which we "do our dwelling" (active). To dwell is more of a middle voice occasion. Dwelling **occurs**, as it were. This middle voice sense of "dwelling," which is the occasion for (active) dwelling in a (passive) dwelling, is played out by Heidegger in the meaning of Tabernacle.

"To dwell" meant to gather together. The Tabernacle was the "tent of meeting" in which God met with Moses and Israel.[30] The "tent of meeting" was the place of dwelling in which those who struggled with one another "meet."[31] The rival siblings of Israel, the twelve tribes of Israel, meet in the tent of meeting. The tabernacle was not a permanent structure. It, too, wandered. It wandered with the people in their years in the wilderness between the Egyptian exile and their return to Canaan. And after the tribes (re-)inhabited the lands of Canaan, the tabernacle wandered among the tribes, staying with each tribe for a set time before it was taken down, carried to another tribe's *nomós*, and there re-constructed. The tabernacle was the *oîkos* of the tribes of Israel. Thus, the "meeting place" in which the tribes of Israel gathered passed from tribe to tribe.

The history of Israel is a history of rivaly between the sons of Israel and the twelve tribes they fathered. Rarely united as one, the tribes were often in contention one with the other, and often collections of tribes would stand in opposition to other collections. The tabernacle--in this history of rivalry and contentiousness--was the meeting place of all the tribes. The tent of meeting was the gathering place of those who stood in opposition. To tabernacle, to dwell, to assemble, to meet was an occasion in which those in opposition dwelt together under one cover.

In the tent of meeting, under cover, hidden from the world at large, hidden from the light of day, God revealed God. In the concealment is disclosure. Undercover Yahweh uncovers.

The *oîkos* was the place of gathering in which those who are in opposition with one another, were assembled undercover, tabernacled. In this place of "concealment," gathered in their opposition, Yahweh discloses. In so gathering, their nomadic character finds terminus for a time. Thus in their sojourn, in their *nomós* they find *oîkos*, shelter, cover, home, for a time.

* * * *

The "doctrine of the mysterious *oikonomia*," the position that the *phusis* of God and humanity are themselves and yet are one in the *oikonomia*, is an absurdity in the metaphysical theology of the Chalcedonian Document precisely because the doctrine is itself "shady." The Chalcedonian Document assumes that the doctrine of the *oikonomia* accomplishes the "uniting" of the natures of God and humanity. But the mysterious *oikonomia*, in concealing, hides how it does what it does, and why.

As such, the mysterious *oikonomia* may be said to accommodate the Imperial Church for its own reasons. While the accommodation may be said to lead to the domination of the

Emperors in christendom as "divinities" whose "peace" violates and seeks to erase all other divinities and peaces, nevertheless, in the mysterious *oikonomia* these differences are recalled and preserved. We have also seen the rather strange way in which the doctrine of the incarnation works a two-fold accommodation. On the one hand, the doctrine accommodates the desires of the Emperors to rule christendom. We have traced how in the creed Marcian and Valentinian Augusti manipulated and came to dominate Christian faith, setting the legal limits of grace, and the penalty for disrupting the peace.

However, the paristic relationship is not so simple. True, the Imperial Church was instituted as an instrument to serve the desires of the Emperors, but the church also in turn fed upon the worldly power and authority of the Roman Empire. The accommodation accommodates a "divine economy" as well.

In hiding how it accomplishes what it does, the mysterious *oikonomia* conceals its difference from metaphysical theism. In its "shade," under its "cover," "hidden from view," differences are gathered and preserved. The *nature* of God and the *nature* of humanity are "gathered and preserved" in the "mysterious *oiko(s)-nomia*." And this "gathering" in which God and man are said to be one is the one who saves. The *oikonomia* is Christ. But this *oikonomia* is no *physus*. It does not enjoy metaphysical reality and therefore is not available to metaphysical epistemology. Thus, within the creed, within the limits of orthodox Christian thought, the *oikonomia* **is not "real" and can not be "known".**

THEOLOGY'S CONUNDRUM

Christian orthodox theology sought to distroy all competing affections, beliefs, and ideas by asserting the sovereignty of one God which then accommodated the Imperial rule by means of metaphysical thought.

The power of monotheism plays upon images in which unity and oneness exercise a strange control. Differences serve the power of monotheism so long as they are subsummed into some movement of unity, some wholeness.

> This kind of power (the power to consolidate and control) is found in a play of images in which unity and oneness exercise a strange control though subsumption of differences into a wholeness of will and law.[32]

However, the movement towards oneness **must** overpower all difference. What differs must be assimulated into the greater whole (suppressing differences) or be annihilated. Monotheism is and has been an extremely violent god. It, or, better, he is unforgiving of infidelity. The one-God (monotheism) promises unity and wholeness, world order and human well-being as ultimate values over against polytheism, disunity and absence of being.[33]

Causal Confusion

The Doctrine of the Incarnation, despite its metaphysical pre-occupations, does not offer an account of causality. In fact, the doctrine of the mysterious incarnation differs from the various doctrines judged unacceptable by the council in that they offer causal account of God, Christ and the world (humanity) while the orthodox position offers an account of God, Christ and world/humanity which is not causal.

It is an irony of Christian theology that the existence of God is defended by orthodox theologians with causal argument while orthodox christology is defended as non-causal. It might be argued that the difference is that the causal arguments for God are concerned with creation while the non-causal account of Christology is concerned with redemption. But there are various problems with such a division. First of all, if christology is non-causal because it is concerned with redemption, then wouldn't it follow that what is being redeemed is the causal relation? And if such is the case, then is christology to be understood as a non-causal event which serves causality? That is, the incarnation serves to restore the causal connection. But such a possibility is clearly rejected in the creed. Christ would be the divinity who mediates God's activity into the world. While such a position has its antecedents in both the biblical, theological and philosophical traditions, such a position is rejected by the council. Such a position would render Christ a second order divinity who is neither God nor human but **between**.

Despite the use of metaphysical language, the creed attempts to trace a thought that is non-metaphysical. One would expect the creed, if it were a coherent metaphysical document, to present a coherent account of causality. But it does not. The physis of God and the physis of humanity relate not as events in a causal system, but as differences which are gathered and maintained as differences in a non-causal gathering which has no physis.

It is surprising that the creed does not state, let alone suggest, who is "responsible" for the "economy." That it occurred is clear. However, in the Chalcedonian Creed no agent is named as the initiator of the economy. It appears to have just "happened."

In order for Christian onto-theo-logy to come to be, logos and physis were divided. The separation of logos and physis is clearly visible in the doctrine of the *mysterious economy*. What we discovered in our detailed reading of the creed is that the *logos*, the *mysterious oikonomia*, is inconceivable given the epistemology of metaphysics. For in the creed, *physeōn* are knowable, but how *physeōn* are together is not traceable, and is unthinkable. In other words, the *phusis* of the creed, in its permanence, its permanent presence, disallows "thinking" and thus renders *logos* as gathering inconceivable. Metaphysics conceals that which is not metaphysical.

As such, the tension and therefore the unity of *phusis* and *logos* is destroyed. The tensive/unity, the *logos* of "*phusis* and *logos*" is lost in the coming to domination of meta-physis in its perpetual manifestation.

(SUPER) NATURAL THEOLOGY AND UN/NATURAL CHRISTOLOGY

God and humanity are natural, each has a physis. They have substance. They enjoy reality and can be known. We might go so far as to say that while God and humanity are both natural, the *phusis* of God exceeds the *phusis* of humanity. God is super natural. Humanity is simply natural.

And Christ, the Incarnation? As the mysterious economy, Christ is not simply the *phusis* of God nor the *phusis* of humanity. But neither is Christ **both** the *phusis* of God **and** the *phusis* of humanity. *The mysterious economy is neither natural nor super* *natural.* The Chalcedonian christology is un/natural. It is a gap which is no *phusis*, which in its absence invokes the ground which is no ground, the order that is not present, which nevertheless grounds and orders the definition of the faith. The mystery of the incarnation is an "aporia," a difficulty, a question, for which the Synod is at a loss. "Incapable" of resolving the conflict, "unable to **manage**" the strain, or solve the riddle, the Synod contends that the incarnation is incomprehensible because Christ is unnatural. Christ is no *phusis*.

As we noted earlier, *oikonomia* was used by many early church fathers to bespeak how it was that the Christian faith could be said to be "monotheistic" and yet have more than one divinity (including Christ and/or the Holy Spirit). The use of *oikonomia* in the creed belies the fundamentality of "mono-theism" in orthodox Christian theology. The mysterious *oikonomia* conceals its difference with metaphysical theism because as a "divinity" which "gathers and preserves" the natures of BOTH "God" and "humanity," *oikonomia* threatens the sovereignty of Christian orthodox "monotheism".

Oikonomia is subversive of the **powers that be**, both the political powers-that-be (the Emperors and the Imperial Church) and the onto-theo-logical powers-that-be. It is a subversion which "accommodates," "conceals," "hides," "shelters," and "gathers" differences in violation of law and order and in definance of reason and reality.

The *oikonomia* thus **accommodates** in the sense that the *oikonomia* gathers and **shelters** God and humanity. God and humanity--in their differentiation--are nevertheless "home" in the *oikonomia*. There is a sense of "return" in that God and humanity "belong" together under the cover, in the shelter of ***oiko(s)**-nomia*.

Earlier, we wondered whether we would find inscribed in the authoritative texts of orthodox Christian theology marks which efface the text and mark the limits of metaphysics' coherence and sovereignty. Clearly we have discovered such marks in the doctrine of the incarnation. The Chalcedonian Creed traces its own limits, effaces its own coherence and sovereignty, thus bringing itself to closure.

Within the Chalcedonian Creed a limit of the ætiological drive for *causa sui* is traced within orthodox Christian theology. The doctrine of the mysterious economy, the **christ**ology of orthodox **Christ**ian **theo**logy, marks a limit of **Christ**ian **theo**logical reflection.

Many things were at stake for the old church fathers in their renunciation of the doctrine of the *logos* by Heraclitus. In one sense orthodoxy itself was at stake. What would have become of the emerging institution/Imperial church if a language of difference rather than a language of identity had dominated Christian self-understanding and thought? Lacking a preoccupation with a language of presence/reality, how would orthodoxy have been perpetuated, let alone generated? Clearly such questions suggest other paths of study and inquiry which are beyond the limits of this thesis. Nevertheless, one of the things at stake was the coalition of forces which subsidized the emerging institution.

One other thing at stake not listed above, but an important feature in the coalition of forces was the emergence of theology, and in particular, **monotheistic** theology. As we have seen, Christian mono-theism accommodated and is accommodated by the mysterious economy. Given its subversiveness with respect to the sovereignty of Christian orthodox **mono-theism**, and its absurdity with respect to the **meta-physics** of orthodox Christian theology, we might wonder why the "doctrine of the mysterious *oikonomia*" is present at all in the ecumenical document of Chalcedon? Possible answers to that question will present themselves in the chapters to follow.

CONCLUSION

THE FOUR-FOLD AND THE DOCTRINE OF THE MYSTERIOUS ECONOMY

The suggestion by Orr and Taylor that the four-fold play traces incarnational themes was true in ways neither anticipated. The mysterious economy of the *phuseon* of God and humanity, and the two-fold play of god(s) and mortals, discloses a difference which is said to be "holy." It is a holy difference which does not fulfill ætiological desire for a *causa sui*. The aspects (God and humanity, gods and mortals) together or individually are not the cause of their togetherness. Gods and mortals, God and humanity, are together without good reason being offered for why or how they are. In both the economy and the four-fold, causality dysfunctions. Ætiological desire for causal connection can not be satisfied.

The four-fold names as holy the coincidental gathering of opposites. In the doctrine of the mysterious economy the holy coincidental gathering of opposites is said to be the one which atones. In other words, Christian salvation is the a/t-oneing of God and humanity in the economy.

POLYTHEISTIC/PANTHEISTIC IMPLICATIONS RECONSIDERED

As we can now conclude, the judgments and/or warnings that the religious implications of Heidegger's thought are pagan by virtue of its pantheistic, or polytheistic implications are not so much wrong as they are unfounded.

Jonas charged that since Heidegger wrote of anticipating the return of the gods or the other gods, and of the two-fold play of gods and mortals in the four-fold, that such an explicit polytheism is pagan. However, as we have seen in our study of the doctrine of the mysterious economy, in particular, and the Chalcedonian Creed in general, the assumption that Christian thought is monotheistic is never clear nor final.[34] In the doctrine of the mysterious economy, not only are there two divinities, but each is different--fundamentally different--from the other. God is natural and Christ is--with respect to nature or *phusis*--unnatural and a mystery. The **two** are different: they are not the same.

However, Jonas' condemnation of Heidegger is not directed so much at the polytheistic implications of his work as it is directed at the explicit pantheism or at least the pantheistic implications of Heidegger's work. Jonas charges that since Heidegger speaks of worlding's four-fold play as "the holy," then Heidegger is a pantheist. And, since pantheism is not monotheism, and therefore not Christian, the implications of Heidegger's work mark him as outside Christian thought. But Jonas has failed to note that christology in Christian thought calls into question the metaphysical identities and division of God and humanity (or God and the world). And in terms of the orthodox doctrine of the mysterious economy, God and the world are said to be in an un/natural union. The metaphysical categories of "God" and "the world" are preserved. They are not confused. And yet, their un/natural union is held to be orthodox Christian belief.

In his condemnation of Heidegger's polytheistic and pantheistic implications, Jonas has wrongly assessed the limits of traditional Christian belief. Our study of the Chalcedonian Creed has made it clear that such assessed limits are wrong.

Without regard for the assessment that the implications of Heidegger's work is beyond the limits of Christian thought, is it the case that his work is polytheistic or pantheistic? Clearly the former assessment is self-evident in the texts.

However, in charging that the religious implications of Heidegger's work yields a pan-theism, Jonas has equivocated Heidegger's talk of "worlding" with the metaphysical category of "the world." Traditionally, pantheism is the metaphysical position that the world is God and God is the world. As such, causality cannot be traced back to a *summa ens* **outside** the world. The world is its own cause, its own God/creator. But as we have seen with respect to Heidegger's work, causality is not a feature of the four-fold. Rather, worlding is a coincidence of the four-fold. And as such, worlding is a middle voice occurrence which enjoys neither an active nor a passive voice. Gods and mortals, sky and earth occur together, and this coincidental (non-causal) opposition is said to be holy. If this is pantheistic then it is a very strange pantheism that fails to offer ætiological explanation.

NOTES

1. *OED*.
2. E. Schwartz, ed.*Acta Conciliorum Oedumenicorum* (Berlin and Leipzig: De Gruyter; 1914ff), Tom II, Vol. 2, Par 2, 12 (104). I have found no earlier evidence of such a practice with respect to the Chalcedonian document though it certainly seems possible that the exchange of the terms might be found in the Fathers.
3. "Definitio Fidei Apud Concilium Chalcedonense," line 69. Bindley, 192.
4. As in the lines "some dare to corrupt the mystery of the Lord's incarnation for us," "those who attempt to corrupt the mystery of the incarnation," and "those who presume to rend the mystery of the incarnation."
5. Klein, 498.
6. In the *Collectio Novariensis de re Eutychis*, dating 458. (Joannes Doiminicus Mansi *Sacrorum Conciliorum Nova et Amphlssima Collectio.* 7: 111-114), the Greek term *Enanthrōpēsin* is rendered *inhumanationeum* in Latin,, and *oikonomias--dispensationis*.
7. Klein, 451.

8. J. H. Reumann, *The Uses Of 'Oikonomia' And Related Terms In Greek Sources To About A.D. 100, As A Background For Patristic Application*, (Dissertation: University of Pennsylvania; 1957), 529. Reumann summarizes his study by proposing that *oikonomia*, as it was employed in Greek thought up to and including the church fathers, may be gathered into four (4) families. He writes: "*Oikonomia* and its related terms occur in Greek sources: 1. In the sense of household management--the ordering, administration, and care of domestic affairs within a household; husbandry which implies thrift, orderly arrangement, frugality, and is, in a word, 'economical....' 2. Applied by extension to *the management of a larger household*--the ordering, administration, and care of: a. *an army or military matters*--'arranging an army' with regard to supplies or for battle; therefore also 'conduct of operations' and 'disposal, distribution of spoils'; b. *a city or political affairs.* A parallel between an estate and a city-state is implicit here, though the political unit in question may range from a city to an empire. Especially, since the term often had commercial or business connotations, with reference to *financial affairs or administration....* Applied to *specific titles in governmental administration....* Also used for officers *in guilds, social organizations, religious groups, and the temple administration* of the Sarapis cult; out of this type of application comes the later ecclesiastical usage, the *oikonomos* in a congregation or monastery, and 'diocese' for an administrative division. 3. Applied by further extension, literally or metaphorically, to *arrangement in general*--management, ordering, direction, or regulation in various specific areas, including: a. *legal arrangements* of many types... also, for the *record or document itself* involved in these transactions: 'deeds,' 'documents for land transfer.' b. *the arrangements of the body or of life generally....* c. *arrangement of materials in the arts*, e.g., in architecture--'arrangement,' 'wise management,' 'disposal of supplies' (*dispersatio*)...; *especially in literature*--of a play, 'production'; or the arrangement of a letter, or a book, or *of history...* regularly in the scholiasts, for 'plot,' 'dramatic arrangement,' 'device'; *and in rhetoric*, sometimes with the added notion of purposeful and *deceitful arrangement*--'economic order,' the arranging of material with an idea of expediency; 'ordering' of material to cover weak arguments with stronger ones; thus in later rhetoricians, 'expedient arrangement' (*dioikasis*) and 'artificial arrangement for a purpose' (oikonomia), in contrast with natural, chronological arrangements (*tazis*). d. and even the *arrangement* of one's *conduct*, again according to inner purposes and sometimes with a deceitful or shady connotation--'the execution of an inner intention'; thus, actual policy in accord with inner purposes, while external conduct may be covered by feigning. Such usage leads to the later sense of 'accommodation' and 'economical behavior.' 4. Applied by ultimate extension to *the management of the largest 'household' imaginable, the universe*--therefore the arrangement, ordering, regulation, direction, or management of the cosmos ... by nature or by God, especially with reference to providence. A parallel between the state and the world is here assumed" (490-494).

9. *OED.*

10. Liddell & Scott, 1179.

11. Charles E. Scott, "Heidegger And The Question Of Ethics," (Graduate Invitational Lecture, Third Annual Lecture, Vanderbilt University Graduate Department of Philosophy, April 9, 1986), in *Research In Phenomenology* (Fall, 1988) 18: 24.

12. J. Derrida, contends that an "'economy of death' is the forgetting and deferral of death in the infinite repetition of the sign, a repetition which reproduces the same without concern for, and thus forgetting the other, any other." "Violence and Metaphysics: An Essay on the Thought of Emmanuel Levinas," *Writing and Difference*, Translated, with an Introduction and Additional Notes, by Alan Bass (Chicago: The University of Chicago Press; 1978), 102.
13. Scott, *The Language of Difference*, 150.
14. Klein and *OED*.
15. *OED*. Latin *absurd-us* inharmonious, tasteless, foolish. From *ab-* off, here intensive plus *surdus* deaf, inaudible, insufferable to the ear.
16. Paul Tillich, one of the few contemporary theologians to catch this play of metaphysics and non-metaphysical themes, asserted that in order for Christ to be mediator and savior, then "It is inadequate and a source of false Christology to say that the mediator is an ontological reality beside God and man." *Systematic Theology* (Chicago: The University of Chicago Press, 1951, 1957, 1963), II: 93.
17. G. L. Prestige, *God In Patristic Thought* (London-Toronto: William Heinemann Ltd.; 1936; 2nd ed., London: Soceity for Promoting Christian Knowledge; 1952), xxv.
18. Ibid., 99.
19. Ibid., 106.
20. Ibid., 107. Emphasis mine.
21. Ibid., 108.
22. Reumann, 386.
23. Epictetus, Arr. Epict. Diss 3.14.7 "Of things which are done, some are done with an express purpose, others on occasion, others *kat' oikonomian*, others required by tact, and others in accordance with a formal plan." Reumann notes that C. R. Haines in the 1916 Loeb translation of Marcus Aurelius Antoninus' *Meditation*, renders *kat' oikonomian*, which is most commonly translated "by arrangement," in "for many things are done "by arrangement" (11.18.5) as "with an eye to circumstances." In the glossary he adds "Management, and so policy, expediency, adaptation to circumstances, ulterior end, secondary purpose, and even *finesse*" (Reumann, 411).
24. John Henry Cardinal Newman writes, "Thus it (e.g., *economy*) is applied by the Fathers, to the history of Christ's humiliation, as exhibited in the doctrine of his incarnation, ministry, atonement, exaltation, and mediatorial sovereignty, and as such distinguishes from the '*theologia*' or the collection of truths relative to his personal indwelling in the bosom of God. Again it might with equal fitness be used for the general system of providence by which the world's course is carried on...." (*The Arians of the Fourth Century* [Westminister, Md.: Christian Classics; 1968], 74 & 75).
25. G. W. H. Lampe, Ed. *A Lexicon of Patristic Greek* (Oxford: At The Clarendon Press, 1940), 940.
26. Reumann writes: "It has long been recognized that the word *oikonomia* has the meaning 'accommodation' in patristic application to moral conduct, especially often in connection with the exegesis of biblical passages where the actions of a patrairch or saint seem on the surface subethical; *oikonomia* here signifies an 'arrangement' which is of doubtful propriety on the surface but which is justified by ultimate purposes or factors, sometimes revealed only later on by God himself or the subsequent, inspired interpreter. This sense of 'economy' has been the despair of translators, and they have adopted a variety of English terms to get at the exact sense,

including 'discretion,' 'concession,' 'reserve,' 'act of policy,' 'connivance in sharp practice,' 'economical behavior,' and 'maneuver'" (587 & 588).

27. Ibid., 589-590.

28. Ibid., 595.

29. The term "house" enjoys a rich history. ME *hus*, *hous*, from OE *hus*, related to OS, ON, OFris, OHG, MHG *hus*, Du. *huis*, G. *Haus*, Goth *-hus* (in the compound *gudhus* 'temple' literally 'the house of God') originally meant 'shelter,' from Indo-European *gues-*, in which -s- is an enlargement of the base *geu-*, 'to cover, hide.' Klein.

30. In the Septuagint, *oikos* was consistently offered in translation for the Hebrew *bayith*, meaning "temple," and for *ohel* meaning "tent or tabernacle." It was on occasion offered for *hekal*, a "palace" (Joseph Henry Thayer, *A Greek-English Lexicon Lexicon of the New Testament: being Grimm's Wilke's Clavis Novi Testamenti; Translated, Revised and Enlarged* [Grand Rapids, Michigan: Baker Book House, 1977], 4th Edition, 441, entry 3624).

31. Israel means "one who fought with God."

32. Charles E. Scott, "Violence and Psyche: A Reflection on Images and Freedom," *Soundings* (Spring, 1985) 68: 44.

33. Scott, *The Language of Difference*, 44.

34. The issue for orthodox Christian theology of how it is that God is one when there are two if not three divinities bespeaks the inability of Christian monotheism to present itself clearly and fully.

PART TWO

THE LANGUAGE OF DIFFERENCE IN THE PAULINE *TEXTUS*

The Christological Closure of Patriarchal Theology

6

HERMENEUTICAL *TEXTUS*

INTRODUCTION

In terms of our inquiry into the end of metaphysics, it could be argued that at the beginning of Christian metaphysical theism, a limit of metaphysics is disclosed as the mysterious *oikonomia*. From the beginning the doctrine of the mysterious "dispensation" or "incarnation" marks the limits of metaphysical Christian theology. Metaphysics is not capable of "presenting" everything, and in this case, **the** central conviction of orthodox Christian thought, the *oikonomia*, is "aporetic."

In the chapters to follow, I will argue that the central conviction of orthodox Christian thought which can not be presented metaphysically in the Chalcedonian Creed is traceable in the "letters" of the predominate Christian writer of the first century. Further, I will attempt to show in my reading of the "letters" that what metaphysical (mono-) theism could not present in the creed--but had to incorporate as its limit (i.e., an internal limit is a gap)--was a different way of thinking about divinity, the acceptance of more than one divinity, and/or the belief that for Christians there is another divinity who was not subordinated to metaphysical theism.

The doctrines of incarnation as *enanthrōpēsin* and as *oikonomia* in the Chalcedonian Creed are said to be developments which are rooted in and true to biblical texts and church traditions. The two biblical passages which appear to be called upon most often to support these claims, mirror the differences in Greek terminology which we have already discussed. Clearly the theme of the *logos* becoming "flesh" in the "Prologue" of the Gospel of John is expressive of the divine *enanthrōpēsin*.

> And the Word became flesh and dwelt among us, full of grace and truth; we have beheld his glory, glory as of the only Son from the Father.
>
> John 1:14

The other verse which is claimed to support the incarnation actually appears to be expressive of the mysterious economy.

> In Christ, God was reconciling the world to himself.
> Or, God was in Christ reconciling the world to himself.
>
> 2 Corinthians 5:19

There is, at least on the surface, or better, on first reading, striking similarity between the *oikonomia* and *katallassōn* (**reconciling** in v 5:19). Just as the *oikonomia* bespeaks the oneness of the natures of God and man in Christ, the Pauline passage bespeaks God and the world reconciling in Christ. And in each instance (whether it is the *phusis* of God and the *phusis* of humanity, or God and the world) the two which are said to be "one" or "reconciling" are in opposition.

Both texts (John 1:14 and 2 Cor 5:19) are difficult to translate and to interpret. We'll not rehearse the difficulties we have encountered in the creed.

However, thus far, the difficulties which 2 Cor 5:19 presents have only been hinted at by its double-reading/translation. The difference between the two readings or translations of v 19 is a subtle play regarding the placement of "in Christ" and the relationship of the third person singular imperfect tense verb "was" (ἦν) and the participle reconciling (*katallessōn*). If we read the verb independently of the participle, we obtain "God **was** in Christ **reconciling**...." That is, one being was in another being restoring relations with yet another being. Reconciling occurs because of an assumed relationship of Christ and the world. God's action of "being in" Christ reconciles God with the world by virtue of the assumed intimacy of Christ and the world. Such a reading mirrors the Johannine "incarnation."

Furnish objects to this reading because "the idea of God's 'being in' Christ is not present elsewhere in Paul's letters, and (he further claims) an **incarnational emphasis** is not otherwise present in the context."[1] By "incarnational" I take it that Furnish means *incarnare*, a divinity taking on flesh and/or *enanthrōpēsin*, a divinity dwelling with or among humans, and **not the mysterious economy.**[2]

Furnish prefers "In Christ, God was reconciling..." reading the relation of the verb (an imperfect tense) with the participle to be an *imperfect paraphrastic construction* (so e.g., Revised Standard Version, Plummer, Bultmann, and Bruce).[3] A paraphrastic construction employs negation, passivity and/or inversion rather than constructing a sentence in a more forthright manner, i.e., positive, active and/or direct construction. As such, the contention that the grammatical construction of the verse is "paraphrastic" only hints at the issue. It is a hint Furnish, Plummer, Bultmann, and Bruce seem altogether unconcerned to explain further, but which we will later return to follow up. I will assume the reading preferred by Furnish, Plummer, Bultmann, and Bruce for reasons which will be presented later.

But we have gotten ahead of ourselves, or at least we have ventured into the Pauline corpus too quickly. If we are to catch the subtle play of opposition between God and the world, in the imperfect paraphasic construction, and understand the significance of the phrase "in Christ," then we must proceed in a less direct manner. In order to proceed, we will first turn to the issues relating to the sort of text we are reading when we read a Pauline epistle.

THE PAULINE TEXTS

The Pauline texts, while often the object of appeal for support to warrant a particular position, present the critical reader with a problem. Upon close inspection it is clear that on a number of issues or positions, a single epistle (let alone the entire corpus) contradicts itself. This complication might not be of interest, except that the conflicts or contradictions have to do with issues which are at the heart of the text and which play a significant role in Paul's christology.

One of these contradictions has to do with the status of women, or better put, the relative status of females and males in the Pauline texts. As we will see, gender differentiation is addressed in the Pauline texts in terms of "causality." And further, causality is consistently disrupted (as is the gender hierarchy) by "christology."

Traditional biblical readers assume that with regards to the status of women, Paul is forthright. Women are to be silent in church and subordinate to their husbands, if not to men in general. Critical readers are "critical" to the extent that they note the discrepancies between what the traditional reader chooses to select from the text and what the traditional reader chooses to leave behind. Critical scholars ask why some verses of the biblical texts which do not cohere or can not be woven into the pattern of church doctrine regarding the status of women, are ignored. Critical readers, returning to the collection of verses in the text, have noted the presence of verses which conflict with, even contradict, the traditional position that women are to be silent in church and subordinate to men.

> ...but, if any woman who prays or prophesies with her head unveiled dishonors her head--it is the same as if her head were shaven.
>
> I Cor 11:5

> ...the women should keep silence in the church. For they are not permitted to speak, but should be subordinate, as even the law says. If there is anything they desire to know, let them ask their husbands at home, for it is shameful for a woman to speak in church.
>
> I Cor 14:34-35

In the first passage (1 Cor 11:5) we note several things. First, it appears that Paul assumes that women pray or prophesy publicly, i.e., preach. Second, if a woman prays or prophesies with her head unveiled, she dishonors her head. And third, such dishonor is comparable to a woman shaving her head. Commentators are quick to point out that a few verses earlier in the eleventh chapter, it had been asserted that "the head of every man is Christ, the head of woman is her husband, and the head of Christ is God."[4] So, we would be instructed that the contention that an unveiled prophetic woman dishonors her head means that the unveiled woman dishonors her husband. The reason why an unveiled woman who speaks in church dishonors her head/husband, and that such dishonor is compared to a woman who shaves her head, is assumed by many scholars to be a reference to the temple prostitutes of Isis located in Corinth who served with shaven heads.

So, we have an explanation of the text. However, it is at this point, when we consider the second passage, that we note the complication.

> ...the women should keep silence in the church. For they are not permitted to speak, but should be subordinate, as even the law says. If there is anything they desire to know, let them ask their husbands at home, for it is shameful for a woman to speak in church.

Women should keep silent in the church.

How do we reconcile our reading of v 11:5 in which women are clearly assumed to pray and prophesy/preach with the passage at 14:34-35 which insists that it is unlawful and shameful for a woman to speak in church?

For the better part of the past century, critical scholars have puzzled over the significance of this (and other) complications in the text. Three types of interpretations have emerged. Some critical scholars have concluded that Paul forthrightly contradicts himself with regard to female participation in the epistle.

Other critical readers, not altogether pleased with the assessment that an author could be self-contradictory (let alone the author of a significant part of the Christian scripture), have sought to discern in the marks of the text, the presence of another author or authors. This position is called in biblical circles the "interpolation hypothesis." It has been assumed by those who propose the "interpolation hypothesis" that if a method can be found which will un-fold (i.e., ex-plicate) the process of interpolation, then the contradictions could be shown to be the result of differences between the authentic Pauline text and the writings of some later writer(s). Critical scholars would thus have the means by which to identify which verses of the text were Paul's and which the interpolator's. Usually such a commentator will resolve the apparent contradiction by asserting that one of the verses is authentic while the other is an interpolation.[5]

Still other critical biblical scholars have sought to understand the text by an analysis which would provide some larger frame of reference in which the contradictions are no longer contradictions but aspects of some extra-textual meaning. A common reading along these lines is that women will be able to speak in the kingdom to come (11:5) but must be silent in this world (14:34-35).

The purpose of our study of gender difference and status will be to provide the means by which we can adjudicate the critical claims that on the issue of female status (relative to male status) the Pauline epistles are self-contradicting, or mis-represented by editorial liberty, or coherent when viewed in the proper context. We will adjudicate these critical claims, and thus provide a coherent reading of these passages (11:5 & 14:34-35) without constructive appeal to any of the aforementioned interpretations. For the **problem** with the critical readings (and the traditional interpretations for that matter) have to do with their approach to the text, an approach which both critical and traditional biblical scholars share in common, and which we will identify and critique.

THE TEXT AS *TEXTUS*

> Etymologically, the text is a cloth: *textus*, from which text derives, means "woven."[6]

As Roland Barthes has reminded us, the term "text" comes from the Latin *textus* which is derived from the past participle (*text-*) of the verb *text-ere*, meaning "to weave, to plait, to fit together". A (Latin) *textus* or (English) "text" is quite literally "that which is woven or fitted together; a texture, structure; context."[7]

The history of interpretation has been dominated by a hermeneutic of "explication." To "ex-pli-cate" means literally to "ex-," ("un-"), "ply," ("fold"). In other words, to "ex-pli-cate means to "un-ply", to "un-twist". Thus, to "explicate" means to un-weave, to un-build. It has been assumed that the "meaning" of the text can be found by unraveling. As such, the process of finding the meaning is a-textual. So long as the text is text-ured, so long as the threads twist and fold and ply, the meaning of the text can be hidden from understanding. The task of the interpreter of texts is to ex-pli-cate, to un-fold, un-plait, un-twist, un-ravel the *textus*. Explicated, the unraveled text lays before the reader like strains of smooth/un-twisted threads. Lines/phrases/words/marks are un-twisted from one another and clearly "un-layered" before the reader. Such a text, a de-text-ured text, is said to be ex-plicated (literally, made level or plain.) A leveled surface lies before the examiner ex-posed (deprived of shelter, protection or care, i.e., abandoned), completely illuminated and present. An explained text is exposed without concern for the texture of the text, without concern for the shades and folds of the *textus*. An explained text is not sheltered from the light of inspection. Fully illuminated, the truth of the text is made present. **Nothing** is hidden. Or, to put it another way, "**everything** is illuminated" and "**no-thing** is hidden."

BIBLICAL A/TEXTUAL HERMENEUTICS

Paradoxically, traditional and critical biblical scholars, who are commonly understood to be at odds, both seek to *explicate* the text. Traditional readers, having un-woven the text in light of inspired illumination, have asserted that the meaning of the text is to be found by discovering those threads which pattern the beliefs or doctrines of the orthodox faith. Critical readers are "critical" to the extent that they note the discrepancies between what the traditional reader chooses to select from the explicated text and what the traditional reader chooses to leave behind. Critical scholars ask why some threads of the explicated biblical texts which do not cohere or cannot be woven into the pattern of church doctrine, are ignored or plucked out. Critical readers, returning to the pile of explicated ravelings from the text, have noted the presence of threads which conflict, even contradict one another.

I have said all of this to show that given the "hermeneutics of explication," biblical scholarship has come to be dominated by readings of the text which assume that the *textus* must first be unwoven in order that the meaning of the text might be unraveled.

The hermeneutics of explication produces (by extraction) a pile of unwoven individual threads which may then be compared and arranged accordingly (depending upon the task at hand). With respect to First Corinthians, explication of the text has led to the conclusion that the text is internally incoherent, or self-contradicting. Several of the threads from the text, when compared, are found to contradict one another, e.g., 11:5 and 14:34 & 35.

But what is extracted in this production is the *textus* of the text. And, given the recent and not so recent history of biblical hermeneutics, many of the unwoven individual threads which do not fit the pattern, are distracted, along with the *textus* of the text.

Biblical Text As Textus

Our inquiry into the *textus* of the text does not lead us to explicate the text, but to explore the weave, the patterns, the plaits, folds and twists of the text itself. Our task is to be sensitive to and curious about the inherent "texture" and tissue of the work. Our task is to feel, to see, and to hear the threads, words, moods, and patterns in the process of coming to presence and twisting into absence which play in the weave of a *textus*.

Our study of the *textus* of Paul's *First Epistle To The Corinthians* is not an endeavor in the hermeneutics of explication. An explicated text is no "text" at all. To explicate (literally, "to unfold, unplait, untwist") Paul's letter would necessitate un-weaving the *textus*. So unwoven, the explicated text would be de-texted, de-textured, made plain, smooth, flat, thin. Thus unraveled, the *textus* of the text would be destroyed, reduced to a heap of threads, a pile of trash.

Nor are we interested in first explicating the text in order to reweave a new text. Rather, we will seek to follow the tapestry, feeling and noting the weave, the plies, the craftsmanship in an effort to understand the text as texture, *teknē*, and *textus*.

In order to come to an understanding of Paul's writing on the issues before us, we will engage the text, not as a heap of individual threads with simple meaning, but as a tapestry whose texture and content produce a single context or work. We will study the weave of the text, how the text is woven. Thus, we shall attend, not to the single threads which have been removed from the text, but to the *textus*, the weave of the "sheets" or "plates" or pages of the text.

As we shall see, the complexity of the text and the apparently contradictory threads (contradictory to those who note that some of the lines/threads do not cohere with other lines/threads) which run through the weave will be better understood, will be better read, not by means of a method of explication, but by first attending to the *textus* of First Corinthians.

THE COMPLICATED WEAVE OF AN EPISTLE

What kind of texts are Paul's texts?

Clearly the Pauline texts are not the presentation of a story the way a gospel is. Paul is not "spinning" a sacred "yarn". Nor are the texts a collection of treatises on church doctrine or theology. The corpus of Pauline texts is a collection of "epistles" from Paul, to the Christian churches of Rome, Corinth, Galatia and Thessalonia.[8] An "epistle" (*epistola*) is a letter, a communication *between* persons who are absent from one another. Such written communication is composed of the "letters" or "characters" of the alpha-bet(a).[9] A letter belongs (i) to both the one who posts it and to those to whom it is posted, and yet, (ii) it enjoys an independence from those for whom it corresponds.[10] For an epistle may be "diverted" from its path and read by one for whom it was not intended. In what ways are the Pauline epistles (collected and edited into a corpus and, then, canonized as Christian scripture) "purloined," put amiss, diverted from their path, **prolonged** by being sanctified?[11]

PURLOINED EPISTLES AND AUTHOR-ITY

"To whom does a letter belong?"

To Jacques Lacan's question we might answer, "To those for whom the letter is a con-text." The letter is an occasion for exchange, or the exchange itself, an inter-subjective relation which expropriates the individual. An epistle is a tracing of the alphabet which in its play of signification traverses and marks the difference and the distance between those who correspond.

The prolonged existence and duplication of the Pauline epistles is an act of thievery. And try as we may, all attempts to discern the meaning of the marks of the epistles is an act of hermeneutic manipulation. Whatever hermeneutic we bring or find (to choose between the two is a false dilemma) in the text is nevertheless a manipulation. To inquire, as we are here, into the *textus* of the epistle, is to manipulate the text or to allow the hermeneutic to manipulate the reader, or to allow a certain reading (manipulation) of the text to occur. Such is not an appeal to some "original" or "authentic" meaning of the text, but a means by which to re-read the text differently. In our case, such a re-reading of the text will provide resolution for several significant quandaries or contradictions generated by critical explanation.

Paul's *First Epistle To The Corinthians* belongs to those for whom it corresponds, for whom it mutually addresses questions. And yet our very naming of the correspondences bespeaks their having been purloined--for the epistles are edited and entitled *First...* and *Second...* suggesting that the second is merely the second installment of a single exchange. However, Paul's *Second Epistle To The Corinthians* is significantly different in structure and style from the *First*. And, further, the *Second Epistle* concerns itself with a very different set of issues.

If the epistle is diverted from its course, what is the path, the trail which the letter traces? What is the letter's proper course? And for whom is the letter a communication?

We thus read a correspondence, which does not correspond with us. As such, we read the epistle without author-ity. The **author**(-ity) of the epistle is not simply the individual whose installment of the exchange we have before us. The **author**(ity) is plural--for all who participate in the exchange author the epistle.

The epistles are for us "literary". They are pseudo-letters to us. And as such, as "literary" (i.e., literally "letters" as characters) the texts are often read as simply "letters" abstracted from the *textus*, without authorial context. When we forget that the Pauline epistles lettered a correspondence, an exchange, we forget the sort of **text** (*textus*, weave) an epistle is.

THE WEAVE OF AN EPISTLE

"What kind of weave or ply is a correspondence?"

The term "ply" (meaning "fold, bend, or layer") has dropped from common use in the English language except in compounds or as a technical terms. We commonly speak of ply-wood (layered wood), com-pli-cate (from the Latin *complicare*, meaning "to fold together"), ap-ply (from the Old French *aplier* and Latin *applicare*, " to fold towards"), ex-plicate (Latin *explicare*, "to un-fold") and im-plicate (Latin *implicare*, "to infold, involve, entangle").[12]

In legal terminology, one "plies" the witness, soliciting response with persistent questions, petitions, etc. (*OED*). In nautical use, "to ply" is "to beat up against the wind, to tack, to work to windward." To tack, to ply, is a going to and fro between certain points. In other words, to ply in this usage is to traverse, ferry, and make passage.

To ply is also "to plaid, braid, interweave." Ply resonates with the Latin *plectere*, which cognates with the Old Indian *prasnah* ("wickerwork, basket") and the Greek terms *plekein* ("to plait") and *plokē* ("network"). As we saw earlier, how a text is woven, that is, the difference which is traversed in the twist, the weaving to and fro, the patterning, is the ply of the threads.

THE RE-PLY

The weave of the First Letter to the Corinthians, the ply of the *textus*, is a "*re*-ply," or re-weave.[13] In the literary sense, a "reply" is a letter which responds to questions, issues or the like raised by another.[14] It is the mutual addressing of issues, the mutual answering of questions, one to another.[15] The English term "reply" is derived from the Middle-English *replien* and the Middle-French terms *replier* and *reploier* meaning "to fold back, to bend back." The late Latin *replicane* also meant "to repeat."[16] Thus, as a military reply is a return of fire for fire, a literary "reply" suggest a return, measure for measure, like for like. In other words, a reply is "to echo" or "copy". To reply is to double, to fold back, to exchange, to repeat. It is a bending and folding back, a layering which may fold together (com-plicate) differences which become involved (im-plicated). In a legal sense a reply would be a "turning the ply back," to respond to persistent solicitation with *counter*-questions, *counter*-arguments, *counter*-petitions, etc.

Significant for our study is the play of "ply" and "re-ply" and the company of terms which accompany the play. A *diploma* was first a two-fold (once-folded) sheet. A diplomat carried an official diploma (a two-fold sheet) of authority (and possibly had a two-fold purpose in exercising such authority). Shipley notes that the Old English *plegan*, which also came to be our modern term "play," came to be the common Modern English term "ply." I'll not go into all the various uses of the term "ply;" they are too many and will not serve to ex-**pla**-in or ex-**pli**-cate the present thesis.

One use of the term that is important to our present discussion is the term "application," which Shipley contends comes to us by way of the French *appliqué*. An *appliqué* is a comply, compliant, or reply named for the blank sheet folded in a letter for responses, said to be included in early letters (by which I take it Shipley means early modern European letters). I have not investigated the possible link between early modern European letters with its blank sheet folded in the folded letter with the art of **diplomacy** and the taking of letters folded and sealed from one head of state by a **diplomat** to another head of state. No doubt such possibilities might be too per**ple**xing for our consideration. *Oxford English Dictionary* notes that the use of "ply" as "to fold," is rare except as it occurs in compounds. In becoming rare we have lost many of the figurative meanings of "ply." Earlier "ply" meant "to bend in disposition"; "to bend or be bent"; and "to yield or to be pliable." In all of these uses of the term, "to ply" suggests a reversal, which is in fact one of the rarer meanings of the term.[17] It is this sense of bending in reverse, "to ply," that we shall develop in the sense of "re-ply." It is the double meaning of "bending in reverse" and "re-sponse" that we shall use the term "re-ply" to interpret the letters of Paul of Tarsus. I will argue that the texts of 1 Corinthians "re-ply," reversing and responding. And further, I will argue that the first fold, the ply which Paul replies, is to be found in the *textus* of the text. The text is a diploma, a two-fold sheet which has been interpolated, either by Paul and his scribe, or by later writers, or by all. Either way, the text is textured, and its textus is that of a "reply" as in the French *appliqué*.

First Corinthians is a text whose lettering traverses the difference between Ephesus and Corinth, Paul and the Corinthian church. It is a text which **plies** the distance and thereby **ferries** the dialogue. The ply of a dialogue, like the lawyer's ply of a witness, is complicated. 1 Corinthians is no simple weave. It is not simply the text of Paul's correspondence **TO** the Corinthians. For in Paul's ply to the Corinthians, in his lettering to them, are traces of their lettering to him. Their ply is woven into his ply, which is his re-ply.

Understood as a reply, we will find woven into Paul's letter to the Corinthian Church the ply, the *textus*, from their correspondence or reports to him, as well as other texts which are called upon to warrant the positions he takes up in reply to a question by the Corinthians. We must keep an eye open or an ear cocked to see and/or hear those places in the text in which Paul might be quoting from or paraphrasing an argument or issue from the Corinthian correspondence to him. Such quotes or paraphrases run counter to his proposal. Paul's replies will mark a difference with the plies from Corinth. To engage 1 Corinthians without a sensitivity for this texture of the text may lead the reader into mistaking what the Corinthians have written and Paul has traced as Paul's writing (i.e., positions). That is, such a reading may lead the reader to forget that the text has a certain texture.

Hurd has noted that within Paul's epistle there are various terms which indicate that Paul is replying. The most common indicators are "now concerning" (*peri de* and *peri gar*) and "do you not know" (*ouk oidate oti*).[18]

Given centuries of reading and study, it is to be expected that the Pauline epistles would have become familiar--common place--assumed. And in that familiarity, in the text's becoming obvious, we have become insensitive to its internal *textus*, its internal intertextuality. The edges of the seams of the various pieces which form the "epistle," have been worn with age and are so frayed that we no longer sense the various edges within the text. The epistle is like a well used patchwork quilt. We no longer see the pieces of a patchwork or feel the seams of the various patches. Instead, the quilt is felt and seen as a whole. So, the epistle text now reads smoothly--without a hitch or bump. The content is assumed to facilitate, to be without seam, for the seams have been leveled off by the fraying of dogmatic interpretation and familiarity.[19]

As we re-read the text, we will note the common indicators of quotations, paraphrase or response. However, as we shall see, there are other more subtle marks in the text which alert the reader to the presence of the Corinthian correspondence to Paul or reports from Corinth. The use of particles in the text mark such texturing. But also, the failure of an argument to flow, or the actual presence of contradictory claims being made within the text are good indicators that there are quotations or paraphrases from the Corinthian correspondence in the reply. If one reads the text, having forgotten the texture of the text, having forgotten the kind of text a letter is, one will misread the text/*textus*.

Tensions At The Seams

> [10]I appeal to you ... that all of you agree and that there be no dissensions among you, but that you be united in the same mind and the same judgement. [11]For it has been reported to me by Chlóe's people that there is quarreling among you, my brethren. [12]What I mean is that each one of you says, "I belong to Paul," or "I belong to Apol'los," or "I belong to Ce'phas," or "I belong to Christ." [13]Is Christ divided? Was Paul crucified for you? Or were you baptized in the name of Paul?
>
> I Corinthians 1:10-13

Having discerned the complicated weave of a reply in First Corinthians, we now read the text as textured by the plies and replies which are woven together. In the above passage we are also introduced to another complication of the text. The traces of the Corinthians' ply in Paul's reply are not of one mind. There are divisions in the church, which are at odds with one another, as well as with Paul.

Since F. C. Baur, it has been common for biblical scholars to identify one of the significant divisions in the church which Paul addressed as the "Judaizers," or **legalists**, who insisted that the church conform to Hebrew legal codes. Another division, the "gnostics" (also called the "freedom party," "proto-gnostics," "individualists," etc.) have been identified since Lutzert. There are other less formidable divisions addressed in the correspondence as well. Such would include Paul's comments aimed at the wealthy in the congregation who were insensitive to the poor in their over-indulgence of food and wine at the eucharistic assembly.

Daniel Patte has provided a detailed analysis of the various conflicts woven into the Pauline corpus. Defining faith as "holding a system of convictions, or better, being held by a system of conviction...," Patte goes on to suggest that such a system of conviction imposes itself upon the believer as self-evident.[20] The conflicts within the Pauline texts (the apparent contradictions, etc.) are tensions between Paul's system of conviction (a meta-system of conviction), and the conflicting systems of conviction of the various factions.[21]

SUMMARY

In the struggle between Paul and the various factions, there is an encounter, an engagement, of the conflicting systems of conviction. The different semantic worlds are engaged in conflict. Their differences are disclosed in their "engagement." Thus, Paul binds himself to each faction in order to differentiate his thinking from theirs. In this sense, Paul's writing is "parasitic." Dependent upon that which he seeks to work against, Paul must first engage himself with that which he seeks to overcome. Mark Taylor reminds us that, "One is forever bound to, woven into, the frameworks that one struggles to subvert."[22]

Given what we said earlier about the *textus* of the text, the ply from the Corinthian church is itself not of one cloth. The weave of Paul's epistle is a patchwork which incorporates the bits and pieces of other texts into a piece which sewn and hemmed, hangs together.

Paul plies his way in the text weaving together the different factions the way one puts together an old fashion Tennessee patchwork quilt. Paul weaves to and fro, threading/stitching his way amid obstacles, traversing the differences--his differences with each of the factions and their differences with one another.

A reply, in folding back, in **counter**-ing, is an en-**counter** which creates a tension in the *textus*. The en-**counter** of **counter**ing places the fabric of the text in a strain. Raising counter arguments and posing counter questions in response to earlier arguments and questions raised by another is the con-*text* for struggle. To explicate the folds of the *textus*, to un-weave and reduce the text to its barest and thinnest threads which are no longer in tension with one another in the weave, is to violate the con-*text* of the text. To relax the struggle and overcome the "**countering**" is to negate the en-**counter**.

When the "Epistle" is read as a *textus*, a "weave," a "ply" which "letters" (corresponds to) another, plying and replying, writing and tracing, the sets of contrasting threads identified by critical biblical scholars no longer present themselves as contradictions, but are read as part of a complex and textual weave which hangs together.

NOTES

1. Victor Paul Furnish, *II Corinthians: The Anchor Bible; Translated with Introduction, Notes and Commentary* (Garden City, New York: Doubleday & Co., Inc.; 1984), 318. Emphasis mine.

2. If we read the verse "God was in Christ reconciling the world to himself" then Christ is the mediator of God's reconciliation, the one through whom God acts upon the world. This is a christological position not unlike that proposed by many of the Apologists. In keeping with the middle-platonism which was coming to dominate western thought at the time, the Apologists identified Christ as the *logos* which mediated between the *eidos* and the *kosmos*. In such a configuration, Christ is the subordinate divinity through whom the superior divinity accomplishes his plans.

3. See especially R. Bultmann, *Primitive Christianity In Its Contemporary Setting*, translated by R. F. Fuller (New York: Meridean Book; 1956), 162, and F. F. Bruce, *1 & 2 Corinthians* (London: Oliphants; 1971), 209.

4. 1 Cor 11:3.

5. Of course the issue of the criteria by which one assesses the authentic from the unauthentic verses is the product of an interpretation which assumes (in the first place) that textual coherence is the standard of authorial identity.

6. Roland Barthes, "From Work to Text," *Textual Strategies: Perspectives in Post-Structural Criticism*, ed. J. V. Harari (Ithaca: Cornell University Press, 1979), 76.

7. *Texere* cognates with terms such as Old Indian *taksati* (he fashions, constructs), *taksan* (carpenter) and *texna* (art); Old Slavic *tesla* (ax, hatchet); Armenian *t'ek'em* (I turn, wind, twist), Old High and Middle German *dahs*, and German *dachs*, and Dutch *das*. Klein contends that these terms share a common ancestry from the Indo-European base *tekht-* and *tekh-*, meaning "to build (of wood, i.e., to carpenter) or to weave." Klein concludes that, "The original meaning of this base probably was 'to plait, to twist." Klein, 1597.

8. The Old English term "epistole," from which we derive "epistle," was directly adopted from the Latin *epistola* which was a phonetic representation of the Greek term *epistolē*. An *epistolē* could be transmitted orally as well as graphically.

9. The English term "letter" was adopted from the Old French and French *lettre*, which was the phonetic descendants of the Latin *littera*. Thus, an epistle is the tracing of the letters of the alphabet in such a way as to form a text.

10. Adopted from the Middle Latin *cor-respondere* (*cor*--together, with each other; and *respondere*--to answer), the etymology of the word suggests that "to correspond" means "to mutually respond, the answering of things to one another."

11. Jacques Lacan, "Seminar On "The Purloined Letter," translated by Jeffrey Melhman, *Yale French Studies* 48 (Yale University: New Haven, Conn.; 1972), 38f.

12. Klein.

13. John C. Hurd, *The Origins of 1 Corinthians* (New York: Seabury Press; 1965), xii. Hurd notes that Charles H. Buck, Jr., introduced his students to the 1 Corinthian Epistle as "The Corinthian Reply." My use was arrived at independently from Hurd or Buck.

14. Immediately following the "greeting" and "salutation" (1:1-9), Paul writes (1 Corinthians 1:10-13):

> I appeal to you ... that all of you agree and that there be no dissensions among you, but that you be united in the same mind and the same judgement. For it has been reported to me by Chlóe's people that there is quarreling among you, my brethren. What I mean is that each one of you says, "I belong to Paul," or "I belong to Apol'los," or "I belong to Cephas," or "I belong to Christ." Is Christ divided? Was Paul crucified for you? Or were you baptized in the name of Paul?

In the verses above, Paul "quotes" or "paraphrases" from the Corinthians (v 1:12) and then returns a "reply" (v 1:13). Paul replies to those who have formed divisions in the church with three rhetorical questions, whose adversarial manner and sarcastic tone cut to the heart of each faction's position.

15. The occasion for Paul's correspondence is clearly visible in the text. His letter is a reply to (1) the reports he has heard about the church from Chlóe's people (v 1:11) and (2) to what he has read (v 7:1) presumably in a letter delivered by Stephanas, Fortunatus and Achaicus from Corinth (v 16:17). It appears that his replies to the oral and written reports recounting the situations at Corinth, were to be carried back to Corinth by Stephanas and company, whom he instructed the congregation to obey.

John C. Hurd, in a detailed analysis, attempts to discern (a) the material in 1 Corinthians written in response to the letter from Corinth, and (b) the material which deals with the word of mouth information concerning the church in Corinth. While I believe his criteria for the distinction is questionable, the distinction itself has no bearing upon our present study.

16. Klein. Shipley contends that "ply" is rooted in the Indo-European term *plek* (*Origins*, 320). *Plek* means to bend, fold; braid, twist, weave. *Plek* has two main offshoots. In one the letter "p," passing through phonetic transformations according to Grimm's law for labials, changes first to the letter "f" and latter to the letter "b". The "f" forms include such Latin terms as: *flectere*, *flexure*, *flex* (your muscles), *circumflex*, *inflexion*, *reflect*, and *retroflex*. Also *flask* (a bottle plaited around as now for Chianti wine) and *flax* (meaning its fibers woven). Shipley further notes that from the Germanic base *fol*, came the English fold, un-fold, mani-fold, re-fold, two-fold, three-fold, and so forth. From the "b" forms come the French *doublure* (doubled, with a lining), *double* and *double entendre* (French *double entente*) meaning "twofold meaning". The other offshoot, and the more common of the two, retained the letter "p". From the Greek Shipley notes a number of rhetorical terms, *ploce* (a weaving of repetitions through a passage), *symploce* (a combination of *anaphora* (repetition at the beginning of successive units) and *epistrophe* (repetition at the end)), and *anadiplosis* (folding back at the beginning of a unit which repeats the preceding end).

17. *OED*. 2.b "to bend in reverse."

18. Hurd provides lists of phrases which he and others take to be the presence of quotations from the Corinthians' letter to Paul or phrases quoted from the oral report(s) to Paul in his correspondence to the Corinthians. Hurd's study is too detailed and lengthy to be represented here. For our purposes, we will employ his comments which have to do with the general sense in which 1 Corinthians is a non-literary reply (that is, 1 Corinthians is a letter directed to a particular destination and is not written as a letter to serve some other purpose) which includes quotations from Corinthians (whether they be oral or written), and his remarks about a particular passage which is of interest to our study.

There are differences of opinion among Pauline scholars as to the extent to which the oral reports from Chlóe's people and the letter from Corinth are traced or paraphrased in Paul's reply. There is little or no argument that the phrase "now concerning" (*peri de*) is one way Paul addresses an issue or answers a question raised to him by the Corinthians. *Peri de* is most often regarded as a lead in to Paul's reply to the "letter" from Corinth as opposed to the oral reports. The phrase *peri de* appears six times in 1 Corinthians (7:1 & 25, 8:1, 12:1, 16:1 & 12) and twice in 1 Thess. (4:9 and 5:1). *Peri gar* is used once in Corinthians (9:1) (Hurd:65-74).

It is also commonly assumed that the negative phrase "do you not know" (*ouk oidate oti*) introduces a question which is "aimed at the Corinthians" (Hurd:85). The question usually addresses some point of general knowledge about the world or some particular knowledge about the Christians faith which Paul assumes the Corinthians should have known without their having to be reminded. But apparently, from the correspondence or the reports to Paul, it is clear that they in fact lack such knowledge. "Do you not know" is thus a lead into items about which they need reminding. Hurd contends that the phrase "do you not know" (*ouk oidate oti*) occurs ten times in 1 Corinthians and once in Romans.

19. I am of course playing with J. Derrida's sense of *bahnung* in "Freud and the Scene of Writing" (*Yale French Studies* #48:73). *Bahnung* is translated by J. Mehlman as frayage. *Bahnung* suggests the wearing down of the 'contact-barriers' which mark the seams between things. Fraying is the violent movement which wears down differences.

20. Daniel Patte, *Paul's Faith and the Power of the Gospel: A Structural Introduction to the Pauline Letters* (Philadelphia: Fortress Press; 1983), 11.

21. I will not attempt to justify Patte's approach, for that is clearly beyond the limits of this thesis. While I will at times disagree with his interpretation of a particular passage, I have pointed out his claim in order to aid our seeing the conflictual manner of Paul's epistles.

22. Taylor, *Erring*, 16.

7

DECENTERING THE ONE

INTRODUCTION

In our earlier study of the doctrine of the mysterious *oikonomia*, I proposed that the *oikonomia* disrupts the metaphysical theology of the creed because *oikonomia* bespeaks a non-metaphysical union of metaphysical entities. The mysterious *oikonomia* bespeaks a different divinity, or way of thinking divinity, which is at variance with and displaced by the metaphysical theism of the orthodox Christian mono-theism presented in the doctrine. As shown in our study of the uses of *oikonomia* in early Christian thought, the term was often employed to name the accommodation of mutually exclusive theological positions (i.e., monotheism and polytheism). Historically *oikonomia* was first used in this connection with the trinitarian controversy.

1 Corinthians 8:1-9 addresses the issue of the number of gods, and does so in terms of cosmological assessment. The Pauline epistles (being some of the oldest surviving Christian texts) are said by the defenders of Christian orthodoxy to substantiate the orthodox claim (i.e., a metaphysical claim) that Christian thought was unquestionably and steadfastly monotheistic from the beginning. Difficulties with expressing this fundamental claim in the centuries which followed were adverbial.

In the chapter to follow, I argue that Paul (1) rejects monotheism, (2) asserts that there are many gods and lords in the cosmos, and (3) that Christians believe in one god and one lord--two divinities--among the many.

THE CONTEXT OF CHRISTIAN THOUGHT

> [1]Now concerning meat sacrificed to idols: we are aware that "we all have knowledge." Knowledge puffs up, but love builds up. [2]If any one imagines that he knows something, then he does not yet know in the proper sense. [3]But if one loves God, one is known by him.[4]Well then, as far as eating meat sacrificed to idols is concerned, we are aware that "that no idol exists in the cosmos and no god exists in the cosmos, but one." [5]For even if so-called gods exist in heaven or on earth--as indeed there are many gods and many lords--[6]yet for us there exists only one God, the Father, from whom are all things and for whom we exist, and one Lord, Jesus Christ, through whom are all things and through whom we exist. [7]But not all possess this knowledge. On the contrary, some having till now been accustomed to idols, eat (the meat) as meat sacrificed to idols, and because their conscience is weak, it is defiled. [8]Meat will not bring us into God's presence. We have neither a disadvantage if we do not eat, nor an advantage if we do eat. [9]But take care that this power of yours does not somehow become a hindrance to the weak!
>
> 1 Corinthians 8:1-9

TEXTURE AND TENSIONS IN THE *TEXTUS*

The text has proven to be difficult reading for critical scholars. Within the text there are such sharp turns and reversals, even contradictions, that markings have been added in modern translations in an attempt to make sense of the content.

> [4]no idol exists in the cosmos and no god exists in the cosmos, but one."
>
> [5]there are many gods and many lords--

Parts of the text have been enclosed in parentheses or set off by hyphens in hopes of showing that when the phrases which diverge from the flow are read as parenthetical, then the text will somehow hang together. Why are such verses read as being parenthetical, spoken under the breath or written off the line? What is it about these verses that renders them somehow "in error?" And "in error" of what? I will argue that v 5 so radically diverges from the flow of the text that attempts to make it "fit" into the weave of the text by simply marking the verses as parenthetical comments fail.

John C. Hurd contends that vv 1-6 contains grammatical and substantive evidence which suggests the presence of the Corinthian letter to Paul in his reply. He notes several quotations in the Epistle from the Corinthian letter to Paul. The assertion (v 8:1b) "we are aware that 'we all have knowledge'" is immediately and definitely qualified by (v 8:1c) "Knowledge puffs up, but love builds ups."[1] Hurd also notes that the lines (v 4b & c) "that no idol exists in the cosmos and no god exists in the cosmos, but one" are similarly modified (v 8:5) by suggesting that they too are quotes from the Corinthian letter to Paul.

I suggest that we begin by considering the first three verses of the text. Having taken into account Hurd's non-controversial reading of vv 1-3, I believe we will receive insight into the *textus* of the controversial passages of vv 4-9.

The left margin contains those verses which trace the Corinthian ply to which the right is Paul's reply. Paul introduces the discussion with,

1Now concerning meat sacrificed to idols:

Corinthian Ply

1b we are aware that "we all have knowledge."

Paul's Reply

1cKnowledge puffs up, but love builds up. 2If any one imagines that he knows something, then he does not yet know in the proper sense. 3But if one loves God,one is known by him.

The text is clear and to the point because the *textus* has not been lost in the processes of translation, interpretation and production. It would be difficult to read "we all have knowledge" as the position Paul is seeking to put forth. The use of quotation marks by translators (markings not present in the ancient texts) suggest that they read the phrase "we all have knowledge" to be a slogan of a faction in Corinth. Paul addresses the problem of "meat sacrificed to idols," quotes the conviction of one faction in the church which asserts that "we all have knowledge" in order to call into question those who so value their knowledge.

The knowledge they have, the content of which is presented in v 4, is theological. **What they know is "God."** Paul's reply reverses the issue of theological knowledge by suggesting in v 3 that what counts is not that **we know God**, but that **we are known by God**. In other words, the knowledge that the faction claims to possess and assumes is "substantive" and "certain," is reversed and relativized by Paul in his reply. Such imaginings are not proper in the convictional world of the Christian community. The knowledge which the faction claims to possess leads them to believe that power comes from knowing something others do not know. Paul counters that such knowledge of God is not the same as being known by God. To the assertion, and therefore as well to the faction in the church which made the assertion, Paul replies with clarity. "Knowledge puffs up." The ply/re-ply structure of the text is obvious. The texture of the passage yields a coherent, understandable text.

PAUL'S RE-PLY TO MONOTHEISM

THE CORINTHIAN MONOTHEIST

> [4]Well then, as far as eating meat sacrificed to idols is concerned, we are aware that "that no idol exists in the cosmos and no god exists in the cosmos, but one." [5]For even if so-called gods exist, in heaven or on earth--as indeed there are many gods and many lords--[6]yet for us there exists only one God, the Father, from whom are all things and for whom we exist, and one Lord, Jesus Christ, through whom are all things and through whom we exist.

Verse 4a ("Well then," *oun*) reintroduces the theme of the larger text, retracing v 1a ("Now concerning meat sacrificed to idols"). This reintroduction of the theme at v 4a, like its counterpart at v 1a, leads into a discussion of positions taken up among the Corinthians. [4b]"We are aware that 'no idol exists in the cosmos' and [4c]'no god exists in the cosmos, but one.'" There is relatively little dissent among biblical scholars that v 4 includes quotes from the Corinthian letter to Paul. However, there is little consensus among biblical scholars as to the intent of Paul's inclusion of these quotes and their relationship to what follows in vv 5 & 6.

Regarding the relation of v 4 and v 5, Hurd contends that

> Paul **certainly** agreed with the twin principles... ("that no idol exists in the cosmos" and "no god exists in the cosmos, but one) ... yet by mentioning other "gods" and "lords" (in v 8:5) he modified and limited their absolute application.[2]

That is, on Hurd's terms, v 5 "modifies and limits the absolute application" of the tenets of monotheism presented in 8:4. Does Hurd suggest that Paul held a modified, less absolute monotheistic position, or that he refrained from a strict *application* of the doctrine of monotheism in real life situations? As we will see, I reject both interpretations and suggest instead that vv 5 and 6 so relativize the monotheistic positions of v 4 as to make them inconsequential.

Hurd is not the only one to stress that Paul "*certainly*" agreed with the basic tenets of monotheism presented in the text at v 8:4. Grant asserts that,

> It is hard to tell what Paul means when he accepts, even for a moment the existence of 'many gods and many lords.' Perhaps he carried over 'so-called' in his mind.[3]

Almost without exception, comments on the passage assert that Paul rejects polytheism either in favor of a strict monotheism or a qualified monotheism. Those who held the latter position pointed out that v 5 was as emphatic a qualification of the tenets of monotheism as Paul could have made as a Christian.[4] What debate there is on the subject (on this verse) has been limited to the above distinction. Either Paul held to a strict monotheistic position or a slightly qualified monotheism. Almost without question, it is assumed that Paul left unquestioned, unchanged, the assumed foundation of Hebrew faith and religion, i.e., monotheism.

The argument being made in v 8:4 is that if there is really only one god (*eis theos*) in the cosmos, then there really are no other gods, only *so-called gods*. If all the other gods are illusions, then meat sacrificed to the idols (*eidōlothutōn*) **is food sacrificed to**

nothing. Thus, those who know there is only one God and that all the many gods do not exist contend that they are free to eat meat sacrificed to idols since the meat has been offered to nothing.

> [5]For even if so-called gods exist, in heaven or on earth--as indeed there are many gods and many lords

First, while v 5 appears not to quote from the Corinthian ply, there is a hint at the beginning of the verse that Paul is paraphrasing the Corinthian ply. This para-phrasing is done in such a way that Paul has already begun to displace, to twist and reply the Corinthian positions. "[5]For even if *so-called* gods exist, in heaven or on earth..." repeats the position of v 4b that the many gods are idols which *do not exist in the cosmos*. But v 5a begins with "for even if" (*kai gar eiper*), which hints that what is to follow will limit the monotheism of v 4: "no idol exists in the cosmos, and no god exists in the cosmos, but one--For even if the so-called gods exist..." then....

With v 5b there are two significant changes. First, v 5b introduces a new term into the discussion. At v 5b the issue is addressed as being about the "many gods" and "many **lords**." In vv 4 and 5a, only "gods" and "god" are discussed. From v 5b through the remainder of the chapter, "gods" and "god" occur with "lords" and "lord." This shift in vocabulary as we shall see is not incidental for it serves to illuminate another theme in the discussion which will come to the forefront in Paul's reply.

There is also a significant shift at v 5b with respect to "the many." In vv 4 and 5a, other gods, other than the one, are called **idols** and are said to have **no existence in the cosmos**. They are **so-called** gods. With v 5b this demeanor towards "the many" is not only missing, but the verse appears to reject the claim that the many Gods (and many Lords) are not real. *"As indeed **there are many** gods and **many** lords...."*

For these two reasons, (1) a change in vocabulary marking the addition of a new term which continues through and therefore provides a context for the confession of v 8:6, and (2) the shift in attitude towards other divinities, I suggest the following reading of the text which pattern the ply/reply structure elucidated earlier.

Corinthian Ply

[4]Well then, as far as eating meat sacrificed to idols is concerned, we are aware "that no idol exists in the cosmos and no god exists in the cosmos, but one."

Para-phrase

[5]For even if so-called gods exist, in heaven or on earth

Paul's Re-ply

--as indeed there are many gods and many lords--

To the two-fold monotheistic claim that (i) there is one god and (ii) all other gods do not exist, Paul replies in v 5b that "indeed" or "in fact" *there are many gods and many lords.*[5] In reply to the theoretical monotheism of v 8:4, Paul reasserts polytheism.[6]

In the reply there is a hint that not only does Paul reject the theoretical monotheism of the Corinthian faction, but he also rejects in a subtle manner the metaphysical distinction between **so-called** and **real** gods (a point we will return to later). The contention that "there **are** many gods and many lords...." stands in opposition to the contention that "no idol exists in the cosmos." In Paul's reply the many gods and many lords **are not called idols**. But this subtle shift may not have anything to do with whether Paul believes that the gods and lords enjoy metaphysical or cosmic existence. As we shall see, he neither affirms nor denies the cosmic **existence** of the divinities. With v 6 and following, Paul's concern is with which gods and lords are "**our**" (i.e., Christians') god and lord. The difference is striking. Paul shifts the discussion from metaphysical speculation to a discussion of the convictional world of the Christian community.

THE PLENITUDE OF DIVINITIES

Having rejected theoretical monotheism in his positive reassertion of polytheism, Paul provides the con-*text* for his tracing of the primitive Christian statement of faith. With the context set, Paul begins to trace the confession of faith, "Yet for us...."

John C. Hurd stands virtually alone among biblical scholars when he "cautiously" suggests that at the beginning of v 8:6 ("yet for us....") Paul is asserting a "*henotheistic* sounding" position which must be understood as qualifying strict monotheism.[7] Hurd is "cautious" in his assessment because his suggestion, though historically and textually credible, runs contrary to the entrenched monotheism of mainline Christian thought.

Given Hurd's reading, it seems all the more likely that over against monotheism, Paul is asserting that Christian faith is not meta-*physical* belief in the illusionary *nature* of other gods, but is faith (i.e., conviction) in one god and one lord. Paul gives voice to, draws out, the conviction that this god and this lord are lord and god *for us* (i.e., of the Christian community). That is, Christian faith is not assent to some special metaphysical knowledge, but is a system of convictions for a community.

The issue for Paul, *contra* gnostics, *contra* legalists, is not whether one should believe in the one god or nothing (i.e., the so-called gods).[8] The issue for Paul is in which god and in which lord among the lords and gods will the Christian community believe.

One Lord and One God

The confession of faith traced at v 8:6 reads:

> Yet for us, there is
> one God the Father,
> from whom are all things and for whom we exist,
> and one Lord, Jesus Christ,
> through whom are all things and through whom we exist.

The confession is said to reach far beyond the present con-*text*. That it exists prior to the letter is probable, that it is pre-Pauline or originates with this or that community of faith or faction within the church at Corinth is a point of speculation. It is however clear that the confession is employed by Paul at this point in the epistle to stand in opposition to the monotheistic positions presented in v 4.[9] And the confession of faith is employed at this point in the epistle as an authority which will warrant what he will have to say later regarding the consumption of meat that has been sacrificed to non-Christian gods.

This confession is important to our present study because it becomes the basis for working out the developed creeds into which the detailed (and itself independent) christological expositions were inserted.[10] It is precisely the "independence" of the detailed christological expositions of the creeds, and how the detailed creedal christologies are different from the primitive confessions which will be addressed later.

Let us retrace the weaves of the text so as to better understand the con-*text* of the confession.

[1]Now concerning meat sacrificed to idols:

Corinthian Ply

[1b] we are aware that "we all have knowledge."

Paul's Reply

[1c]Knowledge puffs up, but love builds up. [2]If any one imagines that he knows something, then he does not yet know in the proper sense. [3]But if one loves God,one is known by him.

Corinthian Ply

[4]Well then, as far as eating meat sacrificed to idols is concerned, we are aware "that no idol exists in the cosmos and no god exists in the cosmos, but one."

Para-phrase

[5a]For even if so-called gods exist, in heaven or on earth

Paul's Re-ply

--[5b]as indeed there are many gods and many lords.

We have already noted how v 5a both continues the themes of v 4, and yet begins the shift, developing a tension in the text which is visible at v 5b. Paul's counter-proposal at v 8:5b serves to open up the closed convictional system of the strict monotheist, possibly to make room for the confession which is traced at v 6. In other words, Paul counters (v 5b) the strict monotheism (v 4) in order to allow for the Christian belief in two divinities, God the Father and the Lord Jesus Christ.

> Yet for us, there is
> one God the Father,
> from whom are all things and for whom we exist,
> and one Lord, Jesus Christ,
> through whom are all things and through whom we exist.

THE PROBLEM OF THE SHEMA

Robert Grant contends that the verse serves two significant theological purposes. First, it is an affirmation of faith in God, and second, it echoes the *Shema*. We will return to the former later, but first, the *Shema*.

It is not uncommon for biblical commentators to note the similarity between 1 Cor 8:6 and the *Shema*, recited in Jewish synagogues and written in the Hebrew scriptures at Deuteronomy 6:4. "Hear O Israel: Yahwey our God is one Yahwey."[11] It is commonly argued that this similarity is expressive of Paul's monotheism, assuming that the *Shema* was a call for Israel to worship the only God.[12] But Conzelmann points out that the *Shema* was a call for Israel to worship **their Lord and God, who was one**. That is, **Israel** had one God, not two or more.[13] The issue of whether the gods of other peoples were real was not an issue for the Hebrew people at the time (or before) of the writing of Deuteronomy. Later, monotheistic meanings came to be attached to the *Shema* as the dispersed Jews in gentile lands sought to distinguish themselves from other religions with their many gods.

While Grant's first point (that v 8:6 is an affirmation of faith in God) is correct, it is nevertheless incomplete. If v 6 is Paul's tracing of the *Shema*, it is retraced with a significant difference from the Deuteronomical text and its later monotheistic interpretation. For in v 6, Paul has clearly **divided** the "one Lord God" of the *Shema* into "**one** Lord" **and** "**one** God".

Whiteley notes that in Romans 10:13, Paul writes, "Everyone who invokes the name of the Lord will be saved."[14] That the term "Lord" here refers to Jesus Christ is made abundantly plain by what precedes at 10:9, "If on your lips is the confession 'Jesus is Lord,' and in your heart the faith that God raised him from the dead, then you will find salvation." The words cited in Romans 10:13 correspond exactly to the Septuagint translation of Joel 3:5 with the addition of the connective "for"; it has never been doubted that the words refer in Joel to Yahweh.[15] Thus, we have an example of Paul, taking verses from the Hebrew scriptures which bespeak the God of Israel, and transferring the attributes to the "Lord Jesus Christ."

Over against the strict monotheism of his own religious traditions and in opposition to various factions in the Christian communities, we find Paul attempting to rethink divinity in terms of multiplicity, free of the preoccupations with "oneness." Conflicting divinities, conflicting understandings of divinity, struggle in the writings of Paul, pulling at the seams and giving texture to the text.

This reading of the text, of course, runs contrary to the doctrinal traditions of Christian institutions. Robert Grant, unburdened by such things as a close engagement with the texts, or even a careful reading of pertinent critical studies, contends that 8:4-6 contrasts "idolatrous polytheism" with "Christian monotheism."[16] He proceeds to point out that 8:4-6 is a key New Testament "bridge" towards the later philosophical doctrines of God developed in the creeds.[17] But what he takes to be "key" actually has little to do with the confession of 8:6. What is taken to be "key" is "key" on Grant's terms precisely because later philosophical (sic) doctrines of God developed in the creeds "fit" or "work" with his "keys". But the issue Grant fails to raise is whether what **he** identifies as "key" is "key" in **Paul's** enterprise. And as I have argued, Grant's "key" is significant for Paul, but only in so far as it is the position he rejects at v 8:5. Grant's "key" turns out not to work with Paul. For what Grant takes to be a "key" is precisely that which Paul **rejects**. And what Paul rejects is later picked up, accepted and played out in the creeds.

* * * *

Given our reading of vv 8:1-6, it is evident that had Paul confirmed the strict monotheism of v 4, the two part confession of v 6 would have stood in contradiction to it. To first propose a position of strict monotheism, and then to contend that for Christians (1) all things come from God through (*di' ou*) the Lord, and (2) that we exist for one divinity (God) and through another (Lord) could not be understood as anything less than a contradiction. There are just too many divinities for such a position to be **mono**-theistic. And it is just as clear, that no matter how Paul could have framed the confession of v 8:6, the two-fold confession of one Lord and one God would be nothing less than blasphemy for a legalistic Jewish/Christian reader.

The Power Play of Knowledge

It is the issue of power which runs like a thread through the text. However, given the history of English translation and the transformations of western societies, the key terms which refer to "power" and "authority" are glossed over and hidden. The issue of power is blatantly expressed in vv 1-4, is disguised and displaced in vv 5b-7b by the standard English translations, but reappears in the final passages of vv 7c-9.

In vv 1-4, the knowledge that puffs up--that there is only one god in the cosmos and that the idols are so-called gods--is a power for those who possess it. For, by virtue of that knowledge, such persons are "free" to eat the meat sacrificed to an idol since such meat has been sacrificed to nothing.

What is implicit in vv 1-4, is made more explicit in the Greek in vv 5 and 6. Commonly translated "lord," *kurios* means "powerful one" or "authority."[18]

Para-phrase

[5a]For even if so-called gods exist, in heaven or on earth

Paul's Re-ply

--[5b]as indeed there are many gods and many lords--

Confession

[6]yet for us there exists only one God, the Father, from whom are all things and for whom we exist, and one Lord/powerful

> one/authority, Jesus Christ, through whom
> are all things and through whom we exist.

In other words, there are many *theoi* and many *kurioi* in the world, "yet for us there is only one *theos* ... and one *kurios*...." We have already touched upon the inter-dependency and relationship of the themes of "power" and "knowledge." Not everyone has the metaphysical knowledge referred to in vv 1-4. And those who lack such knowledge are weak. That is, those who do not possess such knowledge (who do not understand metaphysical monotheism as do the gnostics) do not have the ability (power) to distinguish between the "real" god and the "so-called" gods.

The significance of v 6 thus reasserts itself. In opposition to the **power** of "understanding metaphysical **theo**-logy," Paul repeats that,

> For us there is *one God*, the father,...
> and *one Lord/powerful one*, Jesus Christ....

Patte reminds us that,

> the technical terms 'rule,' 'authority,' and 'power' clearly designate 'enemies' (literally, "those in opposition") which keep human beings under their power....[19]

The "power" of metaphysical speculation stands in opposition (for Paul) to the "power" of Jesus Christ. As such, the "power" of metaphysical belief, exercised over against those "weak" in metaphysical knowledge is relativized by the "Powerful one/Lord" through whom the metaphysically powerful and the metaphysically weak live (as Christians).

This "relativization" is made clear in the verses which follows the confession of faith in v 6.

CONFESSION

> 6Yet for us, there is one God the Father,
> from whom are all things and for whom we
> exist, and one Lord, Jesus Christ, through
> whom are all things and through whom we
> exist.

Paul's Re-ply

[7]But not all possess this knowledge. On the contrary, some having till now been accustomed to idols, eat (the meat) as meat sacrificed to idols, and because their conscience is weak, it is defiled.

Paul's reply at v 7 re-plies the theme of knowledge introduced by the gnostic claim in v 1b ("we all have knowledge") and explicated in v 4. However, Paul's reply at v 7 **twists** the theme of knowledge, re-plying--doubling back upon--the gnostic claims of knowledge. The reply by Paul, "But not all possess **this** knowledge," is not a reference back to the theological and cosmological knowledge explicated in the Corinthian Ply at v 4. Rather, the knowledge that not all possess refers to the "Confession" of v 6. "For us, there is one God the father... and one Lord, Jesus Christ," accents the communal context and purpose of belief in contrast to the cosmic preoccupations of those who possess monotheistic knowledge and employ their cosmological knowledge to accentuate their own power. Those who possess cosmological knowledge assume that they are powerful. Their knowledge that the idols do not exist and that there is really only one God empowers them to eat meat sacrificed to idols without being defiled. Because they have such knowledge they may do as they please, presumable without regard for the opinions and/or judgments of others in the Corinthian Church who do not know as the gnostics themselves know.

Paul's reply is a double cut. First, Paul's reply at v 7 suggests that such cosmological knowledge **is limited, it is not all knowing**. "But not all possess this knowledge." Second, it is assumed by the gnostics that given the **superiority** of their knowledge, they have the power to eat the meat **as** meat sacrificed to idols without being defiled. Superior knowledge--yields superior power--yields a superior moral conscious. Thus, the gnostics have the power to participate in the natural world without being defiled.

Paul's reply is *mockingly sarcastic*. The cosmological knowledge of the gnostics is **not all-knowing** since it does not include the knowledge Paul intends to teach them. Thus, we see that the chain of superiority which proceeds from superior knowledge and yields a superior moral conscious is un-founded. Inferior knowledge thus yields an inferior power which in turns yields an inferior moral conscious. Thus, given that the gnostics are accustomed to eating meat **as** meat sacrificed to idols, are by virtue of their weakness--defiled.

Verse 7b is addressed to the gnostics. Only the gnostics are eating meat, and (on their own terms) they are eating the meat **as meat sacrificed to idols**. It is commonly assumed that Paul regards only the legalists as "weak" in his epistles. But as we see, the meaning of "weakness" is dependent upon an assumed meaning of "power," and vice versa. In this text, those who have a weak conscience are the ones who do not know as they ought to know, who eat meat **as** meat sacrificed to idols.

On the face of it, v 8 appears to be Paul's continued critique of the gnostics.

> 8Meat will not bring us into God's presence. We have neither a disadvantage if we do not eat, nor an advantage if we do eat.

However, the *textus* of the verse may be more complicated. "Meat will not bring us into God's presence" may have been a verse which the gnostics **employed** to justify their practice of eating meat sacrificed to idols. The authority of the verse at 8a may rest with Paul himself. "Meat will not bring us into God's presence" is a clear rejection of dietary rules. Verse 8a may be a paraphrase or a re-phrasing of something Paul said in reply to legalistic dietary regulations. Thus a comment taken out of its context and purloined from whom it was intended, is employed to justify gnostic claims to power. Paul's critique of the legalists exercise of power through dietary regulations is employed by the gnostics to justify their power. Assuming their knowledge that idols do not exist and therefore food sacrificed to idols is sacrificed to nothing, they might have then employed the verse "Meat will not bring us into God's presence" to further justify their freedom to eat meat sacrificed to idols.

With this *textus* in mind, then the remainder of the verse might be read as Paul's reply to the gnostic power play.

Corinthian Ply

8Meat will not bring us into God's presence.

Paul's Reply

We have neither a disadvantage if we do not eat, nor an advantage if we do eat.

The gnostics assumed that their eating meat as meat sacrificed to idols was to their advantage. The practice demonstrated their superiority in the Christian community. Paul's reply so undercuts the power of speculative knowledge that such knowledge is no longer capable of providing support in the factional struggle for control in the Corinthian congregation. Paul's reply provides the occasion by which those who counted themselves "powerful" are now regarded as "weak."

The remainder of the text continues Paul's elucidation of the relationship of the powerful and the weak as regards the eating of meat sacrificed to idols. While Paul's argument and final conclusion is clearly beyond the limits of this study, his conclusion does shed light on our present discussion. Paul's conclusion is that the Corinthians are to purchase and eat the meat of the market without regard to whether it has been sacrificed to other gods. However, if they are at table and the host/hostess makes an effort of pointing out that the meat they are about to eat has been sacrificed, then the Christian is to refrain from eating the meat. Refraining from the eating of meat sacrificed to idols has nothing to do with the divinities per se (Christian or otherwise) in Paul's argument. For **food per se** counts for nothing. One is to refrain (given the situation above) because it might suggest to the host/hostess that the Christian at table believes in the non-Christian gods.

Thus, if the gnostics concluded that Paul's critique of the legalists dietary regulations suggested that not keeping such dietary rules was superior, then they have failed to comprehend the intent of Paul's critique of dietary regulations. The issue is not whether keeping or not keeping dietary regulations is superior. Rather, Paul is calling into question the very play for power which such manners or practices institute.

PHUSIOI AND *OIKODOMEI*

Knowledge puffs up, but love builds up.
gnōsis phusioi, de agapē oikodomei

Earlier at the beginning of our study of 1 Corinthians 8:1-9, we glossed v 1c. We did so at the time, despite the favored status of the phrase in the interpretative corpus, to facilitate our inquiry of Paul's de-structuring of monotheism and his critique of theological power plays. Now, we are better prepared to appreciate the subtlety and the significance of his sarcastic (?) criticism of onto-theological knowledge.

Biblical scholars commonly focus upon the opposition of knowledge and love in the verse at 8:1c. Such established practice is substantiated by the repetition of the opposition at a variety of points in the Corinthian epistles. The most popular repetition of the opposition occurs later in the First Epistle.

> And if I have prophetic powers, and understand all mysteries and all **knowledge**, and if I have faith, so as to remove mountains, but have not **love**, I am nothing.
>
> **Love** never ends...as for **knowledge**, it will pass away.
> 1 Corinthians 13:2 & 8

I will not rehearse the various renditions of the theme in the hermeneutical corpus. Rather, I wish to shift our focus from the oppositional nouns in the verse to the verbs.

It is common practice to translate *phusioi* metaphorically as "puffs up" (as we have thus for in our study) or prosaically as "makes conceited." That knowledge "makes conceited" plays well with the themes of power which we have elucidated. However, to offer "puffs up" or "makes conceited" in translation of *phusioi* is to miss the cruder judgement Paul may be making of such knowledge. To translate *gnōsis phusioi* "knowledge puffs up" is to offer a gentler, more polite selection of terms for the action knowledge accomplishes. The stem *phusa* names a variety of ways air is collected and used. *Phusas* (plural) names "a pair of bellows" that collect and then force air into a stream. *Phusa* also names "a bladder; breath, wind, blast; jet (of fire); and bubble."[20] Thus, the common translation "knowledge **puffs up**" is incomplete. Yes, knowledge does "puff up." But it also "blows out." *Phusa* also names the "wind in the body," or as gentle Southern ladies of days gone by might put it, "the vapors." "**Knowledge breaks wind/gases/fartes!**" Knowledge is full of wind (*phusōdēs*).[21] Knowledge is just gas.

While the common metaphorical translation "puffs up" is correct though incomplete, and the more prosaic "makes conceited" adequately conveys the play of knowledge and power, both practices fail to convey Paul's crude humor and the judgement it levels at the gnostics.

> Knowledge breaks wind.... If any one imagines that he knows something--then he does not yet know.

In other words such knowledge is vacuous, empty and mere imaginings. This knowledge does not yield anything, not even feces, for it was just gas.

Paul's reply in vv 1c-3 undercuts what is most valued by those who possess onto-theological knowledge. They assume that their knowledge is substantive and certain. But note that Paul's reply does not assert that some other speculative knowledge is more substantive and/or certain. Instead, in the reversal from "knowing God" to being "known by God," such theological knowledge is deflated. What was "puffed up" has been "released."

Theological knowledge yields "conceit," "pride," "gas." In opposition to the yield of onto-theological knowledge Paul holds forth *oikodomei*. A compound of *oikos* (a term we have spend considerable time with) and *demō* (to build), *oikodomei* might be translated "builds house," "builds up (house)," "constructs domain," etc. Thus, we might translate *de agapē oikodomei*, "But love builds house," or "But love builds domain." It is customary to employ the metaphorical meaning of *oikodomei* as "to build up" in modern translations. When the verbs are translated metaphorically, the verse reads, "knowledge puffs up, but love builds up." A more prosaic translation might be "knowledge makes conceited (as in tears apart), but love builds." Or following our discussion above, we might render the verse, "Knowledge breaks wind, but love edifies." Edify is commonly understood in modern discourse as "to instruct or improve spiritually." The Middle English *edifien* is from the Middle French *edifier* which is from the Latin *aedificare*. An *aedes* is a temple or dwelling (from *des* and *dis*, meaning "dwelling"). With *-ficare*, "to make," edifies may be translated "To make dwelling," or possible, "to make temple." Given the communal struggles to which the epistle is a reply, the earlier English translation of *oikodomei* as "edifies" plays well. Knowledge makes conceited--knowledge tears apart in the contentious struggle for power--but love edifies--love creates holy community/makes temple.

Clearly we find in the text a critique of *meta-phusis*. The knowledge that distinguishes between real and illusionary gods yields *phusioi*. But, is there also a connection between the activity of love as *oikodomei*, the making of a place/space in which differences are not the occasion for contentiousness, and the mysterious *oikonomia* in which the opposites (God and humanity) are one?

CONCLUSION

THE *TEXTUS* OF 1 CORINTHIANS 8:1-9

1 Now concerning meat sacrificed to idols:

Corinthian Ply

1b we are aware that "we all have knowledge."

Paul's Reply

1c Knowledge makes wind, but love edifies. 2 If any one imagines that he knows something, then he does not yet know in the proper sense. 3 But if one loves God,one is known by him.

Corinthian Ply

4 Well then, as far as eating meat sacrificed to idols is concerned, we are aware "that no idol exists in the cosmos and no god exists in the cosmos, but one."

Para-phrase

5a For even if so-called gods exist, in heaven or on earth

Paul's Re-ply

--[5b]as indeed there are many gods and many lords.

CONFESSION OF FAITH

[6]Yet for us, there is one God the Father, from whom are all things and for whom we exist, and one Lord, Jesus Christ, through whom are all things and through whom we exist.

Paul's Re-ply

[7]But not all possess this knowledge. On the contrary, some having till now been accustomed to idols, eat (the meat) as meat sacrificed to idols, and because their conscience is weak, it is defiled.

Corinthian Ply

[8]Meat will not bring us into God's presence.

Paul's Reply

We have neither a disadvantage if we do not eat, nor an advantage if we do eat. [9]But take care that this power of yours does not somehow become a hindrance to the weak![22]

We have found that the passage commonly employed to warrant Christian orthodox metaphysical monotheism is in fact a detailed argument against the metaphysical monotheism of the gnostic faction in the Corinthian community.

As regards our thesis, we have found that the orthodox assumptions that Christian thought is monotheistic from its earliest texts is unfounded. And while we have yet to consider the identities and relations of *Theos* and *Christos*, it is nevertheless clear that (1) there are "two divinities" **for** the Christian community (according to Paul), (2) the Christian divinities are not assumed to be the only divinities (by Paul) and (3) the Christian divinities do not enjoy metaphysical privilege.

So, how are we to understand *Theos* and *Christos*? How are they related?

Verse 6 of Chapter 8, as we took note earlier, provides content to these questions. However, before we return to v 8:6, we will consider one other extended passage in 1 Corinthians which deals with such philosophical (metaphysical/cosmological speculation) and sociological (the use of such speculation to justify the domination of one faction over another in Corinth) issues.

NOTES

1. J. C. Hurd, *The Origins of 1 Corinthians* (New York: Seabury Press; 1965) 120-121. Hurd follows the standard practice of translating phusioi as "puffs up," as do R.S.V., N.R.S.V..
2. Hurd, 122. Emphasis mine.
3. Grant, "Gods and the One God," *JAAR* (1964) 32:34-40.
4. One exception to this interpretation of the text can be found in Daniel Patte's *Paul's Faith and The Power of the Gospel* (18-20). There he contends that what is in conflict in the text is not monotheism and polytheism per se, but whether "reality" is defined in terms of "existence" (ontology, which is the Corinthian view) or in terms of "power" (which is Paul's view).
5. Wendell Lee Willis is the only scholar I have found who contends that v 8:5b is Paul's qualification of a strict monotheism (*Idol Meat In Corinth: The Pauline Argument in 1 Corinthians 8 and 10* [Chico, California: Dissertation Series #68, Society of Biblical Literature, Scholars Press; 1985] 86).
6. Grillimieu writes, "But this *kyrios* (the sort of *kyrios* Christ is) is also described on the basis of a hellenistic cult-divinity--by means of a contrast. Christ is the **only** (emphasis mine) *Kyrios* set over against the 'gods' and 'lords' that are worshipped in the world (1 Cor 8:5f)" (Grillimieu, 16).

Grillimieu is mistaken in his claim that the text asserts a contrast between Christ as the **only** lord in opposition to the lords of the world. Such a claim has no textual support in 1 Corinthians 8.
7. Hurd, 122.
8. The common practice of distinguishing between gnostics and Jews is a poor division for there were Jewish gnostics, Jewish legalists, gentile gnostics and probably gentile legalists. Thus, I will name the factions who are in conflict in the Corinthian church, gnostics and legalists.
9. See R. A. Horsley, "The Background of the Confessional Formula In 1 Cor 8:6" *ZNW* 69:130-135 (1978); see also Hans Conzelmann, *1 Corinthians: A Commentary on the First Epistle to the Corinthians*, translated by James W. Leitch, edited by George W. MacRae (Philadelphia; Fortress Press; 1975), 144 fn 38, and Willis, *Idol Meat In Corinth*, 83-85.
10. Conzelmann, *1 Corinthians*, 144, fn 38.

11. Other possible readings are "... Yahwey our God, Yahwey is one," or "...Yahwey is our God, Yahwey is one," or "...Yahwey is our God, Yahwey alone."
12. Robert M. Grant, *The Early Christian Doctrine of God*, 5. Hereafter cited as *Doctrine of God*.
13. It would be fruitful for us to consider the possibility that the emphasis on the oneness of the Lord and God might be expressive of the need to call together the "names" of God for the Hebrews (of which there were many names) so as to unify the people by invoking one divinity.
14. Whiteley, 106.
15. M.T., Joel 2:32.
16. Robert Grant, *Doctrine of God*, 5.
17. It is sad to see such a prominent patristic scholar perpetrate a dogmatic reading of such a difficult text with not even a single note on the sea of critical studies on the passage. A sea of critical studies of which most would have challenged his forthright proposal into question on textual grounds alone.
18. *Kurios*, means I. of persons-- having power or authority over; II. of things-- decisive, authorized, legitimate or proper, also the fixed, appointed or regulated time. Substantive, *kurios* means master, lord, head of as in ruler or chief. *O Kurios* is offered in translation of *Yahweh* in the *LXX*. See Liddell-Scott.
19. Patte, 243.
20. Liddell-Scott. *Phusōdēs* translates "full of wind," while *phuskē* names the large intestine or a blister.
21. *Phusiōsis* is translated "inflation, pride, vanity." *Phusaō* also suggests in this connection "to cheat."
22. Translated "freedom" in the R.S.V., *exousia* means "power or authority to do a thing, resources". In other words, (cap)ability.

8

RE-PLYING THE GENDER HIERARCHY

GENDER DIFFERENCE IN 1 COR 10:31-11:16

[10:31]So, whether you eat or drink, or whatever you do, do all to the glory of God. [32]Give no offense to Jews or to Greeks or to the church of God, [33]just as I try to please all men in everything I do, not seeking my own advantage, but that of many, that they may be saved.

[11:1]Be imitators of me, as I am of Christ. [2]I commend you because you remember me in everything and maintain the traditions even as I have delivered them to you. [3]But I want you to understand, that the head of every man is Christ, the head of a woman is her husband, and the head of Christ is God. [4]Any man who prays or prophesies with his head covered dishonors his head, [5]but any woman who prays or prophesies with her head unveiled dishonors her head--it is the same as if her head were shaven. [6]For if a woman will not veil herself, then she should cut off her hair; but if it is disgraceful for a woman to be shorn or shaven, let her wear a veil. [7]For a man ought not to cover his head, since he is the image and glory of God; but woman is the glory of man. [8](For man was not made from woman, but woman from man. [9]Neither was man created for woman, but woman for man.) [10]That is why a woman ought to have a veil on her head, because of the angels. [11](Nevertheless, in the Lord woman is not independent of man nor man of woman; [12]for as woman was made from man, so man is now

> born of woman. But all things are from God.) 13Judge for yourselves; is it proper for a woman to pray to God with her head uncovered? 14Does not nature itself teach you that for a man to wear long hair is degrading to him, 15but if a woman has long hair, it is her pride? For her hair is given to her for a covering. 16But if any one is disposed to be contentious--we have no such custom, nor do the churches of God.[1]

TENSIONS IN THE TEXT

This text has been a bothersome passage for critical biblical scholars for some time. Wayne A. Meeks refers to the text as "one of the most obscure passages in the Pauline letters..." while Moffatt contends that the text contains a multiple argument that is somewhat incoherent.[2]

William O. Walker, Jr., asserts that 11:2-16 is a post-Pauline interpolation which does not fit either in its placement in First Corinthians or as an internally coherent passage in the Pauline corpus.[3] Murphy-O'Connor, replying to Walker's assessment, is quite correct when he asserts that

> such surgical solutions will continue to be proposed as long as we lack a convincing demonstration of the internal coherence of this passage. To a great extent the failure to perceive the force of Paul's *logic* has been due to a misunderstanding of the problem he was facing.[4]

Robin Scroggs writes:

> In its present form this is hardly one of Paul's happier compositions. The logic is obscure at best and contradictory at worst. The word choice is peculiar; the tone, peevish.[5]

Both Scroggs and Murphy-O'Connor are of the opinion that the obscurity or incoherence of the text is expressive of our misunderstanding the problem to which the text is addressed.[6]

I am not all that sure what Scroggs means by, "the **logic** is obscure at best and contradictory at worst." Maybe what he meant was that how the text "coheres" is obscure, or that the text "doesn't cohere," which is only a restatement of earlier observations.

Hans Conzelmann, in his monumental work *1 Corinthians*, more than once ponders the apparently contradictory relationship of the first section of the text (vv 2-10) with vv 11 & 12, in what he identifies as "Paul's *developing* argument."[7] I question Conzelmann's assessment that the text is a "developing argument" for reasons which will be made clearer below. The apparent contradictions in the text are not the occasion for a developing argument, but **are contradictory positions** in the text, a text which, nevertheless, hangs together.

Elizabeth Schüssler Fiorenza regards the passage as "a very **convoluted** argument, which can no longer be unraveled completely...."[8] As we shall see, the argument **is** convoluted, "folding in curved or tortuous windings" to such an extent and in ways that I suspect Fiorenza never anticipated.[9] Thus, *contra* Fiorenza, in order for the text to be understood, it must **not** be "unraveled." In fact, it calls for quite the opposite. *Being concerned with the convolutions of text is the means by which the textus makes sense.*

Daniel Patte contends that in both "the Jewish and Hellenistic systems of convictions women are viewed as having a subordinate status to men...."[10] Thus, given the inferiority of women in relation to men within these systems of conviction, women will have limited rights within Jewish and Hellenistic social institutions. However, warns Patte,

> If our discussion of Paul's convictional view of idolatry is correct, we can expect that Paul would have an ambivalent attitude toward these traditions which belong to idolatrous systems of convictions. He would want to affirm a part of these traditions as fundamentally true, but he would want to reject another part of these traditions as resulting from the absolutization of this truth which makes out of it an idolatry with a power of bondage resulting in a preversion of the relationship between men and women.[11]

Patte argues that the power of the gospel in Paul's faith serves to relativize all systems of conviction which absolutize themselves. Thus, the Christian convictional pattern according to Paul via Patte is a meta-system which calls into question the ultimazation of all systemization. Christian faith occurs in the tension between competing systems of conviction which the gospel both calls together and cuts apart. Thus, Patte suggests that, "In 1 Cor 11:2-16, Paul affirms the traditional view of the subordination of women to men...," and "...in 1 Cor 11:11 & 12 Paul expresses how this subordination is redefined 'in the Lord'."[12] Patte concludes that Paul affirms that women must be veiled when praying or prophesying because (in agreement with the Jewish and Hellenistic traditions) in Christ men have authority over women in that they are the first in relation to God and are thus a more direct image and reflection of God. However, those men who are believers must recognize the authority of women by seeing them as preceding them (which is also in accord with the Jewish and Hellenistic traditions stated in the passage). Patte contends that for Paul, the male believers

> should have toward women the attitude they have toward Christ. This is not a paternalistic attitude; indeed, it considers women as better than themselves. In women, men discover Christ-like manifestations of God. And thus women are in turn in a position of authority over men.[13]

In other words, Patte's reading of the passage suggests that Paul does not disagree with the Jewish and Hellenistic systems of conviction per se. In fact, on Patte's terms, Paul simply elucidates the subtle points of the order of causality and authority that he shares with all concerned. And this elucidation of the subtle points calls into question the "power of bondage" which results in the perversion of the relationship between men and women.[14] We might conclude that the incoherence of the text is the conflict between competing interpretations of a common system of conviction, or at least the incoherence of the text is generated between competing **systems** of conviction which hold a common conviction about causality and authority.

Regarding Murphy-O'Connor and Scroggs' concern for discerning the "logic" employed by Paul, we will come to see that what they no doubt took to be logically obscure was how the text itself cohered. The ply/re-ply of the *textus* is what I take to be the "obscure logic" **of** the text. However, in a way they did not expect, I will argue that Paul employs an obscure "logic" **in his** argument which will be more apparent to us as we come to understand the *textus* of the text.

SOURCE AND RULER: THE GENDER HIERARCHY

The first section of the text begins with the presentation of a hierarchical cosmology which ranks "God," "Christ," "man," and "woman," in descending order. Assuming the hierarchy, the text thus proceeds further to elaborate the relationship of men and women, and to draw certain conclusions as to the proper head attire for women when they participate in worship. The hierarchical text, 11:3, reads,

> But I want you to understand that the head (*kephalē*) of every man is Christ, the head of a woman is her husband, and the head of Christ is God.

Two standard interpretations of *kephalē* (head) in v 3 dominate the critical discourse of the passage. One position is that the Greek term *kephalē* carries the meaning of the biblical Hebrew term *rosh*. The term *rosh* means the "head" of a group or society. Thus, the Greek term *kephalē* (as the translation of the Hebrew term *rosh*) suggests that God is the "ruler," the one who dominates Christ, man and woman. We will label the *kephalē/rosh* configuration to be the "domination interpretation." So, in terms of the "domination interpretation," the hierarchy reads,

> God is the **ruler** of Christ,
> Christ is the **ruler** of man,
> Man is the **ruler** of woman.

The other position contends that with respect to this passage, the Greek *kephalē* is not to be understood in terms of the Hebrew *rosh*. John P. Meier writes:

> Rather, we have here a later Hellenistic use of *kephalē* with metaphysical overtones. The idea of "source" or "origin," especially the origin of something's existence. A chain of sources and emanations is being set up. God is the source of the Messiah, since the Son comes from the Father and is sent into the world by Him, to do His will. Since the Son is God's instrument in creation (a Jewish-Hellenistic Wisdom-motif reflected in 1 Cor 8:6), the male is created immediately by Christ, and so proceeds directly from him.[15]

Given the metaphysical interpretation, the hierarchy reads,

God is the **source** of Christ,
Christ is the **source** of man,
Man is the **source** of woman.

With the "domination interpretation," God is the "ruler" of all, and woman is the "ruler" of **nothing.** Given the "metaphysical interpretation," God is the "source" of all, and woman is the "source" of **nothing.**

We will not attempt to adjudicate this controversy. For as we shall see, neither translation/interpretation of *kaphalē* as "ruler" or "source" dominates the text. Each is presented and elaborated in the text. And together, they interact in such a way as to suggest that the hierarchy is cosmic, both in terms of its ranking, and in terms of its scope. What is central to our study of the text is how the "ruler" and "source" translations/interpretations are played in the *hierarchy itself*. What concerns us is the identity and ranking of "God," "Christ," "man," and "woman" which is played out in terms of "rule" and "source."

Assuming the hierarchical cosmology of v 3, vv 4 through 10 proceed to address the issue of proper head attire for men and women when they participate in worship.

> 4 Any man who prays or prophesies with his head covered dishonors his head, 5 but any woman who prays or prophesies with her head unveiled dishonors her head--it is the same as if her head were shaven. 6 For if a woman will not veil herself, then she should cut off her hair; but if it is disgraceful for a woman to be shorn or shaven, let her wear a veil. 7 For a man ought not to cover his head, since he is the image and glory of God; but woman is the glory of man.[16]

The passage is incoherent at several levels. Or, the passage is convoluted and textured with various tensions pulling in various directions. The most blatant incoherence in the passage occurs between the claim that "man is the image and glory of God" and "woman is the glory of man." In the hierarchy of v 3, God and man are separated by Christ:

God
Christ
Man
Woman.

Christ and man, and man and woman, however, are immediately related. Verse 7 suggests that man has some special relationship to God, who is one degree removed, while woman has no special relationship to Christ though she is also separated by only one degree. The verse would cohere if it were consistent with respect to ranking and relation. If the verse read "man is the image and glory of God, and woman is the glory of *Christ*," or "man is the image and glory of *Christ*, and woman is the glory of man," then v 7 would emulate the hierarchy of v 3.

Verses 8 and 9 offer a summation of the status and relationship of men and women given the hierarchical cosmology.

> [8](For man was not made from woman, but woman from man. [9]Neither was man created for woman, but woman for man.)

Both readings of *kephalē* in v 3 are suggested in vv 8 & 9. Verse 8 contends that man is the source of woman and not vice-versa. Verse 9 asserts that woman was created **for** man, i.e., woman was created to be ruled by man, and not vice-versa. The section concludes that

> [10]That is why a woman ought to have a veil on her head, because of the angels.

As we have seen, vv 2-10 are the presentation of an argument for the veiling of women in worship based upon a hierarchical cosmology. The verses form a solid text, moving in a sense from a major premise (v 3), a minor premise (v 6) to a conclusion (v 10). However, v 11 begins rather oddly.

> [10]That is why a woman ought to have a veil on her head, because of the angels. [11]*Nevertheless....*

With the beginning of v 11 we are led to anticipate a shift. And in fact, vv 11 & 12 shift so completely from the flow of the text which proceeds it, that many modern translations have marked the verses as parenthetical. What is it about vv 11 & 12 that they should be marked as parenthetical? As we saw above in Chapter 7, v 8:5b was also so marked. In a sense their being written as standing in error has to do with the thesis of this study. We will return to the issue of why these verses are troublesome and are read as parenthetical later.

> [11](Nevertheless, in the Lord woman is not independent of man nor man of woman; [12]for as woman was made from man, so man is now born of woman. But all things are from God.)

In v 11 it is asserted that in the Lord, man and woman are co-dependent, and in v 12, that man and woman co-originate from one another, each in its own turn, but that all things are from God.

Meier writes;

> At this point, even Paul begins to fear that he may have gone too far, or at least been too one-sided, in stressing women's subordination. In vv 11-12, without taking back what he has said, Paul stresses the other side of the coin, the indispensable role of woman. If it was true in v 8 that, at the beginning, woman came out of man and not vice versa, it is also true in the natural course of birth today that a man comes into this world through a woman. Thus, one does not exist without the other--first in the order of creation, and *a fortiori* "in the Lord" (v 11).[17]

Conzelmann contends that "the transition with *plēn* (RSV "Nevertheless") marks a note of **retreat**."[18] Assuming that vv 2-16 are the straightforward presentation of an argument, Conzelmann contends that with v 11, Paul appears to first "retreat" from the position taken in vv 3-10, and then "crassly contradict" what he has written in v 8 with v 12a. Yet, no explanation for this apparent self-contradiction or change of heart or mind is offered in the text.

On Conzelmann's account, we are led to believe that somehow Paul held **both** (1) a speculative hierarchical structure (in which God is the head of Christ, Christ is the head of man, and man is the head of woman) **and** (2) asserted the co-dependence/co-origination of man and woman in the Lord.

Conzelmann is right in some regards and in ways he did not anticipate. But he is wrong in his view that the hierarchy Paul held was the speculative cosmological hierarchy of 11:3.

Conzelmann accounts for Paul's holding to mutually exclusive positions by suggesting that Paul is motivated by some "inner tendency." The inner tendency is expressed in his construction of a speculative hierarchy (v 3) which, for some (unknown) reason, Paul immediately abandoned (vv 11 & 12). Why Paul should write in such a way is beyond Conzelmann, unless perhaps Paul is giving expression to his conviction that the order of creation (the hierarchical order) is overcome in Christ (the relational order). According to Conzelmann, Paul begins with a discussion of the order of creation and then radically shifts the discussion by asserting the order of salvation.

Meier notes several problems with reading the text along these lines. First, he questions those who hold that Paul speaks of equality in the Lord (v 11) while holding to distinctions in the order of creation. Meier notes that

> the problem raised in 11:2-16 is not everyday conduct in the world, but prayer and prophecy in the Christian assembly. What could be more 'in the Lord'? Why is there not complete equality here?[19]

Meier concludes that Paul realized that his comments regarding the status of women in v 3 would suggest that women are more distant from God than men are. Such a position must have appeared altogether too harsh for Paul, contends Meier, for Paul adds at the end of v 12 that "all things are from God" in an attempt to soften the blow.[20] That is, after presenting the conflicting orders at v 3 (the natural order of creation) and v 11 & 12a (the order of grace in salvation), Meier contends that Paul concludes the discussion with v 12b ("but all things are from God") in hopes of moderating the harsh position of v 3 in which women appear to be from man and not from God. Meier comments that with v 12b male and female are both from God, though not equally.

Meier never clearly states why he believes v 12b to be a continuation of the "order of nature" expounded in v 3. The one thing v 12b has in common with v 3 is that both affirm God as the *origin*. As we will see, such a similar conviction may serve to support Meier's contention regarding v 3 and v 12b.

What Meier senses, but never seems to put his finger on, is that **both** sets of verses (v 3 and vv 11 & 12) are concerned with the *origin* (i.e., the creation) and *present status* of men and women.

Verses 11 & 12 are not about the re-creation of the creation. Verses 11 & 12 present a different "order of creation" from the "order of creation" presented in v 3. Contra Conzelmann and company, the conflict between these verses can not be overcome by stringing them along some theological time line (creation/ re-creation) or by tracing some dualistic cosmology (the created order and the order of salvation). Both sets of verses offer some explanation about the *origin* and the *order* of the gender difference.

The hierarchy of v 3 encompasses God, Christ, man, and woman in its presentation of "origin" and "order". Verses 11 & 12 encompass God, Christ, man, and woman in **their** reflection on "origins" and "order." And from these different "orders of creation" we are to draw vastly different conclusions about the relative status of men and women.

RE-PLYING THE PLY
DISORDERING THE HIERARCHY

Conzelmann is one of the few critical scholars who understands the grammar and therefore the dynamics of this text. As we shall see, Conzelmann's quandary over how vv 3-10 and vv 11 & 12 relate is expressive of his sensitivity to the texture of the text.

The Greek term *plēn* (RSV & KJV "Nevertheless") commonly notes a joint in the text, serving at the beginning of a sentence "either to restrict, or to unfold and expand what has preceded... according to the requirements of the context...."[21] In 11:2-16, the joint marked by *plēn* at the beginning of 11:11 is so pronounced, cutting the flow of the verse so radically, digressing so completely from the content of 11:3-10, (and vv 13 & 15), that most translators have marked the verses *plēn* introduces (11:11 & 12) to be parenthetical comments.

As a conjunctive, *plēn* notes a break in the text much the way an ἢ "what," "but") or *de* or *alla* cut the flow.[22] Each mark notes a twist, a cut, a fold in the *textus*. Texture is woven in. What was smooth and forthright is now complicated. With the notation *plēn* at 11:11, there is a shift, a break, a doubling upon what has been said.[23]

While *plēn* ("nevertheless") at the beginning of v 11 does mark a break, it does not mark a "retreat" from positions taken up in vv 3-10. *Plēn* does not herald Paul's attempt to soften or balance his overtly one-sided position on women taken up in vv 3-10. *Plēn* is not the pivotal point at which two world orders hinge (i.e., the natural and the salvific).

The term *plēn* marks the beginning of Paul's reply to the positions not his own. I will argue that the text 11:2-10 is a solid piece taken directly or paraphrased from the letter from Corinth to Paul. And that this re-presentation of the positions taken up in Corinth is followed by a refutation in vv 11 & 12a which relativizes the assumptions taken up in vv 8 & 9, and rejects the hierarchy of v 3.

Corinthian Ply	*Paul's Reply*
8For *man was not made from woman* but *woman from man*.	
	12for as *woman was made from man*, so man is now born of woman.
9*Neither was man created for woman*, but *woman for man*.	
	11Nevertheless, in the Lord *woman is not independent of man nor man of woman*.
3the head of every man is Christ, the head of a woman is her husband, and the head of Christ is God.	
10That is why a woman ought to have a veil on her head, because of the angels.	
	16But if any one is disposed to be contentious--we have no such custom, nor do the churches of God.

Having relativized the assumptions of vv 8 & 9, and rejected the hierarchy of v 3, we will find that the conclusion drawn at v 10 is also rejected at v 16.

What marks the beginning of the piece from Corinth that ends at 11:10? Hurd notes that a number of scholars believe that 1 Corinthians 11:2 is an indirect quotation from the Corinthian letter.[24] While the standard introduction, *peri de*, is absent, Hurd notes that Fan contends that the *de* which introduces 11:2 is an abbreviated form of the *peri de* formula. Hurd contends that this suggestion becomes more attractive when it is noted that *de* occurs several times at just those turning points in 1 Corinthians which take on an adversarial posture.[25] Such texts include 1:10, 2:6, 11:17 and 15:12.[26] The particle *de* is a negative conjunctive which marks an opposing or adversative force.

Many translations are attentive to the grammatical shift which occurs at 11:2, and marks a division in the text between 11:1 and 11:2. It has been assumed that the break or shift at 11:2 marks a break with the subject matter of the verses which precede (thus the separation of the verses into different paragraphs). However, the joint or cut is not the demarcation which marks the end of one discourse and the beginning of another.

Evans calls 11:2 "a reference, partly ironical, to expressions in the Corinthians' letter of inquiry, serving as introduction to the next four chapters."[27] Hurd senses that 11:2-16 is dominated by a mood of antagonism. "Paul once again begins his reply by quoting from the Corinthians' letter and then modifying or limiting the quotation."[28] Mistakenly, Hurd took 11:2 to be the full extent of the quote from or paraphrase of the Corinthian letter, and vv 3-16 to be Paul's reply.

On my reading, the shift at 11:2 is the beginning of Paul's tracing (in this case, paraphrasing) from the Corinthian ply. But prior to Paul's quoting from the Corinthian ply which begins at 11:3, Paul introduces the reader to the issue, providing a context in which to understand what is to follow.

> 10:31 So, whether you eat or drink, or whatever you do, do all to
> the glory of God. 32 Give no offense to Jews or to Greeks or to
> the church of God, 33 just as I try to please all men in everything
> I do, not seeking my own advantage, but that of many, that they
> may be saved.

> 11:1Be imitators of me, as I am of Christ. 2I commend (de) you because you remember me in everything and maintain the traditions even as I have delivered them to you. 3But (however/on the other hand) I want you to understand (I would have you understand)....

Paul begins in 10:32 by criticizing those who "seek their own advantage." He proposes that the Corinthians should be imitators of himself as he is an imitator of Christ. But at v 2, given the presence of the particle *de*, there is a shift. If what follows is read as adversarial with sarcastic tone, then we might conclude that what follows is a mocking paraphrase of the faction that claims to remember him in everything and who contend that they are keeping the traditions even as he has delivered them.

But the particle *de* which is in the second position of 11:2 is not the only occurrence of the particle *de* in the passage. Verses 2 and 3 are marked with the particle not once but four times, as well as vv 5, 6, 12a, 15 and 16. At 11:3, Paul begins to re-present the position being asserted by the Corinthian faction. Paul quotes and/or paraphrases from their letter to him. (We are not able to assess which or to what degree because we have no means of documentation.) In 11:3, there is a particle *de* marking each presentation of the sets; man-Christ, woman-man, Christ-God. What is the point of the repetition of the particle *de* in such a short space? Are we to read the verses as becoming more and more in opposition to Paul's thinking that they are to be explicitly read as his adversaries? Are the traces so at odds with Paul's own thinking that there is need to explicitly mark their adversarial character from the beginning, as well as again and again at each of the source/ruler sets?

Paul breaks his tracing of the Corinthian ply with *plēn*, at the beginning of 11:11, where in quick fashion he takes issue with the assumptions of vv 3-10. Paul's counter arguments (11:11 & 12a) lead him, as we shall see, to arrive at a position (11:16) which is exactly the opposite of the conclusion drawn in the Corinthian correspondence to him (v 10).

> 11Nevertheless, in the Lord woman is not independent of man nor man of woman; 12for as woman was made from man, so man is now born of woman.

What we discover in vv 11 & 12a is a point-by-point counter-position offered as a reply to the assumptions present in 11:2-10. The hierarchical cosmology presented in v 3 reads,

> man's head/source is Christ,
> woman's head/source is the man,
> Christ's head/source is God.

The double meaning of *kephalē* in v 3 as both "head" (ruler) and "source" is played upon in vv 8 & 9. Verse 8, "For man was not made from woman, but woman from man," plays upon the metaphysical theme while v 9, "Neither was man created **for** woman, but woman **for** man," continues the ruler theme. Given the double meaning of *kaphalē* in the text, that man is the source of woman, and that man is the head/ruler of woman, we are thus to conclude that "women are to veil themselves in worship."

Verses 11 & 12a counter the positions taken up in vv 3, 8 & 9 point by point.

> [11](Nevertheless, in the Lord woman is not independent of man nor man of woman; [12]for as woman was made from man, so man is now born of woman.

stands in opposition to both the "head/ruler" theme and the "source" theme of vv 3, 8 & 9. "Independence" could be social-political independence (i.e., head/ruler theme) or "cosmic/metaphysical independence" (i.e., source theme). In v 11, *woman is not independent of man,* that is, *she was made "for" man",* and *"from" man*, **and** *man is not independent of woman,* that is, *man was made "for" woman,* and *"from" woman.* In a strange sort of way, v 11 relativizes the gender hierarchy, neither by rejecting "hierarchy per se" nor by simply reversing the hierarchy and thus inverting the positions. Paul relativizes the hierarchy by setting up male and female in hierarchical relationships in which each is the *kaphalē* of the other. Daniel Patte draws a similar conclusion in his study of the passage in *Paul's Faith and the Power of the Gospel.*[29] Nevertheless, my differences with his interpretation developed in *Paul's Faith* will be more evident in the pages to follow. The authority of the passage is not dependent upon whether or not the verse originates with Paul, the letter to Paul from Corinth, or is a quote from some other source. Clearly, it is assumed that the passage is authoritative, and Paul employs that authority to warrant his opposition to the veiling of women at v 16.

The relationship of vv 11 & 12a with 12b has yet to be considered. Are they in conflict with one another? Is there a conflict between "male and female occurring in the Lord," and "all things coming from God"? This issue will be addressed in greater detail in a later chapter.

The remainder of the text, 11:12b-16, is also woven from various plies into a very rough *textus* pieced together at seams which do not match well. The lines of vv 12b-16 are woven together, ply and reply in fast order.

> 12b But all things are from God. 13 Judge for yourselves; is it proper for a woman to pray to God with her head uncovered? 14 Does not nature itself teach you that for a man to wear long hair is degrading to him, 15 but if a woman has long hair, it is her pride? For her hair is given to her for a covering. 16 If any one is disposed to be contentious, we have no such custom, nor do the churches of God.

Meier notes that v 14 begins "with a slight shift in the argument."[30] In v 14, he notes that the author asserts that

> nature itself hints at this need of woman for a covering. After all, if nature, even apart from questions of prayer, provides woman with a natural covering, is not that a hint, a natural indication, that woman also needs a covering in the order of grace, when she prays?[31]

Meier concludes that, "Paul's basic argument here is that woman must follow in prayer the lead nature gives her in daily life." At this point, Meier makes the same point made earlier by Scroggs that,

> it does not seem to occur to Paul that someone might just as easily argue that, since woman's hair is given her by nature "as a covering" (v 15), there is no need for any further covering such as a veil. Paul seems to be using something of a grace-builds-on-and-imitates-nature approach. In v 14, Paul indicates that the same basic principle, though of course in a different way and in the opposite direction, holds true of man too: nature provides him with short hair and so hints at the fittingness of his praying uncovered.[32]

Fiorenza argues,

> Paul concludes that mixture of scriptural and philosophical-midrashic argument (11:2-15) with an **authoritarian** appeal, probably because he himself senses that his reasoning is not very convincing. He insists that he and the churches have no such practice of loose and uncovered hair. This is the point he wants to make.[33]

Paul's reasoning is not persuasive on Fiorenza's terms because she continues to read the text, not as a epistolary dialogue but as a single argument which is convoluted (at best), incoherent or (at worst) inconsistent. An appeal to authority by Paul (as in v 16) is not uncommon in the Epistles. But Fiorenza, whom I believe is correct in noting that Paul rejects the practice of loose and uncovered hair, has missed the point of the text. The point of the dialogue is not about "hair" per se, but about hierarchically ranking gender differentiations.

I suggest that v 12b (which is marked with *de* in the second position of the sentence) breaks with Paul's re-ply of 11:11 & 12a and begins to trace again the Corinthian letter.

> 12b But all things are from God. 13 Judge for yourselves; is it proper for a woman to pray to God with her head uncovered?

There is considerable ambiguity in these lines. Clearly Paul would not simply reject the contention that "All things are from God." However, the phrase beginning with the particle *de*, suggests that what follows stands apart from what is clearly his reply in vv 11 & 12a. And yet, vv 12b & 13 are addressed back to the Corinthians. I contend that vv 12b & 13 are taken from the Corinthian ply and with slight modifications (the addition of *de* in v 12b, and in v 13, "Judge for your-**self**" becomes "Judge for your-**selves**"), are thrown back at the congregation. The shift in argument that Meier's noted at v 14 marks the end of the text which both ends of the correspondence trace as their own. Thus the text at 11:11 breaks the quote from the Corinthian letter, offers a reply (11:11-12a) which relativizes the gender hierarchy of 11:3, 8 & 9. At 11:12b Paul affirms (to an extent) the claim put forth in the Corinthian ply and with v 13 re-plies their call to make a judgement.

Verses 14 and 15 return to trace the Corinthian letter.

> [14]Does not nature itself teach you that for a man to wear long hair is degrading to him, [15]but if a woman has long hair, it is her pride? For her hair is given to her for a covering.

The argument continues the themes of gender subordination, only in vv 14 & 15 it is based upon a (meta-) physical or natural interpretation of the cosmology of 11:3.

Abruptly Paul breaks the flow of vv 14 & 15 with a clean and sharp denunciation of those who seek to fracture the congregation along gender lines.

> [16]If any one is disposed to be contentious, we have no such custom, nor do the churches of God.

Verse 11:16 is Paul's final word on this matter of veiling women in worship. "If any one is disposed to be contentious (*phileikos*) ...," that is, if any one is disposed to be quarrelsome in their love of victory and domination, "...we have no such custom, nor do the churches of God."

THE TEXTUS OF I COR 10:31-11:16

Paul's critique of those who are "seeking their own advantage" (10:30) introduces the discussion of the status of male and female. The hierarchical cosmology is traced (11:3) and rejected (11:11 & 12a). Paul concludes the discussion with, "If any one is disposed to be contentious..." (i.e., disposed to (literally) "seeking their own advantage") "we have no such custom, nor do the churches of God."

Given the co-dependence of women and men in the Lord, and their co-origination from one another (each in its own turn), the attempt to subjugate the women of the church by virtue of a speculative hierarchy and the prevailing cultural rules and etiquette has no place in the churches of God.

If 11:2-10, and vv 14-15 are Paul's tracings from the Corinthians correspondence, and 11:11-12a, and v 16 are his replies, then the significant textual problems are resolved. First, the assumption that 11:2-16 is internally incoherent and contradictory is understood as a tension between texts in the ply/reply of the Epistle's *textus*. The incoherence is the outcome of conflicting systems of conviction which are woven together in correspondence. Thus the appeal of those attempts to explain the text by suggesting some hidden agenda which complicated the text or the corruption of the authentic text by some later writer(s) is nullified. There is nothing to explain. This text hangs together as a multi-*plied* weave.

Paul's Reply

10:31 So, whether you eat or drink, or whatever you do, do
all to the glory of God. 32 Give no offense to Jews or to
Greeks or to the church of God, 33 just as I try to please all
men in everything I do, not seeking my own advantage, but
that of many, that they may be saved. 11:1 Be imitators of
me, as I am of Christ. 2 I commend you because you
remember me in everything and maintain the traditions
even as I have delivered them to you.

Corinthian Ply

3 But I want you to understand, that the head of every man
is Christ, the head of a woman is her husband, and the
head of Christ is God. 4 Any man who prays or prophesies
with his head covered dishonors his head, 5 but any woman
who prays or prophesies with her head unveiled dishonors
her head--it is the same as if her head were shaven. 6 For
if a woman will not veil herself, then she should cut off her
hair; but if it is disgraceful for a woman to be shorn or
shaven, let her wear a veil. 7 For a man ought not to cover
his head, since he is the image and glory of God; but
woman is the glory of man. 8 (For man was not made from
woman, but woman from man. 9 Neither was man created
for woman, but woman for man.) 10 That is why a woman
ought to have a veil on her head, because of the angels.

Paul's Reply

11 (Nevertheless, in the Lord woman is not independent of
man nor man of woman; 12 for as woman was made from
man, so man is now born of woman.

Paraphrase

[12b]But all things are from God. [13]Judge for yourselves; is it proper for a woman to pray to God with her head uncovered?

Corinthian Ply

[14]Does not nature itself teach you that for a man to wear long hair is degrading to him, [15]but if a woman has long hair, it is her pride? For her hair is given to her for a covering.

Paul's Reply

[16]If any one is disposed to be contentious, we have no such custom, nor do the churches of God.

In his relativization of the hierarchical ordering of male and female, Paul makes the counter-proposal that male and female occur in opposition to one another, co-originating and co-dominating one another. Is this reading of 11:11-12a (given its context in 10:30-11:16) characteristic of Paul's convictions about the status of men and women? To address this problem we will consider two other pertinent extended passages in the Epistle which deal with the status of male and female. I will argue that the reading I have put forth of 10:30-11:16 is characteristic of Paul's thinking about the gender difference.

THE QUESTION OF SEXUAL DOMINATION I COR 7:1-7

[1]Now concerning the matters about which you wrote. It is well for a man not to touch a woman. [2]But because of the temptation to immorality, each man should have his own wife and each woman her own husband. [3]The husband should give to his wife her conjugal rights, and likewise the wife to her husband. [4]For the wife does not rule over her own body, but the husband does; likewise the husband does not rule over his own body, but the wife does. [5]Do not refuse one another except perhaps by agreement for a season, that you may devote

> yourselves to prayers; but then come together again, lest Satan tempt you through lack of self-control.

Conzelmann correctly notes that 1 Cor 7:1-7 begins with Paul addressing an issue raised by a faction within the church at Corinth. Paul writes, "Now concerning the question you wrote...," is followed by the position posed to Paul in their correspondence to him. "It is well for a man not to touch a woman." Paul proceeds in a subtle manner which undercuts the assumptions of the position posed to him. The phrase from the Corinthian letter only addresses the conduct of the men.

> [1]Now concerning the question you wrote:
> It is well for a man not to touch a woman.
> [2]But (*dia*)....

The flow of v 1 shifts at the beginning of v 2, breaking from the quote to proceed with an argument for marriage based upon the interdependence and mutual domination of men and women. Paul's response is conspicuously egalitarian.

> [2]But because of the temptation to immorality, each man should have his own wife and each woman her own husband. [3]The husband should give to his wife her conjugal rights, and likewise the wife to her husband. [4]For the wife does not rule over her own body, but the husband does; likewise the husband does not rule over his own body, but the wife does.

Thus, we find Paul replying to the ascetic dictum, "It is well for a man not to touch a woman," with a discourse based on the mutual dependence and mutual rule of husband and wife. Robin Scroggs notes that chapter 7, as a whole, cannot be understood as advocating the supremacy of men and the subordination of women (a traditional interpretation).[34] Scroggs argues that "Paul in almost every instance addressed himself explicitly to **both** men and women in order to show that each sex has the same freedom and the same responsibility."[35]

Verse 7:4 ("For the wife does not rule over her own body, but the husband does, likewise the husband does not rule over his own body, but the wife does.") occurs as the basis for Paul's repudiation of v 7:1b ("It is well for a man not to touch a woman.") with v 7:3 ("The husband should give to his wife her conjugal rights, and likewise the wife to her husband."). Verse 7:4 asserts the co-domination of husband and wife, thereby relativizing the male dominated assumption of 7:1.

LET THE WOMEN SPEAK IN CHURCH
1 COR 14:34-36

One final passage in the epistle text must be addressed in our study of the gender difference in 1 Corinthians. That text is 14:34-36.[36]

> [34]The women should keep silence in the churches, for they are not permitted to speak, but should be subordinate, as even the laws says. [35]If there is anything they desire to know, let them ask their husbands at home. For it is shameful for a woman to speak in church.
>
> [36]What! Did the word of God originate with you, or are you the only ones it has reached?

The passage strains the *textus* of the epistle in several directions. First, it appears that Paul is making a claim that "women should keep silence in the churches." But such a claim contradicts his earlier comments regarding male-female relations in Chapter 7 and Chapter 11. And the silencing of women in church would also contradict what Paul has written elsewhere regarding the status of women. At Romans 16:1 Paul commends to the Roman congregation "Phoebe, a deacon (*diakonon* usually translated into English as "minister" or transposed into its phonetic romanized lettering as above, i.e., deacon) of the church at Cen'chre-ae." And of course one mustn't forget Galatians 3:28.

> There is neither Jew nor Greek, there is neither slave nor free, **there is neither male nor female**; for you are all one in Christ Jesus.

Second, the silencing of women is justified by the presupposition that women should be "subordinate" (*upotassesthōsan*) to their husbands. As we have already noted, in the other two instances in which the gender hierarchy has been presented, it has been re-traced in Paul's epistle from another epistle only to be reversed and relativized. Might the gender hierarchy of v 34 be read as a ply from the Corinthian letter in the *textus* of Paul's reply?

And third, the silencing of women, justified by the pre-supposition that women are to be "subordinate" to their husbands in the gender hierarchy, is warranted by an appeal to Jewish law. "The women should keep silence in the churches. For they are not permitted to speak, but should be subordinate, **as even the law says.**" Only on one occasion in the Pauline corpus does it appear that Paul is justifing a position he is defending by an appeal to the law (Gal 4:21). Even in that case it is not all that clear exactly what is meant by the appeal. Usually, quite to the contrary, Paul states time and again that Christians are not under the law, but are free of it. "For Christ is the *end* (or fulfillment) of the law" (Romans 7:6). Earlier in 1 Corinthians he instructs the Gentile men of Corinth that they are free of the law and are, therefore, not required to be circumcised (1 Cor 7:18-19). Elsewhere, too, Paul has rejected the claim that Gentile Christians should keep the Jewish dietary laws. Therefore, if Gentile Christians are free of the law, then why would Paul instruct that "women should keep silence in church ... *as even the law says*"?

Two critical interpretations have been proposed to resolve the critical problem discussed above. One interpretation concludes that given Paul's egalitarian spirit demonstrated in his letters and/or the Acts of the Apostles, the prohibition against female participation in the worship service of Corinth is an interpolation.[37]

The other critical interpretation finds room for the prohibition by elaborate schemes which attempt to reconcile the text with the body of Pauline literature. Thus, while 1 Cor 14:34-36 possesses certain difficulties in the corpus, it is judged to be an authentic Pauline work.[38]

PLY/RE-PLYING THE SILENCING OF WOMEN

Briefly, I read the text to be a two-fold *textus* tracing a ply from the Corinthian Letter to Paul to which he then replies. The first ply (vv 34 & 35) is a quote from a faction in the church which is asserting that female silence in worship is expressive of women's subordination to men as is dictated in the law. Paul traces from their letter to him in his reply to them for a very good reason. Paul wishes to make clear exactly to which positions he is responding. Paul traces letter for letter, word for word their position.

> [34]The women should keep silence in the churches, for they are not permitted to speak, but should be subordinate, as even the laws says. [35]If there is anything they desire to know, let them ask their husbands at home. For it is shameful for a woman to speak in church.

To this trace from the Corinthian letter addressed to Paul he replies,

> [36]What! Did the word of God originate with you, or are you the only ones it has reached?

To the ply from the Corinthian correspondence, Paul replies with a two-fold negative rhetorical query. It is a two-fold question which is introduced with the particle ἤ. The particle ἤ serves to provide a disjunctive or comparative conjunction between separate ideas or convictions.[39] The particle is capable of conveying a spectrum of negative conjunctions ranging from the simple noting of a difference by comparison to the refutation of one thing by another. The intensity of the disjunctive which any particular ἤ conveys is dependent upon its context. Funk points out that the particle ἤ displays its sharpest disjunctive characteristics in interrogative sentences.[40] In such instances, the particle declares that if one phrase is the case then the other is not. Smyth points out that "an ἤ often introduces an argument *'ex contrario'*."[41] Thayer made the same point when he asserted that an ἤ may appear "before a sentence contrary to the one just preceding, to indicate that if one be denied or refuted the other must stand."[42] Interestingly, one of Thayer's examples of the ἤ functioning in such a manner was 1 Cor 14:36! Unfortunately, Thayer failed to note the full ramifications of his discovery given the content of the passage.

The particle which introduces the interrogative sentence of 14:36 indicates that the rhetorical questions to follow will serve to refute the sentences which preceded it. It is my contention that the ἤ which introduces 1 Cor 14:36 declares that vv 34 & 35 are to be *emphatically* refuted by the two-fold rhetorical query of v 36. The complete passage is not an internally unified, straightforward argument or condemnation of women who participate in the worship of the church. The silencing of women in the name of conformity to tradition and law is neither the last word nor the purpose of the text. The silencing of women in church is to be questioned and refuted by the two-fold negative rhetorical query of v 36.

It is also interesting that in the history of interpretation of this passage, I have never found a single comment regarding the apparent contradiction between the view expressed in v 34, that women are to be *subordinate*, and the reversal and relativization of male domination/female subordination expressed in 7:1-5, and 11:11 and 12. I have already mentioned that those who contend the passage is an interpolation play heavily upon the contradiction between the authority of law in v 34 and its lack of authority elsewhere in the epistle. But, here we have a verse asserting that women are to be "subordinate" and nothing is mentioned about how this passage stands in opposition to 7:1-5, or Galatians 3:28 & 29. The position that women are to be silent because they are to be subordinate, and they are to be subordinate as the law says, is a chain of support. It has been noted that the appeal to the law is an inadequate means of support in the Pauline corpus.

H TO ἤ

One of the things I find interesting about the text is that somehow, in the process of transcription and translation, the particle ἤ was preserved. In the earliest copies of the text, which use pre-Byzantine script, the first term in the sentence would appear as H, capitalized and free of breath and accent markings. An H could be read as the particle ἤ or it could be read as the adverb ἦ which means "truly." To read the H to be the adverb ἦ meaning "truly" would pose a grammatical problem from the start. The difficulty lies in how to reconcile the adverb ἦ which asserts the truth of vv 34 & 35 with the negative rhetorical questions of v 36 which call for a negative answer. What I find remarkable is that when the text was transcribed into Byzantine characters and punctuation, the H which introduces v 36 was *marked* to be a particle ἤ and not an adverb ἦ.

Yet, beginning with the earliest English translations and commentaries, the Greek ἦ, translated "what" is read not as negation but as affirmation.[43] That is, the Greek mark is seen as a particle and was so translated into English, but it has been read as an adverb.[44]

THE AUDIENCE

The full power and justification of the egalitarian interpretation of 1 Cor 14:34-36 is disclosed when we consider "To whom the text is addressed." Traditional interpreters, assuming that the purpose of the passage is to admonish the women of Corinth for speaking in church, have concluded that vv 34-36 are addressed to the women. "Did the word of God originate with you **women** or are you **women** the only ones it has reached?" This interpretation is unsatisfactory on two accounts. First, it assumes that v 36 is the summation of vv 34 & 35. This point we have already discussed. Second, while the pronouns in the verse are ambiguous with respect to their gender (*humōn*, *humas*), the latter in v 36b is modified by the plural **masculine** adjective *monous* (alone). This modification serves to denote that the gender of the second person plural pronoun of v 36b is **masculine**, and **not feminine** as is commonly assumed. Therefore, we can conclude that 14:34-36 is **not addressed exclusively** to the women of Corinth.

At this point, a crucial decision is before us. Are we to translate the masculine modified pronouns as denoting **male** persons or **people** in a gender inclusive sense?

Up until this time, those observant and critical scholars who have noted the masculine modification of the pronoun of v 36b have concluded that the text is addressed to the "whole church at Corinth."[45] The masculine modified pronoun of v 36b is assumed to be gender inclusive. Both the men and the women of Corinth are responsible for the deviation from the common practice of women remaining silent in the churches. By granting equal status to men and women in the ritual of the cult, the church has chosen to traverse from acceptable norms of practice and to forsake the law. The purpose of the two-fold query of v 36 is to reveal to the entire congregation that their actions are based on self-righteous assumptions which are disrespectful of the tradition and the greater community of believers.

The gender inclusive proposal mistakenly assumes that v 36 is the **summation** of vv 34-35. This interpretation fails to take seriously the complete text in that it overlooks the power and disjunctive character of a particle ἠ when it introduces an interrogative sentence.

If the text is addressed to the whole congregation, admonishing all the people for their deviation from the tradition, the law and the larger Christian community in letting women speak in church, then we must conclude that the gender inclusive interpretation fails to offer any new evidence for resolving the alleged inconsistency of 14:34-36 with the Pauline corpus. Thus, the gender inclusive interpretation must accept the judgment that 14:34-36 is an interpolation or room must be found for the text by elaborate schemes which reconcile the text with the body of authentic epistles.

The contention that the masculine modified pronoun denotes "common gender" is mistaken. I propose that we assume that the masculine modified pronoun of v 36b does in fact denote **male persons**. That is, the gender designation of *monous* does in fact declare "to whom 14:34-36 is address."

In rereading the text, we sense that Paul is **not** writing to the women of Corinth. While the style of writing in the third person is a common Pauline practice, it seems clear given v 36b that vv 34-35 are **about** the women addressed **to** the men. "For *they* are not permitted to speak.... If there is anything *they* desire to know, let *them* ask *their* husbands at home."

However, with v 36, we are faced with a dramatic shift of emphasis. The address is no longer **about** the women. Beginning with the ἠ which introduces v 36, Paul writes directly **to** his audience, *the men of Corinth*. "What! Did the word of God originate with you or are you (men) the only ones it has reached." The inquiry of v 36 is a refutation of the self-righteous assumptions of the men voiced in vv 34 & 35. It is with v 36 that the status and full intent of the remarks made to the men about the women are revealed. Verses 34 and 35 give voice to the sexist opinions of at least some of the male believers in the Corinthian church. Some of the men believe that they were the mediators of the faith. By virtue of being born male, the word of God originated with them. Or, at least the word of God came to them first if they ascribe to the hierarchy of 11:3.

No sooner does Paul trace the assumptions of the men of Corinth than he refutes them. What first appeared to be remarks praising the status of men by condemning the women, in the end admonishes the men for their self-righteousness and inconsistency.

The faction to whom this admonishment or critique is aimed are the Legalist. Verses 34 and 35 trace the Legalists' position on female participation in worship. However, even Paul's tracing of the Legalists' text must be read with an ear for tone. The phrase, "as even the law says," hints at the context and something of the purpose of the entire text. The issue of female participation or non-participation in the worship of the Corinthian congregation occurs in the larger debate on the status of the law in the Gentile-Christian communities. "As even the law says" may be a cue to the Gentile reading or hearing the text that all is not right with a perspective which is justifiable according to the law.

For the Gentile men of Corinth, an appeal to the law regarding the status of women in congregational worship opens the door to all the restrictions and ritual which men are required to accomplish *as even the law says*. This may be a subtle allusion to the painful ritual which men are required to fulfill according to the law. This use of the law is a reminder to the Gentile men of Corinth that they are free of the law and are, therefore, not required to be circumcised (1 Cor 7:18 & 19). But, if the women are to be women according to the law, then are not all the men also to be men according to the law? The silencing of the women in worship vindicated by an appeal to the law is linked very subtly to the circumcising of the males. If one is to be observed, then also the other, as even the law says.

The male Christians, being converts to the faith, know that the word of God did not originate with themselves. It was brought to them by Paul and other believers. They also know that they are not the only ones to receive the word of God. The women of their church have also received the word. And Paul's travels have served to spread the word into Asia and Europe. The men of Corinth know that they are not the sole proprietors of the faith. However, Paul's opponents, in this case clearly the Legalist--and possibly the Gnostics--assume that the word of God did in fact originate with them. The

Legalist, given their linkage with Israel, assume that the word of God does originate with themselves--as Hebrews. The Gnostics assume, given the causal hierarchy of their metaphysical theology, that relative to women, the word of God did come to men first (as did creation and authority).

Paul's audience in vv 34-36 is the men of the Corinthian church whom he divides by the two-fold negative query of v 36. Those who answer "no" in agreement with Paul must reject the exclusion of female participation in worship by reason of an appeal to custom or the law.

THE *TEXTUS* OF 1 COR 14:34-36

Corinthian Ply

34The women should keep silence in the churches, for they are not permitted to speak, but should be subordinate, as even the laws says. 35If there is anything they desire to know, let them ask their husbands at home. For it is shameful for a woman to speak in church.

Paul's Reply

36What! Did the word of God originate with you, or are you the only ones it has reached?

THE GENDER DIFFERENCE

R. Jewett contends that Paul "was struggling to maintain two seemingly contradictory points: differentiation of sexual identity on the one hand and equality of honor and role on the other hand".[46] Fiorenza notes that Meeks follows Robin Scroggs who argues "that Paul wanted to elucidate the inequality between the sexes, while the gnostics wanted to elucidate the distinction between the sexes."[47]

Given our study of 7:1-7, 10:33-11:16, and 14:34-36, we have come to see that Paul reverses and relativizes the hierarchical ordering of gender differences, both in terms of a metaphysical speculation about origin, and as a system of domination. Further, such a reversal and relativization of the hierarchy undermines all attempts at a final or complete hierarchy which sets in place male and female in a permanent structure. Paul's critique of the hierarchies asserted by the various factions in Corinth and his relativization of the relationship of male and female is not a rejection of hierarchy per se. Male and female relate to one another in differing positions of domination and subordination. They are not the same in the Pauline epistles. Each one stands in differentiation with the other. Thus Paul suggests that male and female *co-originate* "in the Lord," and that husband and wife *co-dominate* one another.

*It is by virtue of his relativization of the hierarchical identity and ranking of male and female that Paul **REJECTS** the veiling and silencing of women in worship, and the contention that a man should not touch a woman.* Paul's rejection of those who seek to veil and silence women in worship is justified on the grounds that such restrictions of female participation is expressive of those who love the contentious struggle for domination. To those who seek to dominate, Paul's contention that male and female co-originate and co-dominate so relativizes the relationship of male and female, that all who seek to dominate and who do dominate must also accept the domination of those they seek to dominate.

The gender difference is not to be categorized and ordered by degree. Both metaphysical and political hierarchical analogies are relativized and their social implications are rejected. Gender differences are to remain (contra Gnostics), but they are not the occasion for subordination (contra Legalists).[48]

Differences are not to be overcome by the subordination of one by the other or the erasure of one. Such contentiousness is rejected. Man and woman share the same responsibilities: they are given the same advice; each in turn rules the other (7:1, 11:11); each is the source of the other (11:12); and each has received and may speak the word of God which has come to them.

The tensions in the *textus* of 1 Corinthians are the en-counter of Paul with the divisions in Corinth. Paul struggles over-against, or even better put, in the midst of the contentious struggle for domination by the conflicting divisions in Corinth to overcome, not the struggle per se, but to overcome the struggle for gender dominance which does not reverse itself. Cutting and disordering the basic convictions by which the conflicting divisions justify their struggle for domination, Paul relativizes the opposing divisions/convictions.

Paul's reply is no simple rejection of the positions asserted by the Corinthian faction. Paul's "repudiation" is more involved, more convoluted, than a simple abolition of the gender hierarchy. We discovered in our detailed reading of the epistle as purloined and textured, that the male dominated gender hierarchy deconstructed. Man is the *kephalē* of women, **and** woman is the *kephalē* of man. And this relativization of the gender hierarchy, in tandem with Paul's contention that the churches do not recognize any such practices, is the occasion for Paul's "rejection" of the practice of veiling women in worship. The speculative hierarchy of 1 Corinthians 11:3, assumed to warrant the marking of women as inferiors and subordinates to men, is in the end, radically relativized.

Besides the central issue of the veiling of women in worship warranted by the appeal to the cosmological hierarchy, other issues are addressed, less directly but addressed none the less. The cosmological hierarchy ranks God, Christ, and humans, as well as the human gender differences. And yet, in Paul's reply the relationship of the human genders to Christ and God, and the relation of Christ and God, are nonetheless presented although they are not expounded. We will address each of these in turn. It is to the supposed "divine hierarchy" that we next turn, which will be followed by our inquiry into the relation of *Christos* and the human genders.

NOTES

1. The English translation is for the most part from the R.S.V.. The exceptions are as follows: (i) at v 11:12b I translate the beginning of the passage (*ta de panta ek tou theou*) to be disjunctive (But) rather than conjunctive (And) as is the case in R.S.V.. Thus I follow Conzelmann's lead which is followed in the N.R.S.V.. My reasons for the disjunctive will be clarified below. (ii) Verse 16:b is translated in the R.S.V., "we recognize **no other** practice" for *ameis toiautan sunatheian ouk echomen.* I agree with the N.R.S.V. translation which follows Conzelmann's suggestion that the passage be translated "we have **no such** custom" (Conzelmann, *1 Corinthians*, 181).

2. Wayne A. Meeks, *The Writings of St. Paul* (New York: Norton, 1972), 38, and James Moffatt, *The First Epistle of Paul to the Corinthians* (New York: Harper & Brothers, 1938), 149-150.

3. William O. Walker, Jr., "1 Cor 11:2-16 And Paul's Views Regarding Women," *JAAR* (1975) 43:94-110.

4. J. Murphy-O'Connor, "Sex and Logic In 1 Corinthians," *CBQ* (1980) 42:482-3. Emphasis mine.

5. Robin Scroggs, "Paul And The Eschatological Women," *JAAR* (1972) 40:297.

6. Scroggs contends that "All these difficulties (the obscure logic, contradictory claims, peculiar word choice and peevish tone) point to some hidden agenda, hidden probably to the Apostle himself as well as to his readers" (Ibid, 287) Paul's hidden agenda, Scroggs goes on to argue, is actually Paul's fear of homosexuality. The difficulties within the text are generated by the conflict between what is said and what is not said by Paul. Hidden behind what is the apparent issue (women's covering) is the real unspoken issue (homosexuality). Murphy-O'Connor (482 & 483), Charles K. Barrett (*A Commentary On The First Epistle To The Corinthians* (New York: Harper & Row, 1968), 267), and J. P. Meier ("On the Veiling of Hermeneutics (1 Cor 11:2-16)," *CBQ* (1978) 40:223, fn 24) concur with Scroggs' interpretation. As will be made clear below (without a point by point analysis of the arguments for the above interpretation), I reject the homosexuality interpretation.

7. Conzelmann, *1 Corinthians*, 182. Emphasis mine.

8. Elizabeth Schüssler Fiorenza, *In Memory of Her: A Feminist Theological Reconstruction of Christian Origins* (New York: Crossroads, 1985) 228. Emphasis mine.

9. Webster's 7th New Collegiate Dictionary.

10. Patte, 340.

11. Ibid.

12. Ibid., 340 & 41.

13. Ibid., 341.

14. Ibid., 340.

15. J. P. Meier, "On the Veiling of Hermeneutics (1 Cor 11:2-16)," *CBQ* (1978) 40:217.

16. Fiorenza writes that, "Archeological evidence ... shows that female devotees of Isis usually wore long hair 'with a band around the forehead and curls falling on the shoulders,' while the male initiates had their hair shaven." (Fiorenza, 227, see S. Kelly Heyob, *The Cult of Isis Among Women In The Greco-Roman World* [Leiden: Brill, 1975] p. 60)

Fiorenza concludes that "Hence, Paul's sarcastic statement in vv 5f...." As we shall soon see, I take it that the position of vv 4f is not Paul's, but is held by a faction in the Corinthian church. It could be that those who argue for christian women covering their hair in worship are fearful that female christian worshippers with loosened hair might be mistaken for followers of the pagan god Isis. Or, if those who argue for women covering their hair in worship are Jewish in thought and custom, their reasoning might be that loosened hair is a sign of uncleanness (J.A. Fitzmyer, "A Feature of Qumran Angelology and the Angels of 1 Cor 11:10" *NTS* [1958/59] 4:48-58).

17. Meier, 222.

18. Emphasis mine.

19. Meier, 222, fn 21. I believe that Meier employs too narrow a sense of "in the Lord."

20. Ibid., 222.

21. Thayer, 517.

22. Liddell-Scott, 1419.

23. J. D. Dennison, *The Greek Particles* (Oxford: At The Clarendon Press, 1954), 166. "But just as *alla* sometimes is, or appears to be, a weak adversative, so *de* is at times a strong one: particularly in Sophocles, who not infrequently uses *de* in answers, to introduce a project or objection."

24. Hurd, 90.

25. Ibid., 90, fn 2.

26. Of the scholars listed by Hurd in Table 5, Robertson and Plummer, Bousset, Zahn, Parry, Evans, Moffatt, Lietzmann, and Lake believe that a question from the Corinthians motivated 11:2-16.

27. Ernest Evans, *The Epistles of Paul the Apostle to the Corinthians*, "The Clarendon Bible." (Oxford: The Clarendon Press, 1930), 117, quoted in Hurd, 182.

28. Hurd, 185 & 186.

29. Patte, 340 & 41.

30. Meier, 222.

31. Ibid.

32. Meier, 223, fn 24.

33. Fiorenza, 229. Emphasis mine.

34. Scroggs, 298-303.

35. Scroogs, 294 and 297. Hurd concurs, see 65-66.

36. For the recent debate regarding whether 14:33b ("As is all of the Churches of the Saints") is the introduction to vv 34-36, or the conclusion to the passages preceding, see Jerome Murphy-O'Connor, "Interpolations in 1 Corinthians," *Catholic Biblical Quarterly* 48 (1986), 81-94, Charles Talbert, *Reading Corinthians: A Literary and Theological Commentary on 1 & 2 Corinthians* (New York: Crossroad; 1987), and Odell-Scott, "In Defense of an Egalitarian Interpretation of 1 Cor 14:34-36: A Reply To Murphy-O'Connor's Critique," *BTB* 17:3 (July, 1987). I concur in my article with Talbert that v 33b is not the introduction to vv 34-36.

37. E. Schweizer, "The Service Of Worship--An Exposition of 1 Cor 14," *Interpretation* 13 (1959), 400; Conzelmann, 246; and Murphy-O'Connor, 133.

38. F. F. Bruce, *1 & 2 Corinthians.* Trans. J. W. Leitch (Philadelphia: Fortress Press, 1975), 135 & 136; M. E. Thrall, *The First And Second Letters of Paul To The Corinthians* (Cambridge: At The University Press, 1965), 102; W. F. Orr, & J. A. Walther, *1 Corinthians: A New Translation* (Garden City, New York: Doubleday & Company, Inc., 1976), 311-315; C. Holladay, *The First Letter Of Paul To The Corinthians* (Austin, Texas: Sweet Publishing Co., 1979), 188-190.

39. William F. Arndt, & F. Wilbur Gingrich, *A Greek-English Lexicon Of The New Testament And Other Early Christian Literature* (Chicago: The University of Chicago Press, 1957), 342-343; Liddell & Scott, 1761; H. W. Smyth, *Greek Grammar* (Cambridge: Harvard University Press, 1963), 2856; and A. T. Robertson, *A Grammar of the Greek New Testament in the Light of Historical Research* (New York: Hodder & Stoughton, 1914), 1188.

40. Robert W. Funk, *A Greek Grammar* (Chicago: The University of Chicago, 1961), 446.

41. Smyth, 2861.

42. Thayer, 275.

43. This practice of reading the particle ἠ as conveying the sense of "truly" is evident in Robert Young, *Analytical Concordance to the Bible* (Grand Rapids, Michigan: Wm. B. Eerdman's Publishing Co.,; 22nd edition), 1144.

44. We earlier noted that at Romans 16:1, Paul commends to the Roman congregation "Phoebe, a *deacon* of the church at Cen'chre-ae." This is of course a R.S.V. translation of the text. It appears that all pre-twentieth century English translations engaged in a double standard of a sort. When the Greek term *diaconia* appears in the text and was used to describe or name the office a man held in the church, the term was either transcribed into its English phonetic equivalent, i.e., deacon, or it was rendered "minister" (which is a good interpretation of the terms meaning as it appears in the epistle texts). However, when the Greek term *diaconia* appears in the text in conjunction with a woman, then the term is translated into English either as "servant" (which is what a "deacon" **does** at the Table) or as **"widow"** (a rendering for which there is no textual support).

45. F. F. Bruce, *1 & 2 Corinthians* (London: Oliphants, 1971), and W. F. Orr and J. A. Walther, *1 Corinthians: A New Translation* (Garden City, New York: Doubleday & Company, Inc., 1976).

46. R. Jewett, "The Sexual Liberation Of The Apostle Paul," *JAAR Supplement* (1979) 47/1:74.

47. Fiorenza, 203, fn 153.

48. It is a common practice to assert that Gnostics intended to overcome gender differences. They did so on occasion by an appeal to a cosmic hierarchy similar to that of 11:3. In those instances, the Gnostics declared that women must become male in order to overcome the desires of the flesh, and to so end the domination of the flesh over the spirit. In contrast to the Gnostics, who are assumed to seek the overcoming of gender differences by the annihilation of that which is female, it is commonly asserted that there were Jews and Jewish Christians who held to Jewish law and customs (which are in many ways one and the same). It is commonly held that the Jews or Jewish Christians attempted to instate or re-instate Jewish law, which included among other things, dietary rules, circumcision rites, and a gender hierarchy. But such a division along Gnostic/Jewish or Gentile-Gnostic/Jewish lines is mistaken. It has been argued that much of the Gnostic influences in early Christianity were by Jewish Gnostics. Thus the old division does not hold so neatly. I have chosen to speak instead of the "Gnostics" and the "Legalists," without reference to their being Jewish or Gentile or whatever. In a sense, the gender hierarchy was presupposed by both Gnostic and Legalists. In both positions male was either to dominate female, or what was female was to be overcome by what is male. In either case, there is a valuation of male over female. And in Paul's replies, both forms of the gender hierarchy are overcome. For as we have seen the gender differences persist as differences.

9

DIS-ORDERING THE DIVINE HIERARCHY

INTRODUCTION

The texts of 1 Cor 11:3 and 8:6 are commonly called upon to warrant the claim that *Christos* is subordinate to *Theos*. Thus, it could be argued that these Pauline texts support the claim commonly held by the Middle-Platonic Christian theologians of the second century that Christ is the *logos* of God, i.e., that Christ "mediates" between God and the world. If such is the case, then it might further be argued that the mysterious *oikonomia* is a later theme yielded by the emergence of metaphysics but missing in primitive or early (i.e., first century) Christian thought.

I will attempt in the following study to counter the claims common in the interpretative corpus that in the Pauline epistles (1) *Christos* serves as the mediator of *Theos* to the world, (2) that *Christos* is a reconstructed stoic pantheism, and that (3) Paul produced or employed a speculative causal system in which *Christos* and *Theos* serve some particular role.

Instead, I will demonstrate that *Christos* and *Theos* represent different modes of thought or philosophies of religion. *Christos* and *Theos* indicate conflicting divinities which can not be systematized with their differences overcome.

Causality And Difference

Robert Grant contends that at 1 Cor 8:6, we find a causal explanation which incorporates God, Christ and the world.

> [6]Yet for us there is one God the Father, from whom are all things and for whom we exist, and one Lord, Jesus Christ, through whom are all things and through whom we exist.

Grant makes much of the difference in vocabulary between these closely parallelled descriptions of God and Lord. We may summarize by noting that (a) all things are **from** God, (b) **through** the Lord, and (c) that we exist **for** God (d) **through** the Lord. Grant commenting on the passage writes:

> It is philosophical because its structure is provided by a three-point causal system in which God the Father is the first cause and the last and the Lord Jesus Christ is the instrumental cause--both in creation and salvation.[1]

In v 8:6, God is *ex ou* and *eis auton* while the Lord is *di' ou*.[2]

However, in Romans 11:36, Grant points out, Paul writes **of God** as the one *ex, di',* and *eis*.[3] "For from him and through him and to him are all things."[4]

On Grant's terms, the passage from Romans presents **God** as the first, last, and instrumental causes. Christ or Lord are not mentioned at all in the verse. Grant's contention that Paul divides the causal distinctions up among the Christian divinities is unsupported by Romans 11:36. Though Grant notes this discrepancy between 1 Cor 8:6 and Romans 11:36, he nevertheless fails to speak to its implications. While the Romans' passage might appear to be a counter-example to the causal configuration of 1 Cor 8:6, both employ a three-point causal structure in which God is always the first cause.

There is a less obvious counter-example in which God is **not** the first cause. Paul writes at 1 Cor 7:17:

> ...lead the life which the Lord has assigned to him and in which God was called him.

It might be argued that there is no clear causal hierarchy present in the verse. The verbs *emerisen*, "assigned" (or "appropriated") and *keklēken* "called" (or "summoned") are synonyms which "can at one moment name the Lord as the giver, at another moment God."[5] However, such a reading fails to take into account the subtle difference between **assigning** or **appropriating** a life to someone, and **calling** one **into** a life. In this instance, Lord is the first cause, the one who assigns a life **to** someone, and from whom the life comes. God is the instrumental cause, the one who **calls** one **into** a life that has been assigned. God is in this instance identifiable with the life into which one is called. Is there not a pan-theistic overtone to the passage? An overtone which speaks, not of Christ, but of God? The reversal of Lord and God in the causal hierarchy can not be mistaken. It is a reversal which counters the standard interpretation.[6]

This brings us once again to 1 Cor 11, in which it appears that at least two systems of causality are in conflict.

> [3]But I want you to understand, that the head of every man is Christ, the head of a woman is her husband, and the head of Christ is God.

> [11](Nevertheless, *in the Lord* woman is not independent of man nor man of woman; [12]for as woman was made from man, so man is now born of woman. But *all things are from God*.)

The difference between the two plys is obvious in terms of the relative status of male and female. Verse 3 proposes (given one reading of *kephalē*) a causal hierarchy in which God, the first cause, works through intermediate created causes (Christ & man) to create finally that which is the cause of nothing (woman). As we have seen above with respect to the gender differentiation, the causal hierarchy of male and female in v 3 is both presented and reversed in Paul's reply at vv 11 & 12.

The issue before us at this point is whether Paul's disordering of the causal hierarchy is limited to the gender difference, or, whether his disordering of the hierarchy is more pervasive. So, let us consider the next step up the causal ladder of v 3. Having dealt with the causal relation of male and female, what are we to say about the relation of male/female to the Lord?

While the causal line is forthright and clear in the hierarchy of 11:3, causality is ambiguous in vv 11:11 & 12a. In the reply, male and female co-originate. *"In the Lord"* is the context or occasion or happening of the gender origination. Clearly, the co-origination of male and female in the Lord is a new sort of origination, quite unlike a causal source as is presented in 11:3. Male and female are **not** caused by the Lord. They occur in the Lord. And as we shall soon learn, the sense of *in* the Lord is not as the container in which these entities generate one another.

Thus, Paul rejects not only the hierarchical ranking along gender lines, but also chooses a vocabulary to speak about the relation of the Lord and humanity which has no clear line of causality. Male and female occur *in the Lord*, originating one another.

Conzelmann contends at this point that Paul borrows a thesis from cosmology and transplants it into the realm of christology, hinting all the while that the cosmology which Paul has been scavenging is stoic.[7] The issue for us is not (forthrightly) to what extent Paul's christology (or whatever it is) is influenced by stoic thought. That is beyond the limits even of this unruly study. We are, however, forthrightly concerned with understanding how Paul conceives "in the Lord," a turn of phrase about which there is a sea of discussion. It is a concern that we will discuss at length in the following chapter.

Thus far, we have noted that (1) male and female originate one another, and (2) that their co-origination occurs *in the Lord*. In other words, male and female originate one another but are not caused by the Lord. Instead, male and female co-originate and co-dominate one another in a context, a milieu, an environment.

However, Paul concludes his reply at 11:12b with, "And all things are from God." Is *Theos* in the end the first cause? And the Lord, created by *Theos*, the non-causal domain of human co-origination?[8]

In Chapter 8, we discussed the use of the particle *de* with respect to 11:2 & 3. As we noted, the particle *de* may mark a negative conjuction expressing an opposing or adversarial force. What we did not address was the presence of the particle at the beginning of 11:12b.[9]

[11](Nevertheless, *in the Lord* woman is not independent of man nor man of woman; [12]for as woman was made from man, so man is now born of woman. But (*de*) *all things are from God.*)

What are we to make of this opposition of *in the Lord* and *all things are from God?* I suggested that the *de* in the second position in v 12b marks the play of ply/re-ply in the *textus* of the epistle. Verse 12b is a partial return to the position taken in v 11:3 which stands in opposition to Paul's re-ply in 11:11 & 12a. The particle marks the conflict between the Lord and God in the Pauline text.

We may tentatively conclude from our brief survey, that while Paul is in some instances concerned with giving speculative causal explanations, nevertheless, *contra* Grant, there is no clear distinction to be drawn between the various causal classifications and their being accomplished from or through the Lord or God. Furthermore, it is clear that Paul has no single "causal system" of explanation in which he merely moves the divinities around to fulfill various tasks of causality.

The commentaries and critical studies of causality in the Pauline corpus fail precisely because they attempt to discern or to frame all the various allusions to causality in the text to fit a single causal structure. But, as we have seen, there is no single causal structure. And furthermore, in the systems of causality evident in the texts, non-causal "spaces" disrupt the line of causality. So what are we to make of these conflicting systems of causality, and the disruptions which violate such systematization?

Could it be that our confusion over how to understand these texts is born of our desire to show that the texts present a uniform coherent causal claim or position? The disruptive presence of a non-originating context in the midst of the line of causality bespeaks not simply the incoherence of Paul's causal speculation. The causal incoherence which the text presents is expressive of the inherent difference between *Theos* and *Christos*. The inherent difference between *Theos* and *Christos* is one which we have characterized in our present discussion as the difference between "causality" and "context." In terms of the broader issues of this thesis, the difference between *Theos* and *Christos*, between "causality" and "context," is the difference of metaphysics and logos.

This observation, as we have already noted, is not novel. However, those theologians who have seen the conflict, have sought to resolve the difference by means of some systemization that overcomes the breach between the two divinities.

Christological Subordination Reconsidered

How are we thus to understand the relation of *Theos* and *Christos* in the Pauline epistles? We have already noted above in our reading of the various causal passages that no one system of causality dominates the text. And that in fact the systems differ to such an extent that in one instance the divinities are reversed in their order of primacy. We have also noted Paul's rejection, reversal, of the hierarchy of v 11:3 with a most unusual passage (v 11:11) which asserts the co-origination and co-domination of male and female "in the Lord."

While christological subordination continues to be suggested as a viable assessment of the relation of *Theos* and *Christos* in the Pauline texts by some scholars, the claim is heavily dependent upon the hierarchy presented in 11:3 and the creedal formula of v 8:6.[10] In one case, (v 11:3) we have noted that the hierarchy is disordered. In the other (v 8:6) we have discerned that the position being proposed is no mere subordinationist position. We have also noted that (1) in the same epistle there are numerous counter-examples to christological subordination (vv 7:17, 11:11 & 12), and (2) that the notion that the preposition "through" (*dia*) is applied by Paul as well in Romans 11:36 to *Theos* in the creation of the world.

Conzelmann's claim that "christological subordination *emerges* in the reference back to God" fails to take into account the various counter-examples in the text to which we have alluded.[11] If Conzelmann means by "emerges" that later writers work "out of" the passages without regard for the counter-examples, then I believe his assertion is valid. But it is clear elsewhere that he does not hold such a position (as is seen at Gal 1:4, Phil 2:11, cf. 15:28).[12]

Conzelmann contends that there is one other passage (besides 8:6 and 11:3) that is expressive of Paul's systematic and essential christological subordination, as opposed to a merely rhetorical schematic presence in the text. The text is 1 Cor 1:18-25. Conzelmann takes special notice of v 24b.

> [18]For the word of the cross is folly to those who are perishing, but to us who are being saved it is the power of God. [19]For it is written,
>
> "I will destroy the wisdom of the wise, and
> the cleverness of the clever I will thwart."
>
> [20]Where is the wise man? Where is the scribe? Where is the debater of this age? Has not God made foolish the wisdom of the world? [21]For since, in the wisdom of God, the world did not know God through wisdom, it pleased God through the folly of what we preach to save those who believe. [22]For Jews demand signs and Greeks seek wisdom, [23]but we preach Christ crucified, a stumbling block to Jews and folly to Gentiles, [24]but to those who are called, both Jews and Greeks, Christ the power of God and the wisdom of God. [25]For the foolishness of God is wiser than men, and the weakness of God is stronger than men.

The claim is made that in v 24b ("...Christ the power of God and wisdom of God"), **Christ refers back to God**. That Christ, by virtue of being the power and wisdom **of** God, derives power and wisdom **from** God. Thus, as Christ is "dependent" upon God for the attributes of power and wisdom, so *Christos* is subordinate to *Theos*.

While the verse clearly makes reference back to God in that Christ is the extension of God's power and wisdom, Conzelmann fails to note what sort of reference is made or how the content of the verse cuts and deflates the reference **back to** *Theos*. To suggest that "the power and wisdom of God" is present, finds expression, or is complete in *Christos* does **NOT** entail in this passage "the subordination of Christ to God." For the Christ who is the "power" and "wisdom" of God is the **crucified** Christ! To suggest that the one who has been **crucified** (painfully executed at the hands of a pagan occupational army at the urging of the institutional leaders [the powers that be] of the Temple) **is the power** and **wisdom** of **God**--*is to mock the power and wisdom of God*. That is, if the meaning of power and wisdom are clear, then **the crucified Christ is a "mockery" of the power and wisdom of God**. If on the other hand "power" and "wisdom" are subordinate to the "crucified Christ," such that power and wisdom are taken to be expressed in the crucifixion, then to contend that "the crucified Christ is the power and wisdom **of God**" is to reverse what we commonly mean by "power" and "wisdom." At any rate, the passage may be said to express christological subordination only if one erases crucifixion and reads the verse as

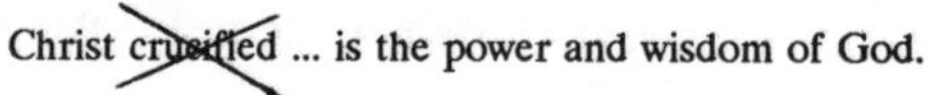

DIVINE CONFLICT: PANTHEISM AND MONOTHEISM IN CONFUSION

It is not uncommon for Pauline scholars to suggest that Paul works with (more or less) pantheistic concepts which he presses into "christological" service. Conzelmann concurs, but goes a step further and proposes that while Paul **begins** with a pantheistically influenced christology, he nevertheless concludes his theological enterprise in monotheism. This development from pantheism to monotheism Conzelmann calls "the monotheistic transformation."[13]

The hypothesis that a change occurs during the first and second centuries (C.E.) during which the predominantly stoic pantheistic world view is displaced or transformed by a neo-platonic world view is a rather common theme played by intellectual historians. It is not uncommon for historians of the period to note that in various works of the period tensions between these competing ways of thinking are evident, and that in some works, there is a considerable confusion and/or mixing of these different world views. However, Conzelmann contends that one can discern this cosmological change (which he suggests is a development) not only in the broad sweeps of western intellectual history, but also in certain individual works.[14] He contends that certain writings of the period contain traces of both pantheism and monotheism. And further, that one can discern in these individual works a movement which begins with a "pantheistic starting point" but ends transformed, i.e., in the end pantheism gives way and is transformed in the developmental process into "monotheism." We will not rehearse Conzelmann's argument or retrace his sources. For our purposes it will be enough to note that he believes that Paul is engaged in the developmental reshaping of stoic pantheism into monotheism.

I argue that Conzelmann, having (rightly or wrongly) discerned the "development" from pantheism to monotheism in some of the writings of the period, has too hastily concluded that such a development is discernible in the Pauline corpus. There may be tensions and even contradictions with respect to Paul's conception of divinity, or there may be conflicting divinities or philosophies of religion in the corpus. But Conzelmann's generalization that such tensions, contradictions or conflicts can be made sense of by way of a developmental theory or that there is a clear development from pantheism to monotheism is highly questionable.

Are we to conclude from Conzelmann's contention that Paul's pantheistically influenced christology is "dismantled and scavenged for reuseable parts," or "overcome" or "consumed by" the developmental transformation from pantheism to monotheism? And what are we to say about the *Christos* in this development? Are the two now one?

Perhaps a more plausible argument could be made that in the Pauline texts there is movement **FROM MONOTHEISM TO PANTHEISM**, parallel to the movement from monotheism to polytheism.

Earlier we noted that Paul rejected monotheism in his acceptance of "the many Lords and many Gods," and held the conviction that "for us, there is one God ... and one Lord...." In effect, Paul doubly rejected the monotheism of his Jewish religious heritage. First, he rejects the strict claims of monotheism for the pluralism of polytheism. He accepts the existence of "other Gods and other Lords" in heaven and on earth. Second, in this context of polytheism, Paul asserts that "for us," there is "**one God and one Lord.**" In other words, among the many Lords and many Gods, there are one Lord and one God who are Lord and God "**for us**." And third, remembering that the text is a purloined epistle, we must not simply assume that when Paul contends that "**for us,** there is one God ... and one Lord...," that he is making an authoritative claim for *ALL* Christian communities. Clearly, "for us" bespeaks at least those gathered in the exchange. To accept the exchange between Paul and the Corinithian Church as appling *"for **all** of us"* who read the text entails another move justified by other authorities and authors.

Just as Paul moved away from a monotheistic position and affirmed the existence of many Lords and many Gods in the cosmos, so it might be suggested that with his acceptance of a second divinity (i.e., *Christos*), Paul has also moved away from a strict monotheism to a more pantheistic theology. However, I suggest that **movement per se** from monotheism to pantheism (or from pantheism to monotheism for that matter) is not discernible, and that in the Pauline texts there is persistent ambiguity and conflict regarding *Christos* and *Theos*.

This ambiguity and conflict is not occasioned by the uncertainty of where to place or how to rank two individual concepts, *Christos* and *Theos*, in relation to one another on some causal latter, hierarchy, or series. The persistence of the ambiguity and conflict is occasioned (in one sense) by the lack of a clearly stated causal system (note the singularity of the term "system") to which the divinities relate. Causality is not an issue for Paul. The discernment of or presentation of a systematic/ theological causal explanation is not a fundamental feature of his enterprise.

ALL AND ONE

Even if we bracket for a time the conflict over *Theos* and *Christos* as well as Paul's rejection of the contentious belief that there is really only one God, how Paul discerns the relation of the divine and the non-divine still persists. It is characteristic of a monotheistic position to speak of **one God and ONE COSMOS**." There is **the creator** and **the creation**, God and **the world**. If there is a development from *pan*-theism to *mono*-theism, we might also expect to find a transformation discernable from "the all," or "all things," **TO** "world," "universe," and like terms.

However, in the Pauline epistles we find no clear indication that such a movement is underway. There are instances in which Paul speaks of the "all" (*pan*-), the "world" (*kosmos*), and in some instances "all the world" (Rom 3:19) or "all the earth" (Rom 10:18). From the earliest to the latest written epistle (spanning a decade) there is no clear point that one vocabulary is exclusively used.

It is also clear that *contra* Conzelmann, the pantheistic sounding comments about "the all" are not exclusively christological. As we have seen at 1 Cor 11:12b, and the various Romans passages, Paul makes various allusions to God and the All.[15]

After having read widely in the Pauline commentaries, one is left with the impression that either the pantheistically influenced christology is giving way to monotheism in Paul's thought or his theological endeavor is confusing and incomplete.

To assess the enterprise from a position that assumes that "monotheism," by virtue of its "oneness," enjoys a clarity and completeness that lacks diversity and multiplicity, is presumptuous. Given that such an assessment has to do with Christian thought, it is clearly dogmatic (in the worst sense of the term) when the diversity of theological thought must always appease "oneness."

Conclusion

We have considered the proposal that Paul attempts to provide a theology in which the "pantheistic" elements of his "christology" can be of service to "monotheism." It is traditionally assumed that monotheism is a fundamental conviction of Paul's faith and that "pantheism," i.e., christology, is secondary or subordinate. This position is substantiated in the literature by appeal to Paul's use of a speculative causal system employed to explain the creation and/or ordering of the cosmos, and the gender hierarchy.

In Chapter 8, we noted that the gender hierarchy is asserted, reversed and relativized. In the chapter above we noted that Paul does not present a **single** causal system, but several systems, and that with regard to any one system, Paul will in the course of his corpus, freely move the divinities about on the causal latter.

The replacement of one divinity by another in any one system of explanation and the presentation of several speculative causal systems so relativizes the idea of causality that the idea of causality can no longer be appealed to as an authoritative support.

We found no support for the claim that monotheism is a fundamental conviction in the Pauline text and that "pantheism," i.e., *Christos*, is subordinate to *Theos*. Instead, we discovered that *Christos* and *Theos* are ambiguously presented with respect to identity, context, and relations.

Thus I conclude that Christ and God represent different and differing modes of thought and philosophies of religion. Further, I conclude that *Christos* and *Theos* are conflicting divinities who are nevertheless woven together into a corpus of texts. Their conflict, their differences, can not be overcome by an appeal to a hermeneutic intent on forwarding some form of systemization.

NOTES

1. Grant, *Doctrine of God*, 6; and "Causation and the Ancient World View," *JBL* (1964) 83:34-40.
2. Grant, "Causation," 34.
3. Ibid., 35.
4. The verse is closely paralleled later by Marcus Aurelius. "From thee, in thee and to thee are all things." *Meditations* IV:23. Interestingly Marcus is speaking about "nature" as the causality from, in and to which are all things. Augustine of Hippo drew the title for his most noted work *Civitas Dei* from the next verse of Marcus' *Meditations*.
5. Conzelmann, 125-126.
6. Interestingly, in the King James translation of the passage, "Lord" and "God" are exchanged. God is the assigner and Lord the one who calls. Why the terms were exchanged? No reason is given in the text, nor are there textual/linguistic reasons for the exchange. Clearly the translators did not believe that assigning and calling were synonymous otherwise the divinities would have been left in their respective places as per the greek texts. Something about the ordering was seen as being in error. The reversal of the divinities was done not on textual grounds, but for theological/ philosophical reasons. The text failed to pattern the established causal structure.
7. Conzelmann, 190, and 144.
8. "'All things are from God' (*ta panta ek tou theos*) appears at 2 Cor 5:18 and 1 Cor 11:12b, and with a slightly different rendering ("For from him and through him and to him are all things") at Romans 11:36. These passages echo a doxological formula "apparently adapted by the early church from the Hellenistic synagogue, which had in turn, adapted it from a formula of stoic pantheism. For Stoic Formula see especially Marcus Aurelius IV, 23 (speaking of nature)" (Furnish, 316).

"In Judaism this doctrine was modified in accord with belief in a Creator who stands over creation; see, e.g., Sir 43, especially vv 26, 27, 33 and cf. Philo *Special Laws* I, 208; *Who Is The Heir* 36; *On Dreams* I,241; *On The Cherubin* 125-126. The formula is also echoed in 1 Cor 8:6, 11:12b, Eph 3:9, 4:5, Col 1:16 & 17, Hev 1:3 (R.S.V. 1:2), 2:10, and Rev 4:11. The Hellenistic background of the formula is discussed by Norden 1913:240-250, 347-54; cf. Ricke *TDNT* V:892-3" (Furnish, 316).

9. *"Ta de panta ek tou theou."*
10. Conzelmann, 80-81.
11. Ibid. Emphasis mine.
12. Ibid., 81, fn 22.
13. Conzelmann, 145, fns 46 & 47.
14. cf. 1 Cor 8:4.
15. Compare Romans 4:16 "Abraham who is the father of us all," and 9:17 "name might be declared throughout all," with 1 Cor 11:12 "All things are from God," and 2 Cor 1:3 "Father of mankind and the God of all."

10

BAPTISM IN CHRIST

Before we proceed, let us summarize the conclusions we have drawn thus far in our study of the Pauline texts. It is in this context, assuming the study which proceeds, that the readings which I will next put forward are understandable. What follows both assumes what precedes and answers the questions raised in the earlier chapters.

First, in relation to the text of 1 Cor 8:1-9, we considered the number and the relation of the Christian divinities. Our conclusions were that Paul (1) rejected monotheism, asserting the existence of many gods and lords in heaven and on earth, and that (2) Christians share a convictional system; they have faith in one God and one lord among the many. Further, I argued against those critical scholars who having discerned the positions above, nevertheless attempted to assert that there is in the Pauline epistles a developmental movement from polytheism to monotheism. I concluded that (3) movement per se, from polytheism to monotheism or from monotheism to polytheism for that matter, is not evident in the text. And that in the end, monotheistic interpretations of the Pauline epistles fail due to their lack of textual support.

In the two chapters which followed we considered an extended, complicated text (1 Cor 10:31-11:16) in which a comprehensive hierarchy was presented and deconstructed. The hierarchy of

God
Christ
Man
Woman

was presented. This was followed by a passage which asserted, reversed, and relativized the hierarchy, thus displacing the power and authority of the hierarchy to serve as the means by which women were to be marked (as veiled) as inferior to men.

> [11]Nevertheless, in the Lord woman is not independent of man nor man of woman; [12]for as woman was made from man, so man is now born of woman. And all things are from God.

The gender hierarchy was re-asserted,

Man
Woman,

then reversed,

Woman
Man,

thus relativizing the hierarchy. And, having relativized the hierarchy, the lines of causality and domination were undercut.

In keeping with the "hermeneutical *textus*" of the epistle, we considered how Paul deconstructed the hierarchical ranking of "male" and "female" in his reply. After an extended study of several pertinent passages (pertinent to the gender difference), we noted that for Paul, male and female were presented as (1) opposites, and that in their opposition they (2) co-originated and (3) co-dominated one another. We also noted at the time (4) the peculiarities of the phrase "in the Lord." It is peculiar in that male and female were not caused or dominated by the "Lord," but, in their opposition, were occurring "in the Lord," as the *place* in which the opposites male and female co-originate and co-dominate one another.

Then we returned to the text of 8:5 & 6 to reconsider, in light of the deconstruction of the gender hierarchy and the interruption of the lines of causality and domination "in the Lord" (which occurs in the text of 10:31-11:16), and in conjunction with other pertinent passages, Paul's uses of *Christos* and *Theos*. I concluded that a single formula (causal or otherwise) for understanding "divinity" in the Pauline texts is not discernable. In the epistles, *Christos* and *Theos* are ambiguously presented with respect to identity, context and relations. Thus *Christos* and *Theos* suggest different philosophies of religion, conflicting divinities and/or differing modes of thought.

Having noted this difference, we have wondered about the persistent reappearance in the Pauline texts of the theme, phrase or concept (or formula if you prefer) of various things said to be "in Christ" or "in the Lord." In our reading of 1 Cor 11:11 & 12 we discerned that the opposites "male and female" co-originate and co-dominate one another *in the Lord*. It is this "christological" theme on which we now focus our attention.

In Christ

In the New Testament the formulae "in Christ," "in the Lord," etc., rarely occur outside the Pauline corpus. Oepke in *The Dictionary of the New Testament* contends that they "are not found prior to Paul" and that "he is perhaps their author."[1]

Oepke notes that biblical scholars tend to divide into two camps of thought as regards the significance of *en* in the Pauline christological formula. It is held by many that Paul's use of "in Christ" and other parallel formulae can be explained as a Hebraism based on the *Septuagint* equation of the Greek *en* and the Hebrew *B* (which is instrumental). It is argued that since the Greek term *en* does not convey an instrumental meaning in the Greek language per se (whatever per se means), that by virtue of being adopted to explain/exchange/displace the Hebrew term *B*, *en* in this sense is a paraphrasis. On the other hand, *en* can be explained in terms of what Oepke calls "a mystically local conception of *dwelling* in a pneuma element comparable to the air."[2]

Oepke identifies five (5) different ways the "in Christ/Lord" formulae are used in the Pauline corpus. The first three (3) are said to be expressive of the "instrumental meaning" of *en*, while the fourth and fifth are expressive of the "mystical union."

> (A) In general they denote membership of Christ and the church...
> (B) They may also characterize an activity or state as Christian...
> (C) They can also be value judgments circumscribing the sphere of reference.
> (D) They sometimes denote the objective basis of fellowship with God, with *charis*... and
> (E) Comprehensively it notes the gathering of the many into one.[3]

In this and the chapter to follow, we will proceed in the following way. First, as regards the "baptismal passages," I will make the following arguments. One, I will argue against the claim that the baptismal passages simply employ an "instrumental meaning" of *en* in the formula "in the Lord." While it may be the case that the baptismal passages "denote membership in the church," nevertheless such inclusion is not so simple (or simply "instrumental") as Oepke would have us believe. I will argue that the "baptismal passages" are expressive of a more comprehensive convictional system with its own logic. Second, I will argue that Oepke's claim that "in the Lord," and "in Christ" note the comprehensive gathering of *the many into one* is correct, althought incomplete. As we have already learned from our reading of 1 Cor 11:11 & 12a, with respect to the gender difference the opposites of male and female are "in the Lord." I will argue that in the baptismal passages, **OPPOSITES** (the many) are gathered "in Christ" (are one) as **OPPOSITES**.

Secondly, in the chapter to follow, having developed the interpretation of "in Christ" as the gathering of opposites, we will return to the "reconciliation fragment" and consider the meaning of the phrase that "In Christ, God was reconciling the world to himself...."

BAPTISM IN CHRIST

Commonly labeled "Baptismal Passages," 1 Cor 12:12 & 13 and Galatians 3:27 & 28 are two very obvious texts in which Paul makes a great deal of oppositional pairs occurring **in** Christ. These texts will usher us into the discussion of the peculiar phrase "in the Lord."[4]

> [12]For just as the body is one and has many members, and all the members of the body, though many, are one body, so it is with Christ. [13]For by one spirit we were all baptized into one body--Jews or Greeks, slaves or free--and all were made to drink of one spirit.[5]
>
> I Corinthians 12

> [27]For as many of you as were baptized into Christ have put on Christ. [28]There is neither Jew nor Greek, there is neither slave nor free, there is neither male nor female; for you are all one in Christ Jesus.[6]
>
> Galatians 3

Our first selection asserts at v 13 that just as the body is one and has many members, and just as all the members, though many, are one body, then the various differences existing in opposition to one another (Jews and Greeks, slaves and free) are baptized into one body. That is, Christ is one body into which the many members are baptized. The oppositional differences persist in their opposition as different members **in** one body.

On the other hand, it appears that Gal 3:28 asserts that a variety of social distinctions are to be negated. "There is **neither** Jew **nor** Greek, **neither** male **nor** female, **neither** slave **nor** free." The passage concludes that *all of these differences* (the differences which have just been negated) *are one in Christ*. That is, "for (meaning in this instance, "since") *you are all one in Christ Jesus...*" "there is neither jew nor greek... slave nor free ... male nor female...." That "*many are one*" assumes that *there are many which are one*, **not** that *the many are no more* in Christ.

ESCHATOLOGICAL END: DIFFERENCES TERMINATED IN CHRIST

Karl Barth contends that the order of nature (the conflicting differences) and the order of salvation (oneness in Christ) must be kept distinct. The order of salvation does not abrogate the order of the world or vice versa. The oneness of "natural" opposites occurs in the "eschatological abrogation" taking place "in Christ." Bultman concurs, asserting that it cannot be said, "natural relations mean nothing to us, so let us ignore them!"[7] Conzelmann concludes that baptism brings about the eschatological abrogation of human differences which no longer exist in Christ, i.e., in Christ's body which is the church.[8]

Among other things, the above reading of the "baptismal passages" must introduce a division between what is and what is to come, or what is and what is potential. Both passages lack any mention of "eschatology," let alone the assumed bifurcation of the "natural" and "eschatological" (supernatural). The eschatological interpretation bids we lay out the "natural" and the "super-natural" along a theological time line on which the "super-natural" will appear at the "end" of the world or **nature**. And at the temporal end of things, the various differences shall be "abrogated" in the body of Christ.

Differences In Christ

As we saw in our (first) rereading of the texts above, the "differences" are not collapsed into "oneness" in the *Christos*. They are, instead, gathered and preserved in their differentiation. And this reading resonates with Paul's instructions in 1 Cor 7:17-24 to the different groups in the church at Corinth.

> 17Only, let every one lead the life which the Lord has assigned
> to him, and in which God has called him. This is my rule in all
> the churches. 18Was any one at the time of his call already
> circumcised? Let him not seek to remove the marks of
> circumcision. Was any one at the time of his call
> uncircumcised? Let him not seek circumcision. 19For neither
> circumcision counts for anything nor uncircumcision, but keeping
> the commandments of God. 20Every one should remain in the
> state in which he was called. 21Were you a slave when called?
> Never mind. But if you can gain your freedom, avail yourself of
> the opportunity. 22For he who was called in the Lord as a slave
> is a freedman of the Lord. Likewise he who was free when
> called is a slave of Christ. 23You were bought with a price; do
> not become slaves of men. 24So, brethren, in whatever state
> each was called, there let him remain with God.

Not only does Paul **not** collapse the various differences addressed in the text, he instructs each to remain as they are. Hebrews are to remain Hebrews, gentiles...gentiles, so on and so forth. There is no move to annihilate the difference. *The differences* are to continue *as differences. Differences are differences!* For Paul contends "...the Lord has assigned... and ...God has called..." these different lives into being, concluding "This is how I--order/ or rule--in all the churches."[9]

Betz contends that Galatians 3:27 & 28 (and 1 Cor 12:12 & 13 as well) are not about the eschatological annihilation of the natural orders. Instead, the baptismal passages continue Paul's abolition (by means of a reversal which relativizes and displaces) of all "claims to privilege" by any and all groups in the church.[10] The triple negation of v 3:28 is not an *annihilation* of the differences into oneness. *Neither one nor the other has a prerogative. Nor is one the origin of the other.* Priorities and dominations are presented and reversed thus relativizing priority and domination. Differences persist in their tension with one another, each remaining what or who or how it is. Paul rejects the various attempts to overcome the differentiations (racial, economic and gender). And he accomplishes this, not by rejecting the use of hierarchy by some appeal to the "sameness" of the various differences, but by (re-)asserting each contentious ranking of the differences and then reversing the hierarchy. Thus, one might conclude that Paul, by (re-)asserting and reversing each of the hierarchies, negates all differentiation. And that such a method of critique leaves us with "nothing." For in the end, the hierarchies cancel one another out leaving neither ranking nor differences. But such an assessment fails to take into account how Paul employs the reversal as a means of relativizing differences, and of rejecting all attempts to subordinate one aspect to the other in a contentious ranking.

DYEING IN CHRIST

Derived from the Greek *baptizō*, to baptize means quite literally "to dip," "to immerse," "to bury" in a liquid. In its pre-litergical, pre-Christian usuage, *baptizō* refered almost exclusively to "dipping cloth in dye."[11] It was identified so much so that *baptein* came to mean "to steep, dye or color" as well as "to dip." And *Baptisia* or *Baphia* names a genus of plants of the pea family used to dye cloth.

Despite this dominant pre-liturgical, pre-Christian usuage of *baptizō*, baptism has come to be understood in the hermeneutical tradition of the institutional church to name the "entry" of the person being "baptized" into the church which is the body of Christ. And among many protestant interpreters baptism is understood as a ritual cleasing which restores the purity of the person.

However, I believe that to conclude that this is the dominant meaning of baptism in the Pauline texts before us, is *mistaken*. As we shall see, the verse at Galatians 3:27 plays heavily upon the pre-liturgical themes of "immersion and dye."

> [27]For as many of you as were *baptized* into *Christ* have put on Christ.

First, "have put on" is offered in translation of *enedusasthe*. From the root *en-duō*, meaning "to put on, to envelop in, to hide in" and thus commonly "to cloth," *enedusasthe* is a Aorist middle (2nd Aorist) indicative, "you hide yourselves," or "you clothed yourselves." Thus the verse might read

> For as many of you as were baptized into Christ--hid yourselves/ clothed yourselves--in Christ.

If we play upon the themes of "immersion and dye" we might read the verse as "For as many of you as were immersed in Christ--colored yourselves in Christ" or "For as many of you as were dyed in Christ--covered yourselves in Christ". But this play continues. For that in which "many of you were **baptized**" and with which "you--clothed/ covered/ colored--yourselves" is *Christos*. Offered in the Septuigint in translation of the Hebrew *messiah* (meaning "annointed one," "one annointed with holy olive oil") *Christos* (from *chrisma* meant "an unguent" or "holy oil," from the verb *chriō* "to annoint") is the one who is "covered" or "annointed."[12]

There is a sense in v 27 that in being dipped in (immersed in) the annointed, one envelops/dyes/covers oneself with the annointed. All who are immersed in *Christos* have endowed (*enduō*) themselves with *Christos*. They are steeped **in** *Christos*; soaked, saturated, stained. Paul makes much of the notion of being "covered" in Christ throughout the corpus of his epistles.[13]

MIDDLE VOICE

In our reading of Gal 3:27 we noted that *enedusasthe* is an Aorist middle (2nd Aorist) indicative which notes a self-reflexive action. Anyone who is baptized in Christ "endowed **one's self** with Christ." Let us take note at this point that *Christos* is neither the agent who **baptizes**, nor the one who "endowed." ***Christos* is that into which one is baptized and with which one endowed oneself in having been baptized**, but, *Christos* enjoys no causal status in the event. ***Christos* is the medium, the place in which baptism happens.** As we shall see with respect to the reconciliation fragment, *Christos* bespeaks a **non/self-reflexive middle voice.**

* * * *

In the Pauline texts, "baptism in Christ" is not the means by which some hidden characteristic which the various groups have in common is disclosed. Baptism is not the restoration of some hidden quality, the washing away of that which covers and conceals some common nature shared by the various differences.

Baptism in Christ is an occasion of closure, concealment and disclosure which gathers and preserves those in opposition as opposites. Those in opposition are preserved, sheltered, covered/baptism/dyed in Christ. Their differences are gathered in their differentiation and are preserved as differences. And those in opposition are said to be one in Christ because they have been immersed or concealed in *Christos*. Once having been immersed in *Christos*, those who have been baptised in Christ are said to emerge saturated, dyed, steeped, soaked, changed. Dipped in their differentiation, they are gathered by the covering of *Christos* which conceals them all.

IDENTITY OR DIFFERENCE
ECCLESIOLOGY OR CHRISTOLOGY

For the theologian, a foreboding sense of ambiguity has been lurking just out of sight, sensed but not heard, in our discourse of

Paul's "baptismal passages." Under the dominance of systematic theology and its compartmentalization, most theologians would at least hesitate, if not halt at this point of the discussion, to inquire "Is Paul developing his 'christology' or his 'ecclesiology' in the baptismal passages?" In other words, are the baptismal passages first and foremost about entry into the membership of an institution, "church," or are they symbolic expressions about the identity of "Christ"?

Conzelmann has noted that Paul makes no clear distinction (or even gives a hint that there need be) between Christ and the *ekklēsia*. As ambiguous as this may appear to the systematic theologian, Paul plays fast and free with the notion of "body". Those who are baptized are baptized into one body, the ecclesia, the gathering, and that *ekklēsia* is (the body) Christ. Members of the *ekklēsia* are members of Christ's *sōma*, flesh, body.

In the Pauline epistles, *Christos* is that divinity who negating himself, emptied of rank and position, is humiliated and crucified.[14] Selfless, humiliated and crucified, Paul's *Christos* is the gathering of the differences which preserves them as such **in it-self**, a self which is no self at all.

Thus, in the *ekklēsia*, the body of Christ, there is a "meeting," or at least the possibility of "meeting" between those who are in opposition. For they "meet" in opposition as differences **in** a divine milieu, in an empty space. And the empty space/domain/milieu is determined as an empty place by the presence of those who meet in their opposition to one another. Crucified and absent, *Christos* is an opening in which differences are illuminated as differences, in which those in opposition meet, in which **dif-**ferances are (dif-) **ferried**.

For Paul, the *ekklēsia*, the body of *Christos*, is the meeting--the gathering of differences--in the name of the one whose presence is deferred and whose absence is the occasion for those who are present being present. To say that for Paul *Christos* is a "milieu" is to say that that which is absent (*Christos*) is presented as absent. Such an absence is determined by those things which are present. Paradoxically the absence is the occasion which allows those things which occur--to occur. *Christos* is the meeting, yielding space to the opposites while those in opposition, by virtue of their standing in opposition, yield the *Christos*.

As such, *Christos* does not name an identity. *Christos* is that which covers those who are immersed in Christ. The *Christos* covers, stains and conceals, but is itself not something.

As we have seen, Christ **atones**. Shortened from the phrase "at one," atone names the activity of gathering together those who differ.[15] *Christos* **a/t-ones** by covering and concealing. Those who are in opposition are "at one" in Christ.

In the Old Testament, "atonement," offered in translation of the Hebrew *kaphar*, names the oneness of those who are covered. Such covering might include the gathering of the different tribes in the tent (covering) of meeting. The covering which **a/t-ones** might be the blood of a sacrifice which is poured on the altar and sprinkled upon those in the congregation. Such covering was said to please God and to bring pardon and forgiveness. Thus, the blood of the sacrifice which covered the altar and covered the people, was said to **a/t-one** the people and God. Those who were **a/t-oned** were "together" and "reconciled."

In a related sense, *kaphar* quite literally names the covering which gathers a family or village. It names the "at homeness" of those who gather undercover.

SUMMARY

How are we to think Paul's christology (if we don't insist too much that his thought "fit" the systematic scheme too neatly) in light of our reading of the "baptismal passages" and the "disordering of the hierarchy"? In the disordering of the hierarchy we discerned that male and female co-originate and co-dominate one another **as other** in their coming into being and in their sexual relationship. And that such co-domination and co-origination occur "**in** the Lord."

In the Corinthian baptismal passage we have read that those in opposition became members of one body in baptism. And in the Galatians baptismal passages we discerned that those in opposition are separated and together "**in** the *Christos*."

In *Christos* those who having been in opposition to one another in their contentious struggle for domination are preserved in their differentiation. The tension, between those in opposition, and between the two self-contradicting hierarchies, is preserved in its tension as tension. The privilege of each is preserved. No simple hierarchy rules. The differences are not allowed to rest in some settled state of affairs. With the privilege of each preserved, there is the preservation of constant tension. The differences occur **in** *Christos* **AS** "opposition".

This tension, does not lead to the simple negation of one by the other, but is the negation of an essentialistic sense of identity. The gender difference is preserved in the oppositional interplay of male and female. So too with slave and free, and Jewish and Gentile.[16]

The oppositional pairs are set in exclusive opposition to one another. They occur, by definition, in opposition to one another. Each is defined by the other **as** other. Their identities are determined by their "difference", their opposition. The difference which their opposition marks and in which they are held in tension one with the other, the gathering place of opposition, is the *Christos*.

The differences are gathered in their opposition not by an appeal to some common nature or essence. They are a/t-oned in their opposition in the immersion into *Christos*. In being a/t-oned, concealed, covered, and stained by *Christos*, they are a/t-oned (i.e., forgiven and pardoned).

CONCLUSIONS

The doctrine of the **mysterious** *oikonomia* and **baptism in** ***Christos*** are strikingly similar in many regards. Both are concerned with how "dif-**ferences**" **ferry**, with how opposites are a/t-one. In both the doctrine of the *oikonomia* and in **baptism**, the a/t-onement of the opposition occurs in *Christos*.

Yet, the striking difference between the doctrine of the **mysterious** ***oikonomia*** and **baptism in** ***Christos*** is that while the latter is concerned with how the various mundane sets of opposites are **a/t-oned**, the former is concered with the **a/t-onement of God and humanity**. In the doctrine of the *oikonomia*, it is the (at-)**one**ness of the opposites God and humanity **in Christ** that atones. It is an atoning which given its double meaning, is **incomprehensible**.

The play of *ekklēsia* and in *Christos* in the Pauline corpus violates not only the attempts to systematize Paul's texts into ecclesiological and christological categories, but it also violates ecclesiastical institutionalization. A gathering of differences, an accommodation of opposites, violates institutional coherence/identity and yields institutional anarchy. As such, the *Christos/ekklēsia* in the Pauline texts is powerless and thus incapable of harboring conclusions which yield force and violence. The full significance of such a christo-ecclesiology are beyond the limits of the present study but will be forthcoming in a later work.

NOTES

1. Oepke, "*En*," *TDNT*, II:541.
2. Oepke, 541 & 542. Emphasis mine.
3. Oepke, 541. In his brief analysis, Oepke contends that the underlying spatial concept gives us the clue to the true significance of the formula *en Christos Iēsous* and its parallels, in both the "local" and the "instrumental" meaning (542). Preoccupied as he is with the historical Jesus, Oepke states his bias clearly when he contends that "At root is the view of Christ as a universal personality. This is to be construed *cosmically* and eschatologically rather than *mystically* in the current Hellenistic sense" (emphasis mine). One of the problems with Oepke's attempt to conceive Paul's christology cosmically is that it is not altogether clear whether or not Christ is in the world or the world is in Christ in Paul's epistles. While our study is not engaged with the issue pertaining to the biblical hermeneutic commonly called "the search for the historical Jesus," it is nevertheless clear that those who are, tend to pick and choose as they please from the verses in the Pauline epistle or, like Von Harnack, to simply dismiss the Pauline corpus as so much addendum to the Christian faith, i.e., the rethinking of the faith in terms of Greek philosophical speculation.
4. I assume in my reading of each of these passages a broader reading of the *textus* which for the sake of time, is not included here.
5. Lietzmann contends that the phrase "whether Jewish or Greek," etc., disturbingly interrupts the course of the argument of 1 Cor 12:12. The reason being, asserts Lietzmann, that the intent of the section is about unity. But on his terms, v 12 is about differences. While Conzelmann contends that Lietzmann misunderstands the intend of the passage, it is not very clear what Conzelmann takes to be the intent (Conzelmann, 212, fn 14). As we shall see, Lietzmann is correct in his identification of the presence of difference and unity, but his conclusion as to its not fitting has more to do with his presupposition regarding the relationship of difference and unity than with the logic of the text.
6. Biblical scholars commonly observe the strong similarities in the content, vocabulary and structure of the two passages. Many believe that the Corinthian and Galatian epistles were written within the two year period Paul lived in Ephesus.
7. Bultmann, *Faith And Understanding*, 1:77/(48); quoted in Conzelmann 188, fns 75 & 76.
8. Conzelmann, 212.

9. *"Kai outos en tais ekklēsiais pasais diatassomai."*

10. See Romans 2:25-29, 3:1-20, 4:9-12, 9:3-5, 10:2; Gal 5:6, 6:15; 1 Cor 7:19 and Phil 3:3.

11. The Greek *baptein* "to dip, steep, dye, color," comes from *baphē* "a dyeing." It cognates with the ON *kuefia* "to plunge," and "OSwed *Kvaf*, "a deep place." See Klein, 147.

12. The Indo-European root of *chriō* ("to annoint") is possibly *ghrei* or *ghri*, which are enlargements of the base *gher* which means "to rub." If *chriō* is "to rub," the *christos* is "the rubbed one." The base *gher* carries such meanings as (I) "scratch, scrape away" (as in an ointment which rises to the top in the process of boiling), and (IV) "seige; embrace, enclose, enclosure." The Greek *choros* was "an enclosed place for dancing." And *chonos*, time, "embraces all things." See Klein.

13. Rom 13:12, 13:14; 1 Cor 15:53, 54; 2 Cor 5:2, 3, & 4; Gal 3:27.

14. Phil. 2:7

15. Klein.

16. The Jewish/Gentile difference is a play in one sense upon the racial difference, but it is also a play upon the set of oppositional terms "civilized" and "*un*-civilized."

11.

THE RECONCILIATION FRAGMENT

THE *TEXTUS* OF THE RECONCILIATION FRAGMENT

16From now on, therefore, we regard no one from a human point of view; even though we once regarded Christ from a human point of view, we regard him no longer. 17Therefore, if any one is in Christ, he is a new creation (or creature); the old has passed away, behold, the new has come. 18All this is from God, who through Christ reconciled us to himself and gave us the ministry of reconciliation; 19**as it is written** (*ōs oti*)

In Christ, God was reconciling the world to himself

not counting their trespasses against them, and entrusting to us the message of reconciliation. 20So we are ambassadors for Christ, God making his appeal through us. We beseech you on behalf of Christ, be reconciled to God. 21For our sake he made him to be sin who knew no sin, so that in him we might become the righteousness of God.

2 Cor 5:17-21[1]

At last we return to the passage with which we began our inquiry into the Pauline corpus. Only now, we read the verse in its con-text. We understand the difference the texture of an epistle makes.

We have returned to the "reconciliation passage," now mindful of the "place" *Christos* plays in the *textus*, of the space it marks and displaces in the midst of opposition, or how it marks the difference between slave-free, Jew-Gentile, male-female. Whereas these oppositional sets are mundane, social, political and/or biological, the "reconciling passage" encompasses an opposition of a grand scale; "God and the world." Note that this is not a cosmology.

Verse 18a "All this is from God," traces a common theological theme in the Pauline epistlesy[2]. In this verse, the phrase "All this is from God" marks the beginning of a theological explanation for the conclusions stated in vv 16 & 17;

> [16]...therefore, we regard no one from a human point of view....
> [17]Therefore, if any one is in Christ, he is a new creation....

Both (1) the regarding no one from a human point of view and (2) being a new creation "in Christ" are "...from God." Verse 18 provides the reasons for these conclusions. "All this is from God" because (1) "God...reconciled us to himself...through Christ," and, (2) it was "God...who...gave us the ministry of reconciliation."

I suggest that we keep these two themes separated. It is argued by many that Paul's intent in the passage is to justify his own ministry and message. If this is the case, then we must be alert to the difference between his purpose (the justification of his own ministry/message) and the **means** by which he justifies his purpose to the reader. We'll begin with noting the structural similarities of vv 18 and 19.

> [18a]All this is from God
> [18b]who through Christ reconciled us to himself
> [18c]and gave us the ministry of reconciliation.
>
> [19a]As it is said (*ōs oti*)
> [19b]In Christ, God was reconciling the world to himself
> [19c]not counting their trespasses against them
> [19d]and entrusting to us the message of reconciliation.

There are two sets of repetitions in vv 18 and 19. Verse 18b ("...God, who through Christ reconciled us to himself") and v 19b ("In Christ, God was reconciling the world to himself") appear to be repetitive, as are vv 18c ("...and gave us the ministry of reconciliation") and 19d ("and entrusting to us the ministry of reconciliation"). In each verse, Paul begins by making an appeal to God's activity of reconciliation "in Christ." No argument is made in the text for the validity of the reconciliation. Paul assumes that his reader will readily identify and accept the reconciliation theme.

Thus, assuming that the reader accepts the validity of God's activity of reconciliation through/in Christ, Paul suggests that **his** (Paul's) ministry/message of reconciliation is a continuation of God's reconciliation. As God reconciled himself to us and the world through Christ and entrusted the message/ministry of reconciliation to us, so "we are ambassadors for Christ (in the world), God making his appeal through us (to the world). We (i.e., Paul and company) beseech you on behalf of Christ, be reconciled to God."

THE INTER-TEXTUAL AUTHORITY OF A FRAGMENT

While it is clear that the purpose of the text is to support Paul's ministry/message, and that vv 18 and 19 have strikingly similar structures, v 19a introduces a twist: *ōs oti*. Often translated "As it is said....", *ōs oti* introduces a text or verse **independent of the Corinthian exchange**, which is now included in the Epistle so as to provide support for Paul's ministry/message.[3] Given its independence from the exchange between Paul and the Corinthian correspondance, we may assume that the "fragment" is placed in the text as a warrant for the positions Paul is taking.[4]

While Paul's use of the verse in the text is employed, called upon to support his own agenda, the verse stands out in the *textus* as a fragment. This fragment occurs in the Pauline text as a fragment, a piece pulled from another context and woven into the tapestry of the epistle as something which simultaneously belongs and doesn't. It is this tension of the piece both fitting and not fitting in the *textus* that textures the epistle and discloses the fragmentedness of the verse in its displaced/placement.

It is the tension, the weaving of the fragment *as displaced* (coming from another context) but *placed* in the Corinthian epistle, that the fragment "warrants" the claims being made in the epistle. As a fragment, the verse occupies the place of authority in the weave. It is called upon as authoritative to support Paul's agenda.[5]

We cannot avoid considering how the fragment occurs in the context of the epistle. That is to say, it is the tension of the fragment--drawn from a different context and yet woven into a this *textus*--which provides us with a strategy for reading the verse. Or, to put it another way, our reading the *fragment **as** a fragment* which "warrants" other claims will be insightful.

The similarities between vv 18b ("who through Christ reconciled us to himself") and 19b ("In Christ, God was reconciling the world to himself") now fades. Our reading was too hasty, we passed over "As it is said" (*ōs oti*) too quickly, failing to note that the writer intends for us to assume that vv 18b and 19b are the same, though they are not. In both verses God is engaged in reconciling. In both verses, the act is self-reflexive with the subject. God reconciles to himself. However subtle or minute, what "God reconciles to himself" is different between the two verses. In v 18 "God reconciles **us** to himself." In v 19 "God reconciles the **world** to himself." Paul's identification in v 18b that "**we**" are the ones "God reconciles to himself" plays well with his second point that 18c "God...gave **us** (i.e., Paul and company) the ministry of reconciliation."

And v 18c is duplicated at v 19d ("God...entrusted to us the message of reconciliation") so as to finish the frame, or complete the series. It is assumed that by being woven in at v 19b, the fragment will be read as duplicating v 18b, and will support the conclusion at v 19d as v 18b supports v 18c. Thus, vv 18 and 19 will be read as **not** different.

But the fragment--*fragments* the progression and coherence of the text. While Paul is preoccupied with God reconciling **us** (i.e., Paul and company) to himself, which in turn justifies their ministry and message, the fragment bespeaks "God's reconciling **the world** to himself." The move from v 18b to v 18c is not duplicated in v 19. From "the world" to "us" is incomplete.

KATALLASSŌN

[19]In Christ, God was reconciling the world to himself....

Translated "reconciling," the verb *katallassōn*, and the related noun *katallagē*, are used exclusively in the New Testament by Paul.[6] In its theological application in the Judeo-Christian tradition, *katallassō* suggests "the changing of persons from enmity to friendship."[7] Thus, the English translation "reconciling" (viz Latin *re-* "again," *con-* "together," and *-ciliare* "to call"), meaning "calling-together-again" is a good interpretation of the Greek.[8] Reconciling suggests a "bringing into unity," "meeting," "encounter," of those who are at odds with one another. "To reconcile" is to reconcile differences, as in overcoming the differences or to meet and come to an understanding about the opposition. Friends do not need to be reconciled. Enemies are reconciled. To say that reconciling has occurred is to simultaneously recall (*-con*) the earlier (*re-*) being together (*-ciliare*), the division, and the return.

Katallassō has also been translated into English as **to atone**. This practice, while never common, was more prevelant in the earliest English translations and progressively less the case in the past two centuries. The decline in the exchange parallels the shortening of **at-one** (the loss of the hyphen) to **atone** and the subsequent loss of the sense of oneness evident in the earlier spelling. With the shortening, atone comes to mean simply "justification."

If we translate *katallassō* as "**at-one**," then the passage would read, "*In Christ, God was* ***at-oning*** *the world to himself....*" So rendered, the verse continues the play we discovered in **reconciling**, though as **at-oning** the verse emphasises more directly the issue of the **oneness of opposites**.

We have already come upon one instance in which *katallassō* appears. 1 Cor 7:11 reads "but if she does, let her remain single or else be reconciled to her husband--and that the husband should not divorce his wife." This is the only instance in the Pauline corpus where reconciling is employed to bespeak the "coming-together-again" of exclusively human individuals. Romans 11:15 plays upon the multidimensional reconciling of God and the world which is also presented as the reconciliation of Jews and Gentiles. "For if their rejection means the reconciliation (*katallagē*) of the world, what will their acceptance mean but life for the dead."

In Romans 5:6-11, the estrangement between *theos* and *anthrōpos* is described as an enmity (cf. Rom 11:28). *Theos* and *anthrōpos* are at odds, in opposition, divided. Humanity has broken with God in their sinning. And the metaphor used is that *Theos* and *anthrōpos* are separated by a "dividing wall of hostility." It is a wall which is brought down in the death of Christ.

> 6While we were yet helpless, at the right time Christ died for the ungodly (*asebōn*, impious, ungodly, sinful). 7Why, one will hardly die for a righteous man--though perhaps for a good man one will dare even to die. 8But God shows his love for us in that while we were yet sinners Christ died for us. 9Since, therefore, we are now justified by his blood, much more shall we be saved by him from the wrath of God. 10For if while we were enemies we were reconciled to God by the death of his Son, much more, now that we are reconciled, shall we be saved by his life. 11Not only so, but we also rejoice in God through our Lord Jesus Christ, through whom we have now received our reconciliation.
>
> 18Then as one man's trespass led to condemnation for all men, so one man's act of righteousness leads to acquittal and life for all humans.[9]

Earlier we distinguished between those passages in 2 Cor 5:18 & 19 which bespoke God's reconciling us/world to himself (vv 18b & 19b) from those which justified Paul's ministry/message of reconciliation (vv 18c & 19d). Another way of distinguishing these different themes of reconciliation ("God's reconciling ..." from Paul's "message/ministry of reconciliation) is to note their grammatical difference. Paul's message/ministry of **reconciliation** (*Katallagē*) is nominal. God's **reconciling** us/world to himself is active. *Katallassō* is a verb.[10]

In each of the reconciliation texts, enemies stand in opposition:

God-humanity
God-sinners
Godly-ungodly
God-world
God-us.

All things are from God, and so God "**re-calls**" them back "together." In a self-reflexive act God calls those who stand in opposition to return. The invocation yields an **a/t-oning**. Thus, we might re-read 2 Cor 5:19b as "God was re-calling the world to himself," or "God was calling the world to meet with him again," or "God was calling-together-again the world to himself," or "God was **a/t-oning** the world to himself."

Thus far we have played with the **traditional** reading/translation of "reconciliation" and *katallassō*. The non-theological or, better, pre-Christian use of *katallassō* and *katallagē* meant "exchange" or "to exchange," and was used especially to denote the exchange of money.[11] In other ancient Greek texts it also named the "money-changer's profit" and on occasion "freight, or merchandise."[12] And it is suggested that in rare instances, *katallassō* named a "change" or "difference."[13]

In all these uses of *katallassō*, the related themes of "change" and "exchange" are dominate. It has been suggested that in the act of "changing" enemies into friends, there is an exchange, from the eleborate exchange of gifts by heads of state, the exchange of signitures that occurs in the signing of a treaty, to the simple exchange of hands (or arms) in the hand shake. All of these play upon the themes of change and ex-change which **a/t-one** those in opposition. Such an **a/t-oning** does not make all the same, but "ferries" those who differ, gathering and preserving those who are in opposition.

MONOTHEISM/PANTHEISM AND THE RECONCILIATION FRAGMENT

> How are we to think the reconciling, the *katallassō*, the a/t-oning, of *Theos* and *kosmos* in *Christos*?

Theos and *kosmos* are in opposition, divided, enemies. This enmity is changed by *Theos* who was reconciling the world to himself, calling the world to meet with him again, calling-together-again the world to himself, **a/t-oning** the world and God. The opposition of "God and the world," and the self-reflexive activity of God in reconciling the world (to himself) appears to be monotheistic. God originates the activity upon a passive object, the world, which God returns to "himself."

And yet, despite how neatly this fits monotheistic definitions, "in Christ" occurs as a spoiler to the systematization. The activity of reconcilation occurred "in *Christos*." The opposites, *kosmos* and *Theos*, are gathered "in *Christos*." That is, one divinity (*Theos*) in opposition to the world, re-gathers the world to himself in another divinity (*Christos*).

This calling to council, this self-reflexive activity by God **happens** "in Christ." Christ is not the agent of reconciliation nor the mediator of *Theos* to the world. In the fragment, the reconciling does not occur *in the world*. The reconciling of the world to God occurs "in Christ."[14]

The gathering in Christ might appear to be pan-theistic, but only if one mistakenly assumes that is pan-theistic by virtue of "what" is gathered: *pan* and *theos*. That is, the gathering "in *Christos*" is "pan-theistic" because the opposites--world (*pan*-) and God (-*theos*)--are gathered. But such a movement forgets the opposition, the enemity of God and the world which is being addressed and reconciled in the fragment. God and world **are** reconciling, are regathering, are **a/t-oning**. The re-calling together, what it means to be "in *Christos*," is not discernable in the preoccupation with "world" and "God". The re-conciliation of "world" and "God" "in *Christos*" is not the overcoming of the difference of God and world. The world is not God nor is God the world "in *Christos*."[15] The difference of God and world is gathered and preserved as difference.

While God is the self-reflexive agent, Christ is the non-reflexive place of meeting in which God calls the cosmos to meet with him again. *Christos* is not reconciled to *Theos*, nor with the cosmos for that matter. In the fragment, *Christos* is not the agent of reconciliation but is the domain, the place, the dwelling. And in this dwelling, in this meeting, "in *Christos*," *Theos* does not cease being *Theos*, nor does the world cease being the world. In their differentiation one reconciles the other, and in being reconciled, both are gathered and preserved in the meeting, "in *Christos*."

I have argued above that "in Christ" is neither the "instrument" by which God relates to the world, nor is "in *Christos*" the residue of some pantheistic cosmology which Paul employs in his "christology". In the reconciliation fragment, *Christos* is not *Theos*. Nor is *Christos* the *kosmos*.

The fragment does not serve some pantheistic purpose nor is it the product of a pantheistic speculation. For one thing, *pan* and *Theos* are not the same. They are different. And it is their **dif-**(ferance) that is (dif-) **ferried** in the *Christos*.

The a/t-onement is not metaphysical. What are a/t-oned are not-the-same. The atoning "in *Christos*" is the at-oning of differences in their being gathered and preserved **AS** differences. It is a gathering and preserving which conceals itself in its **a/t-oning**.

THEOS AND CHRISTOS
A DIVINE CONFLICT

PARAPHRASTIC RECONCILIATION RECONSIDERED

The assessment by Furnish, Bultmann, Bruce and company that the reconciliation fragment is a paraphrastic construction appears to be the result of their focus upon the "activity of God" depicted in the fragment. In other words, the fragment is paraphrasitic because God acts indirectly upon the world through another instead of reconciling the world to himself directly.[16]

However, we have found in our study that *Christos* fails to provide "causal" connection between God and the world (or any segment of the world). *Christos* is not the means by which nor the agent of causality. And so, our search for lines of causality frustrated our endeavor.

While I concur with the paraphrastic assessment by Furnish, Bultmann, Bruce and company, I do not agree with their reading of *en*. Therefore, I reject the argument that the passage is paraphrastic in that God acted upon the world through a third party, an instrument, *Christos*, in order to accomplish something with a second party.

Paraphrastic constructions often increase in a language when grammatical devises and structures fade from use. In some cases, an older structure simply disappears (as with the optative case in Modern Greek). In other instances, a particular case or voice is no longer used, but the structure persists paraphrastically (as in the case of the future tense in Modern Greek).[17]

The Greek middle voice, so evident in the Heraclitean fragments, faded in its use by the beginning of the Christian era.[18] However, while the grammatical devises and endings which marked the middle voice were fading from Greek texts by the beginning of the Christian era, they nevertheless are evident in texts of the period. Occassionaly middle voice endings are used in texts of the period, though more frequently the language retained the middle voice and expressed it paraphrastically, primarily through the passive voice.[19]

The paraphrasis (*periphrasis*) of the fragment is exemplified not by God's indirect action through an instrument, but by the reconciliation that **happens in Christ**. Reconciliation happens in Christ as something which Christ **does not cause**. Reconciliation is in-directly (*peri-*) dis-closed (*phrasis*) **in Christ**, but **not by Christ**.[20]

If we work with the notions of "round about" or "indirection," and attempt to understand how each might be expressed given the different metaphors of disclosure, we might better understand the meaning of "in *Christos*" in the reconciliation fragment. If reconciliation is verbally disclosed, is "declared" or "told" indirectly, then the message of reconciliation travels round about. Reconciliation is "declared" by God to the world **through** Christ.

However, if we think paraphrasis as visual disclosure,--"to show forth," "to reveal," "to bring to light,"--then paraphrasticicly something is "brought to light in the dark," or is "uncovered undercover," or is "disclosed in being concealed." Reconciliation is thus "revealed" by God to the world in the dark, is disclosed in the concealment, uncovered undercover. The a/t-oning is revealed in the opposition.

Such a reading of visual disclosure plays upon themes we considered earlier in terms of "tabernacle." God's self revealing in the tabernacle to the tribes of Israel, occured paraphrasicly: God uncovered God's self undercover (of the tent). In the concealment of the tabernacle, God disclosed.

But this theme of paraphrastic visual disclosure is also evident in our study of baptism in two ways. First, those who are baptized are immersed, buried, or saturated in Christ, and are forever covered in Christ through not **by** Christ. And, those in opposition who are baptised, are one "**in Christ**" but are also still "**in opposition.**" That is, those who are in opposition are at-one.

CENTRICITY AND CHRISTOS

It is commonly assessed that Paul's "theology" is "christocentric." The hierarchy of 1 Cor 11:3 is often alluded to as a significant example of the centrality of "*Christos*" in Paul's thought. In v 11:3 Christ is the central agent which mediates cause and rule between God and humanity. But, as we have already seen, the hierarchy of 1 Cor 11:3 is reversed and relativized in the *textus*, and Paul's reply cuts the chain of cause and authority. The reconciliation passage is also assessed as expressive of the christocentricity of Paul's "theology." Read with an instrumental emphasis, Christ is at the center between God and the world. But, as we have seen, such a reading fails both grammatically and in terms of the content. The traditional assessment that Paul's "theology" is "christocentric" is dependent upon the common reading of the texts which has already displaced the gap or lapse or space *Christos* marks in the text.

Christos, emptied, humiliated and crucified, traces a space, an opening in the very texture of Paul's textus; a gap at the very center of Paul's thinking. In the "rupture" of the traditional reading of these texts, in re-reading or double-reading, in the de-structuring and confusing of the old order, other readings occur which seek to trace and thus include the gaps, ruptures and confusions of the old order. They are the gaps, ruptures and confusions which have been overlooked, skipped over or filled in by the old order.

As we have seen in our reading of the baptismal passages and the reconciliation fragment, in the old reading "in Christ" occurs as such a "lapse". In the *textus*, "in Christ" traces a space, a place, a gap. However, in the old reading the gap was filled in, covered over, forgotten. Yet, in a gap which is no longer gapping, a place that has no space, nothing can meet or dwell.

To contend that the Pauline epistles are "**theo**-logy" is to have already erased *Christos*, the traces which mark the space whose gap is the center of Paul's text. In the erasure of *Christos*, *Theos* is written, filling and displacing the empty center.

The common assessment that Paul's "theo-logy" is christocentric (a *Christos* which no longer traces a space in the text, but is now an extension of *Theos*) finds itself bewildered at the very moment of its assessment. For now, having displaced the lapse traced by *Christos*, theology wonders how Paul's christology, incomplete as it now appears under the domination of theology, can do all it sets out to do, or appears to do in the Pauline text. And so theology concludes that Paul's **christo**-centric **theo**-logy (a christology which in service to *theos*, is already displaced) is paradoxically both **theo**-centric and **anthropo**-centric.

This dilemma, that the "center" of the "center" is not singular but paradoxically "theos-" and "anthropos-" centric, is born of a hermeneutic which does not recognize spaces as spaces. The gap which *Christos* traces must be displaced because a gap is no-thing.

IDENTITY

The deliberation over the "center" of the "center" is a search for that thing which is essential in and to Paul's theology. In one sense, the dilemma is the result of an inquiry which seeks to locate "the center" or "essence" around which everything else turns and twists and must related (but which itself transcends the turns, twists and relations) in Paul's theology when Paul's writing may not have such a "center." Thus, the dilemma is a dilemma precisely because a hermeneutic seeks to discern something in the text that doesn't exist. Or, to put it in other words, a hermeneutic which seeks to identify "essential identities" in a text which does not contain or present identities as essences, will always be frustrated about and mystified by the lack of clear and identifiable essences.

IN CHRISTOS AND THE *OIKONOMIA*

We found that the reconciliation fragment does possess themes which are played upon in the doctrine of the mysterious economy. Yet, the themes which are commonly identified as shared by the two are not the themes we discovered in our reading of the epistle text as a reply. In the Chalcedonian Ecumenical Creed and the Corinthian Epistles, the dominate christological theme is that those who are in opposition are said to be **a/t-one**. In the Pauline passages those factions in opposition are said to be one in Christ by baptism, and in Christ the world and God are **a/t-oned** by God. In the doctrine of the mysterious economy, the *phusis* of *theos* and the *phusis* of *anthrōpos* are one in Christ, and it is this oneness of the *phuseon* that **a/t-ones**.

In tandem with this theme of "**a/t-oneness**" is the problematic claim that the oneness in Christ preserves the differences of the various opposites AS differences. In fact, in both the doctrine of the economy and the Pauline "in *Christos*" passages, only those persons, natures, or whatever that are said to be in opposition are said to be one in Christ. Nothing is made of sameness per se. Differences mark the **a/t-oning** which marks the difference which mark the **a/t-oning**. *Christos*--empty, lacking, humiliated and crucified--is no ground. *Christos* traverses the perimeters in both unity and difference and fails to be an identity.

The conflict between *Theos* and *Christos* in the Pauline epistles is not a conflict between the one God and an intermediate god, but between two differing concepts of divinity or (to put it non-reflexively) between two divinities. *Christos* and *Theos* are different and differing divinities. *Christos* is not *Theos*, nor is *Christos* the *kosmos*. Instead, *Christos* marks the difference of *Theos* and *kosmos*, nor unlike the way the mysterious economy marks the difference of God and humanity in the Doctrine of the Incarnation.

The ambiguous relationship, the unresolved conflict between *Theos* and *Christos*, is expressive of Paul's "failure" (?) to clearly delimit the identity and status of each divinity from one another and with respect to everything else. Paul's "failure" to accomplish this task is a "failure" on his part to systematize. As such, the reader is left with a writing that lacks clear delimitation. Or put another way, we are left to read a letter whose texture is not simple. We are left with a work in which there is an on-going conflict which does not come to resolution and which escapes our hermeneutical attempts to bring it to resolution either by appeal to some foundation or by assessing the universality of some hierarchy.

I have argued that "in *Christos*" is neither the "instrument" by which *Theos* relates to the world, nor is it the residue of a pantheistic (stoic or otherwise) cosmology. What we find in Paul's letters regarding *Christos* is not metaphysical speculation (neo-platonic, aristotelian or stoic), but an endeavor to understand or conceive of the *Christos* as divine in terms of the "gathering" of opposites. I have suggested that "in *Christos*, as developed in the Baptismal passages, the reconciliation fragment and with regards to the gender difference, is the occasion for and is delimited by the play of opposition. *Christos* is unlike the opposites which are said to occur, to meet, to moot, to gather "in Christ." *Christos* is a "divine milieu" (Mark Taylor), "the forceful play of difference that forms the nonoriginal origin of everything...."[21] *Christos*, the milieu, marks a middle way, it is the place of crossing/gathering/opposition which inverts and subverts the privilage of the contrasts.

Christos accommodates *Theos*, providing a place for *Theos* to reconcile the world. In the Pauline epistles, only *Christos* is capable of accommodating such guests. However, in so accommodating God, the sovereignty of God is compromised. In accommodating, Christ provides for the accommodation (compromise) of God with the world.

"Christ" does not enjoy a clear sense of identity in the epistle. For one thing, *Christos* is marked by its difference from those in opposition which gather and are gathered. And in the gathering-- *Christos* is absent. Christ is not one of those who is gathered in opposition. *Christos* is not presented in the Pauline texts as having an opposite.[22]

> *Christos* is the gap
> which is nothing.

It is a milieu which is delimited by the opposites who meet. And in meeting, those in opposition make present the meeting place. If one must speak of the identity of the milieu, then it is the *coincidentia* (co-incidental, non-causal) *oppositorum* (opposition) alla Taylor and Derrida. *Christos* is the *coincidentia oppositorum*, a nonidentity or difference which overcomes itself in the play of the difference of identity and the identity of difference.

NOTES

1. Emphasis mine.

2. 2 Cor 5:18 "All things are from God," 1 Cor 11:12 "and all things are from God," etc.

3. In other Pauline texts, *ōs oti* introduces the content of something said (11:21) or written (2 Thess 2:2) which is traced in Paul's epistle. Käsemann suggests that *ōs* is "transitional" and that *oti* introduces a quote (Käsemann, 53, in Furnish, 318).

4. Verse 19b is introduced by "as it is said" (*ōs oti*). I argue that v 19b, "In Christ, God was reconciling the world to himself," has a life of its own, independent of the epistle. Furnish has pointed out that it has been suggested that the verse is the work of the Corinthian congregation under the influence of Paul (Collange), or that the formula originated with Paul and having been quoted back at him in the Corinthian correspondence to him, is being used by Paul in his reply (I.H. Marshall), or that the citation is from "a pre-Pauline hymnic fragment (Käsemann)" (Furnish, 334).

These and other assessments of the origin of the verse are textually speculative for there are no surviving records which might aid in such a historical reconstruction, nor a hint in the text that such is probable. While the origin of the verse is a historical topic about which little can actually be said at present, it is nevertheless clear that Paul believes the "verse" will exercise authority among his readers. And so, Paul uses the verse to support his argument.

5. Is it not strange that in the history of biblical hermeneutics, the scriptures occupy the places of authority in many western texts (theological, philosophical, literary, historical, institutionally) AS fragments which in their displacement are (placed) woven into texts?

6. The term *apo-katallassein* (a compound of *katallassō* [which appears in the Pauline epistles]) is used in the Pastoral Epistles (Eph. 2:16, Col 1:20, 22). The Pastoral Epistles often seek to imitate the content and style of the Pauline epistles, thus the use of *apo-katallessein* suggests such an imitation with a slight variation.

7. Thayer, 2644. Theological application of the terminology occurs in only a few texts of hellenistic Judaism (notably 2 Mac 1:4 & 5, 5:20, 7:33 and 8:29).

8. Klein.

9. This theme is echoed in the pseudo-Paul epistles. Ephesians 2:12-16,18 speaks of the division between Gentile and Hebrew as the difference between *theos* and *atheos*.

> "12Remember that you were at that time separated from Christ, alienated from the commonwealth of Israel, and strangers to the covenants of promise, having no hope and without God (*atheoi*) in the world. 13But now in Christ Jesus you who once were far off have been brought near (to the circumcised) in the blood of Christ. 14For he is our peace, who has made us both one, and has broken down the dividing wall of hostility... 16and might reconcile us both to God in one body through the cross, thereby bringing the hostility to an end.

[18]...for through him we both have access in one Spirit to the Father.

And a cosmic reconciliation is the theme in Col 1:20 although the term *kosmos* (world) is not employed. God wills "...to reconcile to himself **all things** (*ta panta*), whether on earth or in heaven...."

10. "Reconciliation" denotes the state of having been reconciled. It is a settled affair. Reconciling is an activity which unsettles what has been settled.

11. Thayer, 2643; LS, 899. In a psudo-aristotelian work *Oikonomia*, *katallagē* named the "exchange of money" (*Oikonomia* 1346b 24). See also P. Hib 1.100.4 (iii b.c.).

12. Ag 10, D.50.30, Diph. 66.14 and Euphro 3.4.

13. Phld. *Mus.* 74k.

14. Käsemann seeks to resolve the subtle difference by means of a developmental hypothesis. Furnish writes:

> Käsemann suggests that the citation is drawn in this situation from 'a pre-Pauline hymnic fragment,' and that it extends from v 19 through v 21. In his view, the earliest form of the tradition would be found in Rom 5:11; Col 1:20 and Eph 2:16 - where the emphasis is upon a reconciliation *within* the world (*kosmos*). The notion (found in the present passage v 19) that the world itself is reconciled would then be a later development, and the idea of the reconciliation of humanity to God (v 18) would be later still" (Furnish, 334).

Furnish is not convinced however of Käsemann's reconstruction of the **development** of the tradition. Furnish notes an anthropological aspect already in the pre-Pauline formula. Thus, Furnish concludes that Paul's citation of the tradition is probably confined to v 19b. It is a citation which Paul weaves into his text, embedding it within the text as a support for his own argument while at the same time giving the citation an interpretation.

15. Having considered several of the other prominent passages which have been declared down through the ages to express Paul's monotheism, the formula of the reconciliation does not strike us as monotheistic. The equivocation between "all" and "us" in verse 18 (not to mention "world" in the fragment) bespeaks an undeveloped and ambiguous construction in terms of strict monotheism. And we need only recall the stoic formula which we considered earlier which asserted that "All things come from thee (*phusis*), subsist in thee (*phusis*), go back to thee (*phusis*)." The stoic verse, assessed as the epitome of pantheism, employs only **one** term for the divine, that being *phusis*. Paul, on the other hand, commonly defended as a monotheist, commonly divides the formula between *theos* and *christos*: "from *theos*, through *christos*, to *theos*."

16. This reading of the fragment assumes that the paraphrasis of the text has to do with the authors use of the Greek *en* to stand for the Hebrew *b*.

17. Funk, #65.

18. The Stoic grammarians wrote of a neuter voice as neither active nor passive, meaning the middle (Roberts, 331, Dion. *Thr* 886, cf. Farrar *Gk. Synt* 40 (1876)).

19. Funk notes that "The syntax of voices in general remainded the same in the Hellenistic period (including the N.T.) as in the classical period of the language. Modifications have arisen mainly because of the tendency to merge the middle and passive into a single voice" (Funk, 307).

20. *Phrasis* is from *-phrazō* meaning "to show forth, tell, declare."

21. Taylor, *Erring*, 113.

22. A possible exception might be that Christ stands in opposition to Adam.

12.

ENDINGS AGAIN

THEOLOGIA AND OIKONOMIA

THE TEXT'S TEXTS IN THE *TEXTUS*

Conflicting texts are brought into a unity and remain in a more or less stable coherence by the power of some authority. That authority dominates so long as the unity holds together; so long as the inter-textual coherence is maintained. Thus, the critique of authority is a critique of some existing structure which can be traced in the (inter-) textual coherence. The inter-textuality is not discernable so long as the authority which maintains the coherence is powerful. The **inter**-textuality of a world is visible only in the creation of the unity or when the unity is seriously challenged. In the beginnings and endings the coherence is seen as coming to be or as coming to an end. And in each instance, the text's seams (re-)appear as seams. The coherence is (called) in(to) question. The domination of the authority falters as the text's "texts" reassert their independence from the overriding structure. Thus, the hermeneutic's limits are disclosed, not by its horizons, but by gaps within itself. Like the New Madrid fault which fractures the heartland of North America, disclosing old plates from which the continent is constructed, and which reassert themselves in quakes and shifts, a hermeneutic's limits are disclosed not by its shoreline but by the shakes and quakes along the seams/fractures internal to the perimeters and forgotten by the self-identity.

It has been argued by contemporary protestant theologians that the "doctrine of the Incarnation" is simply a metaphysical construction which plays/prays/preys upon few if any of the earlier christological themes evident in the books of the New Testament. They conclude--assuming the primacy of scripture over orthodoxy--that the doctrine is authoritative only to the extent that it adequately represents early Christian faith. Thus the overcoming of metaphysical theology (to which the doctrine of the incarnation belongs) is one of the ways by which one returns to authentic Christian faith evident in the scriptures. The Doctrine of the Incarnation is merely a metaphysical doctrine.

Others have argued, usually Catholic theologians, that the creeds merely make explicit what is implicit in the biblical texts. Thus, the creeds are the means by which the message is clarified. Having thus clarified the true message, judgment may be made as to whether a particular position is true (orthodox). The doctrine of the incarnation is not simply a metaphysical doctrine. Rather, it is the essence of the faith presented in a clear and concise manner. Thus, the doctrine of the incarnation is merely the truth of the faith drawn from the biblical text in clear and concise language.

Both standard approaches are flawed. Both fail to present the metaphysical gap which the mysterious economy traces in the midst of the metaphysical theology of the creed. As we have seen, this gap traces a theme of difference which may be said to have historical (textual) antecedents in Paul's epistle to the Corinthians: contra protestant theologians. On the other hand--contra Catholic theologians--the "doctrine of the incarnation" does not simply make explicit what is implied in the biblical text. Commonly, Catholic theologians appeal to those Pauline passages which appear to support metaphysical theology. But as we have seen, the passages appealed to for support either do not offer support for metaphysical theology, or they are the very positions which Paul quotes or paraphrases in order to overcome. The mysterious economy happens in the Chalcedonian text as a "gap" which under cuts the sovereignty of both metaphysical thought and the orthodoxy of the Imperial Church.

Taylor contends that the place of the radical co-dependence, the divine milieu, is "scripturing." For the epistle writer, this place of opposition is no place in particular other than the transitory gathering which is woven in the *textus* of the epistle. Paul traced the co-dependency of all things which negates the possibility of an absolute primal origin from which everything descends as **in Christ** in the script of his replies. For Paul, *Christos* negates the possibility of **origin** and **hierarchy**. And this negation happens **as** a destructing and a deconstruction in the epistles.

The deconstruction of origin and hierarchy has the effect of making room for differences between cultures, genders, races and economic classes. However, to suggest that Paul is leading a "movement," as has been suggested by some recent liberal biblical scholars, or that he has a community in mind which fulfills his deconstruction, or to suggest that such an *ekklēsia* is a societal possibility, is to regard the epistle as something other than an epistle. In this instance, to make such suggestions is to forget that the text is a purloined letter(s) which engages and calls into question what has been "addressed" to Paul. As such, the epistle is a **reply** to and **critique** of the Corinthian gathering.

So, we come to understand that there is no rest in the *textus*, that the divinities (Lord and God) continue to be in conflict, or that there are notions of divinity, or philosophies of religion which compete, compliment and work at cross purposes in the epistle texts.

Mystery Of The Middle Voice

In the course of our inquiry we found that the *oikonomia* was a mystery. Given the metaphysics of the creed, the *oikonomia* was inconceivable, unknowable and illegible in the text. The Doctrine of the *oikonomia* traced a non-metaphysical conviction or thought in a document dominated by metaphysical epistemology. The conviction or thought that counters the metaphysical-theological assumptions of the Chalcedonian text is "inconceivable" because, quite literally, it is un-real. The "incarnate one" has no *phusis* and is not present/legible. And yet, we saw that a denial of the mysterious economy would constitute self-annihilation of Christian thought.

In the epochal transformation and displacement, *theo*-logy (the logic of *Theos*) displaced *Christos*. Theoretically, we might contend that one manner of thinking displaced another. In the displacement, *Christos* could not be "assimilated" into *Theos*. Nevertheless, *Christos* persisted as a conundrum, a mystery, in theology.

However, the "mystery" is not simply how one theological conviction persists as a problem in a different theological framework. The problem is not the relative difference between different onto-theo-logical epochs. Rather, the doctrine of the *oikonomia* is remembered as a mystery because it traces a manner of language which is no longer legible in the language or grammar of the Creed. No longer within the limits of metaphysical order and grammar, persists a language of difference and a different language. In Chapter I, we discussed the ends of metaphysics in terms of what Charles Scott has called the non-reflexive middle voice. We have discussed the middle voice with respect to the paraphrastic grammatical construction of the reconciliation fragment, and have suggested that we so read and understand the baptismal passages.

At the conclusion of the last chapter, I suggested that there are a number of connections between Paul's christology and the doctrine of the mysterious economy. Now, I wish to carry this discussion one step further in terms of the interrelated themes of grammar and illegibility.

I suggested in our study of the "reconciliation fragment" and the "baptismal passages" that the phrase "in Christ" appears to name a non-reflexive middle voiced occurrence (by means of a paraphrastic grammatical construction) of oppositional gathering. That a periphrasis is evident in the "reconciliation fragment" seems to be if not a majority opinion among critical biblical scholars, surely one of the dominant understandings of the text. Might it be that the doctrine of the mysterious economy is a mystery, illegible in the creedal text, because the doctrine that is being defended is the ever so faint traces of a middle voiced grammar that has been crushed out of sight? To think with the middle voice, to work within such a grammar is **nonsense** to a thinking or in a grammar preoccupied with the action of subjects and the passivity of objects. Might it be in the creed, that even the common paraphrastic traces of the long ago lost middle voice have disappeared, and that all that can be said of such grammar/language/thinking, is that it is a mystery that can not present itself? In other words, the doctrine of the mysterious *oikonomia* traces the traces of a thinking/writing/grammar which appear to be everywhere crushed out of sight, erased; yet remembered simply as an erasure. And that, as such, a pre-metaphysical manner of understanding, a grammar not preoccupied with ætiological linguistics, is remembered as other, as divine mystery, as spiritual.

Thus, we have traced the *closure* of the Chalcedonian Document in the central doctrine of orthodox Christian theology which it reports to present and purposes to defend. The Doctrine of the Incarnation or Dispensation turns out to name a mysterious *oikonomia* which traces a grammar/language/thinking which is all but crushed out of sight in orthodox Christian theology. And further, the mysterious *oikonomia* reasserts a divinity **un/like (un/natural)** either *Theos* or humanity.

The ends of Christian theology have been traced in texts which are at the heart of orthodox Christian theology. Within the cannon, a language of difference and different divinities play the plies of the texts and so, simultaneously, open the texts to their own non-metaphysical traces not unlike bringing to closure the onto-theological doctrine of Christian thought.

Theologia comes to an end in christological accommodation (in *Christos*, *oikonomia*). The ætiological coherence of *theologia* falters in a language of difference. *Theologia* is unraveled by the *oikonomia*.

CHRISTO-ECCLESIOLOGY

Earlier we traced Heidegger's unanswered inquiry into what was at stake for the Old Church Fathers in their rejection of the Heraclitean *logos* as they sought to establish Christian onto-theological discourse. What we discovered in our study of the Doctrine of the Incarnation was that the rejection of the *logos* as gathering and the privileging of onto-theology were necessary if the Imperial Church was to be established. What was at stake for the Old Church Fathers was **institutional establishment or destruction, institutional coherence or anarchy**. Without force the church would be powerless and vulnerable to violence, death and annihilation. And without coherence and identity the church could not accommodate nor use the (institutional/ ontological) powers-that-be. However, what was at stake--what was valued and sought--eclipsed different manners of thinking and gathering. The domination of onto-theology in the Chalcedonian Creed happened in tandem with the instituting of the Imperial Church. Likewise, as the *oikonomia* came to name the mysterious saving event which could no longer be traced, the kind of gathering yielded by the mysterious economy could not be instituted. We might say that one church displaced another church. Or, better, the synthesis of force and rightness in the Imperial Church violated and forced out of sight (driving underground--subverting, damming or making invisible) all powerless and deviant communities and their Lord.

We have found in Paul's epistles what Heidegger calls in reference to Heraclitus, that origining and unique process commonly named in philosophy as the one-in-many (*en-panta*), the origining and unique process of "the dif-ference." We find this process (this logic, if you will) to be central in Paul's thought. *Christos* marks the difference. And this "difference" is also called "the *ekklēsia*" which is an oppositional gathering.

It is beyond the limits of this study to trace out and track down in detail the historical/textual antecedents of Paul's christology. Their paths are too many and too complex and the lack of clear historical evidence to substantiate a causal influence is too involved and too weak to be adequately presented let alone successfully executed here. However, I do suggest that such tracks might be traced, and that it is possible that there are causal (historical) connections between Paul's thinking and that of Heraclitus. Possibly this connection is through Stoic writings which were influenced by Heraclitus and are evident in the Pauline epistles.

The play of *ekklēsia* and in *Christos* in the Pauline corpus violates not only the attempts to systematize Paul's texts into ecclesiological and christological categories, but it also violates ecclesiastical institutionalization. A gathering of differences, an accommodation of opposites, violates institutional coherence/identity and yields institutional anarchy. As such, *Christos/ekklēsia* in the Pauline texts are powerless and thus incapable of harboring conclusions which yield force and violence. My claim is that the christo-ecclesia discourse in the Pauline epistles is not the (re-)source for the orthodox (institutional) christo-ecclesiological tradition.

The full significance of the inter-connection and co-dependency of christological positions and ecclesiologies are beyond the limits of the present study but are forthcoming in a work in progress.

HEIDEGGER AGAIN

The negative assessment of Heidegger's (explicit or implicit) philosophy of religion is rarely the outcome of a purely philosophical analysis. Most if not all such negative assessments are the conclusions reached after Heidegger's work is considered as a means of interpreting western religious texts, experience, thought and/or doctrine, and in particular, whether Heidegger's work is adequate as a means of interpreting **Christian** texts, experience, thought and/or doctrine.

One might suggest that the present work (concerned as it is with an orthodox Christian theological document and a canonized epistle) is simply a religious or theological study which provides historical support for a manner of religious and/or theological thinking which Heidegger elucidates in terms of philosophy. Thus, the reason the four-fold appears to be "incarnational" (and thus appears to play upon the christological themes in Paul's epistle to the Corinthians) is because Heidegger's thinking is the working out of such religious themes in terms of philosophical discourse. Who knows? That there are complex movements and traces between these texts is clear, though causality is not.

Christian thought, as Heidegger pointed out in brief, often cryptic comments, is not easily at home in the onto-theo-logical enterprise. And yet, ironically, so it seems, Christian institutions have been the powers that employed and preserved metaphysics. The domination of the onto-theo-logical in Christian thought made possible Christian *theo*-logy. For with or by the emergence of metaphysics as a theme in Christian thought, *Theos* came to dominate the enterprise.

In the ending of onto-theo-logical thought, the onto-theos gives way to other gods who (re-)appear. I have argued that the Christian divinity *Christos*, no longer subjugated by onto-theos and displaced by the "incarnation," reappears in its difference from onto-theos. My contention is that metaphysical theology concealed the pre-metaphysical understanding of logos as difference. Or in more traditional theological language, we might say that metaphysical theology led christendom to forget the saving occurrence, the *Christos*, the a/t-onement. Thus, pre-metaphysical christological thinking was overcome by onto-theo-logy which came to dominate Christian thinking in post-nicene theology. Thus, in a post-modern rereading of the texts of Christian faith the traces of *Christos* may be traced more openly. The *oikonomia* is much less a mystery. It appears to be logical and intelligible.

Heidegger has suggested that in the end of philosophy as metaphysics there is an end to the onto-theo-logical network, that as in the ending of philosophy, theology ends as well. To the extent to which Heidegger's thinking is philosophy, a philosophy unlike the mainstream of traditional western academic philosophy, can we begin to think, or rethink (to deconstruct) "theologically?" Or, given our study of the Doctrine of the *oikonomia* and **in** *Christos*, might we call a deconstructed Christian *theo*-logy an "accommodation," or simply "Christology?" Or might it be better to say that with the two fold closure of philosophy and theology, thinking happens and difference occurs. To speak of the happening of thinking or the occurrence of difference as philosophical or theological would be misleading to the extent that such labels reinscribe onto-theo-logy into that which is said to happen at or in the ending.

So, might we muse with Heidegger that Christian *theologia* "experienced in virtue of the dawning of the origin,... is, however, at the same time past in the sense that it has entered its ending. The ending lasts longer than the previous history of..." Christian onto-theo-logy.

Such leaves us in a quandary. It is of course the quandary with which we started. For if the end of metaphysics is disclosed from its beginning and lingers to its conclusion, then it might be said that philosophy and theology have been in perpetual closure. And to suggest that might lead us to conclude that in the closure of their identity (as onto-theo-logy), philosophy and theology--defer. My claim is that in the Christian tradition they defer to an experience of *Christos* without the *Theos* of western metaphysics.

BIBLIOGRAPHY

Altizer, T. J. S. "The Triumph of the Theology of the Word." *Journal of the American Academy of Religion* 54 (Fall, 1986):525-29.

Aristotle. *The Metaphysics*. Translated by H. Tredennick. The Loab Classical Library. Cambridge: Harvard University Press, 1933. 2 Volumes.

Arndt, William F. & F. Wilbur Gingrich. *A Greek-English Lexicon Of The New Testament And Other Early Christian Literarture*. Chicago: The University of Chicago Press, 1957.

Aurelius, Marcus. *Meditations*.

Baird, William. *The Corinthians*. New York: Abingdon Press, 1964.

Barrett, Charles K. *A Commentary On The First Epistle To The Corinthians*. New York: Harper & Row, 1968.

Barth, Karl. *Church Dogmatics*. Translated by G. W. Bromiley & T. F. Torrance. Edinburgh: T. & T. Clark, 1936-1939.

Barthes, Roland, "From Work to Text." *Textual Strategies: Perspectives in Post-Structural Criticism*. Edited by J. V. Harari. Ithaca: Cornell University Press, 1979.

Betz, H. D. *Galatians: A Commentary on Paul's letter to the Churches in Galatia*. Philadelphia: Fortress Press, 1979.

Bernasconi, Robert. "The Transformation of Language At Another Beginning." *Research in Phenomenology* 13 (1983):1-23.

Bindley, T. Herbert. *The Oecuminical Documents of The Faith*. Edited with Introduction and Notes. London: Methuen & Co. LTD., 1950

Bruce, F. F. *1 & 2 Corinthians*. Trans. J. W. Leitch. Philadelphia: Fortress Press, 1975.

Bultmann, Ruldolf. *Faith And Understanding*. Edited with Introduction by Robert Funk. Translated by L. P. Smith. London: S. C. M., 1969.

_______. *The Gospel of John: A Commentary*. Translated by G. R. Beasley-Murry. General Editor R. W. N. Hoare and J. K. Riches. Philadelphia: Westminister Press, 1971.

_______. *Primitive Christianity In Its Contemprary Setting*. Translated by R. F. Fuller. New York: Meridean Book, 1956.

_______. *The Second Letter To The Corinthians*. Translated by Roy A Harrisville. Minneapolis: Augsburg Publishing House, 1985.

_______. *Theology of the New Testament*. Translated by Kendrick Grobel. New York: Scribner, 1951-1955.

Caputo, John. *Heidegger and Aquinas: As Essay on Overcoming Metaphysics*. New York: Fordham University Press, 1982.

Clark, Elizabeth A. *Women In The Early Church*. Wilmington, Del.: Michael Glazier, Inc., 1983.

Conzelmann, Hans. *1 Corinthians: A Commentary on the First Epistle to the Corinthians*. Translated by James W. Leitch, edited by George W. MacRae. Philadelphia: Fortress Press, 1975.

Craddock, Fred B. *Christology And Cosmology: An Investigation of Colossians 1:15-20.* Ph.D. Diss., Vanderbilt University, 1964.

_______. *The Pre-Existence of Christ in the New Testament*. Nashville: Abingdon Press, 1968.

Cüllmann, O. *The Earliest Christian Confessions*. Translated by J. K. S. Reid. London: Lutterworth Press, 1949.

Curtis, W. A. *A History of Creeds and Confessions of Faith*. Edinburgh: T. & T. Clark, 1911.

Deely, John N. "The Situation of Heidegger in the Tradition of Christian Theology." *The Thomist* 31 (April, 1967):159-244.

Demske, James M. "Heidegger's Quadrate and the Revelation of Being." *Philsosophy Today* 7 (1963):245-257.

Denniston, J. D. *The Greek Particles*. Oxford: At The Clarendon Press, 1954.

Derrida, Jacques. *Disseminations*. Translated, with an Introduction and Additional Notes, by Barbara Johnson. Chicago: The University of Chicago Press, 1981.

_______. *Of Grammatology*. Baltimore: John Hopkins University Press, 1974, 1976.

_______. *Margins of Philosophy*. Translated, with Additional Notes, by Alan Bass. Chicago: The University of Chicago, 1982.

_______. *Positions*. Translated and Annotated by Alan Bass. Chicago, The University of Chicago Press, 1981.

_______. *Writing and Difference*. Translated, with an Introduction and Additional Notes, by Alan Bass. Chicago: The University of Chicago Press, 1978.

Detweiler, Robert. "Theological Trends of Postmodern Fiction." *Journal of the American Academy of Religion* 44/2 (1976):225-237.

Dunn, James D. G. *Christology In The Making: A New Testament Inquiry into the Origins of the Doctrine of the Incarnation*. Philadelphia: Westminister Press, 1980.

_______. *Unity And Diversity In The New Testament*. Philadelphia: Westminister Press, 1977.

Eusebius of Caesarea. *Eusebii Pamphili Evangelicae Praeparationis Libri XV*. Edited by E. H. Gifford. Oxford: Oxford University Press, 1903.

Evans, Ernest. *The Epistles of Paul the Apostle to the Corinthians*, "The Clarendon Bible." Oxford: The Clarendon Press, 1930.

Fabro, Cornelio. *God In Exile: Modern Atheism*. Translated and Edited by Authur Gibson. Westminister, Md.: Newman Press, 1968.

Fell, Joseph P. "Heidegger's Mortals and Gods." *Research in Phenomenology* 15 (1985):29-42.

Fiorenza, Elizabeth Schüssler. *In Memory of Her: A Feminist Theological Reconstruction of Christian Origins*. New York: Crossroads, 1985.

Flanagan, N. & Snyder, E. Hunter. "Did Paul Put Down Women In 1 Cor 14:34-36?" *Biblical Theology Bulletin* 11 (1981):10-11.

Funk, Robert W. *A Greek Grammar of the New Testament and Other Early Christian Literature: A Translation and Revision of the Ninth-Tenth German Edition (by F. Blass). Incorporting Supplementary Notes of A. Debrunner*. Chicago: The University of Chicago Press, 1961.

Furnish, Victor Paul. *II Corinthians: The Anchor Bible; Translated with Introdution, Notes and Commentary*. Garden City, New York: Doubleday & Co., Inc., 1984.

Girosheide, F. W. *Commentary On The First Epistle To The Corinthains*. Grand Rapids, Michigan: Eerdmans Publishing Co., 1953.

Grant, Robert. "Causation and "The Ancient World View." *Journal of Biblical Literature* 83/1 (1964):34-40.

_______. "Gods and the One God." *Journal of the American Academy of Religion* 32 (1964):34-40.

_______. *The Early Christian Doctrine of God*. Charlottesville, Va.: University Press of Virginia, 1966.

Gray, William N. "The Myth of the Word Discarnate." *Theology* 88 (March, 1985):112-117.

Green, Michael. Editor. *The Truth of God Incarnate*. Grand Rapids, Michigan: Wm. B. Eerdmans Publishing Co., 1977.

Grillimieu, Aloys. *Christ In Christian Tradition: Volume One; From the Apostolic Age to Chalcedon (451)*. Translated by John Bowden. Atlanta: John Knox Press, 1975.

Gryson, Roger. *The Ministry of Women In The Early Church*. Translated by Jean Laporte and Mary Louise Hall. Collegeville, Minn.: The Liturgical Press, 1980.

Guthrie, W. K. C. *A History of Greek Philosophy*. Cambridge: At The University Press, 1962.

Hahn, Ferndard. *The Titles of Jesus In Christology*. Translated by H. Knight and G. Ogg. New York: World Publishing Co., 1969.

Hall, F. J. *The Being And Attributes of God*. New York: Longmans, 1909.

Hardy, E. R., and C. Richardson, Editors. *Christology of the Later Fathers*. Volume 3 of *The Library of Christian Classics*. Philadelphia: The Westminister Press, 1956.

Harvey, Irene E. "Derrida and the Concept of Metaphysics." *Research in Phenomenology* 13 (1983):113-48.

Heidegger, Martin. *Being and Time*. Translated by John Macquarrie & Edward Robinson (New York: Harper & Row, Publishers; 1962).

_______. *Early Greek Thought*. Translated by David Farrell Krell and Frank A Capuzzi. New York: Harper & Row, Publishers, 1975.

_______. *The End of Philosophy*. Translated by Joan Stambaugh. New York: Harper & Row, Publishers, 1973.

_______. *Essays In Metaphysics: Identity And Difference*. Translated by Kurt F. Leidecker. New York: Philosophical Library, Inc., 1960.

_______. and Eugene Funk. *Heraclitus Seminar 1966/67*. Translated by Charles H. Seibert. University, Alabama: The University of Alabama Press, 1979.

_______. *An Introduction To Metaphysics*. Translated by Ralph Manheim. New Haven: Yale University Press, 1959.

_______. *On The Way To Language*. Translated by Peter D. Hertz. New York: Harper & Row, Publishers, 1971.

_______. *On Time And Being*. Translated by Joan Stambaugh, New York: Harper & Row, Publishers, 1972.

_______. "The Pathway." Edited and translated by Thomas F. O'Meare, O.P., *Listening* 2 (1967):89-91.

_______. "Phenomenology and Theology." Translated by James Hart and John Maraldo in *The Piety of Thinking*. Bloomington: Indiana University Press, 1976.

_______. *Poetry, Language, Thought*. Translated and Introduction by Albert Hofstadter. New York: Harper & Row, Publishers, 1971.

_______. "The Way Back Into The Ground Of Metaphysics." *Existentialism from Dostoevsky to Sartre*. Walter Kaufmann New York: Meridian Books, New American Library, 1975.

_______. *Unterwegs Zur Sprache*. Tubingen: Verlag Gunther Neske Pfullingen, 1959.

Hengel, Martin. *The Son Of God: The Origin of Christology and the History of Jewish-Hellenistic Religion*. Translated by John Bowden. London: S. C. M. Press, 1976.

Herring, Jean. *The First Epistle Of Saint Paul To The Corinthians*. London: The Epworth Press, 1962.

Heyob, S. Kelly. *The Cult of Isis Among Women In The Greco-Roman World*. Leiden: Brill, 1975.

Hick, John. Editor. *The Myth of God Incarnate*. Philadelphia: The Westminister Press, 1977.

Hodgson, Peter C. *Jesus--Word and Presence: An Essay In Christology*. Philadelphia: Fortress Press, 1971.

Holladay, C. *The First Letter Of Paul To The Corinthians*. Austin, Texas: Sweet Publishing Co., 1979.

Horsley, R. A. "The Background of the Confessional Formula In 1 Cor 8:6." *ZNW* 69 (1978):130-135.

Hurd, J. C. *The Origins of 1 Corinthians*. New York: Seabury Press, 1965.

Hurley, James B. "Did Paul Require Veils or the Silence of Women? A Construction of 1 Cor. 11:1-16 and 1 Cor. 14:33b-36." *The Westminster Theological Journal* 35 (1972):190-220.

Jaeger, Werner. *Early Christianity and Greek Paideia*. Cambridge: Belknap Press of Harvard University Press, 1961.

________. *The Theology of the Early Greek Philosophers*. Translated by E. S. Robinson. Oxford: Clarendon Press, 1947.

Jewett, R. "The Sexual Liberation Of The Apostle Paul." *Journal of the American Academy of Religion Supplement* 47/1 (1979):55-87.

Jonas, Hans. "Heidegger And Theology." *The Phenomenon of Life*. New York: Harpers, 1966.

Kahn, Charles H. *The Art and Thought of Heraclitus*. New York: At the University Press, 1979.

Käsemann, Hans. *Perspectives on Paul*. Translated by M. Kohl. Philadelphia: Fortress Press, 1971.

Kelly, J. N. D. *Early Christian Creeds*. New York: Longmans, Green and Co., 1952.

Kittel, Gerhard. *Theological Dictionary of the New Testament*. Translated and edited by Geoffrey W. Bromiley. Grand Rapids, Michigan: Eerdmans, 1964-1976.

Kirk, G. S. *Heraclitus: The Cosmic Fragments*. Cambridge: At The University Press, 1954.

Klein, E. *A Comprehensive Etymological Dictionary of The English Language*. New York: Elsevier Publishing Co., 1960.

Knox, John. *The Humanity and Divinity of Christ: A Study of Pattern in Christology*. Cambridge: At The University Press, 1975.

Lacan, Jacques. "Seminar On "The Purloined Letter." Translated by Jeffrey Melhman. *Yale French Studies* 48 (1972).

Lampe, G. W. H., Editor. *A Patristic Greek Lexicon*. Oxford: At The Clarendon Press, 1961, 1965.

Liddell, Henry G. & Robert Scott. *A Greek-English Lexicon*. Oxford: At The Clarendon Press, 1940.

Lloyd, G.E.R. *Polarity and Analogy: Two Types of Argumentation in Early Greek Thought*. Cambridge: At The University Press, 1987.

MacDonald, Dennis Ronald. *There Is No Male and Female*. Cambridge, Mass.: Harvard Dissertations in Religion 20. Philadelphia: Fortress Press, 1987.

Macquarrie, John. *An Existentialist Theology: A Comparison of Heideggar and Bultmann*. London: SCM Press, 1955.

Mansi, Joannes Doiminicus, *Sacrorum Conciliorum Nova et Amphlssima Collectio*.

Meeks, Wayne. "The Image of the Androgyne: Some Uses of a Symbol in Earliest Christianity." *History of Religions* 13.4 (February, 1974):165-208.

_______. Editor. *The Writings of St. Paul*. New York: Norton, 1972.

Meier, J. P. "On the Veiling of Hermeneutics (1 Cor 11:2-16)," *Catholic Biblical Quarterly* 40 (1978):212-226.

Moffatt, James. *The First Epistle of Paul to the Corinthians*. New York: Harper & Brothers, 1938.

Moule, C. F. D. *An Idom Book Of New Testament Greek*. Cambridge: At The University Press, 1953, 1960.

_______. *The Origins of Christology*. Cambridge: At The University Press, 1977.

Murphy-O'Connor, J. *1 Corinthians*. Wilmington, Delaware: Michael Glazier, 1979.

_______. "Interpolations In 1 Corinthians." *Catholic Biblical Quarterly* 48 (1986):81-94.

_______. "The Non-Pauline Character of 1 Corinthians 11:2-16?" *Journal of Biblical Literature* 95 (1976):615-21.

_______. "Sex and Logic In 1 Corinthians 11:2-16." *Catholic Biblical Quarterly* 42 (1980):482-500.

Newman, John Henry Cardinal. *The Arians of the Fourth Century*. Westminister, Md.: Christian Classics, 1968.

Norris, Richard A., Jr. Translated and Edited. *The Christological Controversy*. Sources of Early Christian Thought Series, ed. William G. Rusch, Philadelphia, Fortress Press, 1980.

_______. *God And World In Early Christian Theology*. New York: Seabury Press, 1965.

Odell-Scott, David W. "In Defense of an Egalitarian Interpretation of 1 Cor 14:34-36: A Reply to Murphy-O'Connor's Critique." *Biblical Theology Bulletin* 17 (1987):100-103.

_______. "Let The Women Speak In Church: An Egalitarian Interpretation of 1 Cor 14:33b-36." *Biblical Theology Bulletin* 13 (1983):90-93.

O'Leary, Joseph Stephen *Questioning Back: The Overcoming of Metaphysics in Christian Tradition*. Minneapolis: A Seabury Book, Winston Press, 1985.

Orr, Robert P. *The Meaning of Transcendence: A Heideggerian Reflection*. American Academy of Religion Dissertation Series, Number 35. Edited by Wendell Dietrich. Chico, California: Scholars Press, 1981.

Orr, W. F. & Walther, J. A. *1 Corinthians: A New Translation*. Garden City, New York: Doubleday & Company, Inc., 1976.

Owen, H. P. *Concepts of Diety*. Philosophy of Religion Series. London: Macmillian, 1971.

The Oxford English Dictionary. C. T. Onions, General Editor. Oxford: At The Clarendon Press, 1966.

Patrick, G.T.W. *The Fragments Of The Work Of Heraclitus Of Ephesus "On Nature"*. Baltimore: N. Murray, 1889.

Patte, Daniel. *Paul's Faith and the Power of the Gospel: A Structural Introduction to the Pauline Letters*. Philadelphia: Fortress Press, 1983.

Perotti, James. *Heidegger On The Divine: The Thinker, The Poet and God*. Athens: Ohio University Press, 1974.

Portier, William L. "*Ancilla invita*: Heidegger, the theologians, and God." *Sciences Religieuses/Studies In Religion* 14/2 (1985):161-180.

Powell, Ralph A. "Has Heidegger Destructured Metaphysics?" *Listening* 2 (1967):52-59.

Prestige, G. L. *God In Patristic Thought*. London-Toronto: William Heinemann Ltd., 1936. 2nd ed., London: Soceity for Promoting Christian Knowledge, 1952.

Prier, Raymond A. *Archaic Logic*. The Hague-Paris: Mouton, 1976.

Reumann, J. H. "Stewards of God." *Journal of Biblical Literature* 77 (1958):339-49.

_______. *The Uses Of 'oikonomia' And Related Terms In Greek Sources To About A.D. 100, As A Background For Patristic Application*. Dissertation: University of Pennsylvania, 1957.

Richardson, Alan. *Creeds In The Making: A Short Introduction to the History of Christian Doctrine*. London: Student Christian Movement Press, 1935.

Richardson, William J. *Heidegger: Through Phenomenology to Thought*. The Hague: Martinus Nijhoff, 1974.

Robertson, Archibald, and Alfred Plummer. *International Critical Commentary, A Critical and Exegetical Commentary on the First Epistle of St. Paul to the Corinthians*. New York: Charles Scribner's Sons, 1911.

Robertson, A. T. *A Grammar of the Greek New Testament in the Light of Historical Research*. New York: Hodder & Stoughton, 1914.

Robertson, E. H. *Corinthians 1 And 2*. New York: MacMillian Publishing Co., 1973.

Sallis, John, and Kenneth Maly. Editors. *Heraclitean Fragments: A Companion Volume To The Heidegger/Fink Seminary On Heraclitus*. University, Alabama: The University of Alabama Press, 1980.

Scharlemann, Robert P. "The Being of God When God Is Not Being God: Deconstructing the History of Theism." *De-Construction and Theology*, ed. Thomas J. J. Altizer, Max A. Myers, Carl A. Raschke, Robert P. Scharlemann, Mark C. Taylor, Charles E. Winquist. New York: Crossroad, 1982.

Schmithals, W. *Gnosticism in Corinth: An Investigation of the Leter to the Corinthians*. Translated by John E. Steely. Nashville: Abingdon Press, 1971. SchÜrmann, Reiner. "Principles Precarious: On The Origin of the Political in Heidegger." *Heidegger: The Man And The Thinker*. Edited by Thomas Sheehan. Chicago: Precedent Publishing, Inc., 1986.

Schwartz, E. ed. *Acta Conciliorum Oedumenicorum*. Berlin and Leipzig: De Gruyter, 1914ff.

Schweizer, E. "The Service Of Worship--An Exposition of 1 Cor 14," *Interpretations* 13 (1959):400-408.

Scott, Charles E. "Foucalt's Practice of Thinking." *Research In Phenomenology* XIV (1984):75-85.

_______. "Heidegger And The Question Of Ethics." Graduate Invitational Lecture, Third Annual Lecture, Vanderbilt University Graduate Department of Philosophy, April 9, 1986. *Research In Phenomenology* 18 (Fall, 1988):23-40.

_______. *The Language of Difference*. Atlantic Heights, N.J.: Humanities Press International, Inc., 1987. Contemporary Studies in Philosophy and the Human Sciences, edited by John Sallis.

_______. "Violence and Psyche." *Soundings* 68 (Spring, 1985):42-51.

Scroggs, Robin. "Paul And The Eschatological Women." *Journal of the American Academy of Religion* 40 (1972).

Sellers, R. V. *The Council of Chalcedon: A Historical and Doctrinal Survey*. London: S.P.C.K., 1953.

Sheehan, Thomas. Editor. *Heidegger: The Man and the Thinker*. Chicago: Precedent Publishing, Inc., 1981.

Shipley, Joseph T. *The Origins of English Words: A Discursive Dictionary of Indo-European Roots*. Baltimore: The Johns Hopkins University Press, 1984.

Smyth, H. W. *Greek Grammar*. Cambridge: Harvard University Press, 1963.

Sophocles, E. A. *Greek Lexicon of the Roman and Byzantian Periods From B.C. 146-A.D. 1100*. New York: Frederick Ungar Pub., Co., 1887.

Stokes, Michael C. *One and Many In Presocratic Philosophy*. Cambridge, Mass.: Harvard University Press, 1971.

_______. "Heraclitus of Ephesus." *The Encyclopedia of Philosophy* 3:477-481.

Sykes, S. W. and Clayton, J. P. *Christ, Faith and History: Cambridge Studies in Christology*. London: Cambridge University Press, 1972.

Talbert, Charles. *Reading Corinthians: A Literary and Theological Commentary on 1 & 2 Corinthians*. New York: Crossroad, 1987.

Taylor, Mark C. *Deconstructing Theology*. Chico, CA.: Crossroad and Scholars Press, 1982.

_______. *Erring: A Postmodern A/theology*. Chicago: The University of Chicago, 1984.

_______. "Masking: Domino Effect" Symposium *Journal of the American Academy of Religion* 54:3 (Fall, 1986):547-560.

Thayer, Joseph Henry. *A Greek-English Lexicon of the New Testament: being Grimm's Wilke's Clavis Novi Testamenti; Translated, Revised and Enlarged*. Grand Rapids, Michigan: Baker Book House, 1977. 4th edition.

Thiselton, A. C. "Radical Eschatology At Corinth." *New Testiment Studies* 24 (1977-1978):520-21.

Thrall, M. E. *The First And Second Letters of Paul To The Corinthians*. Cambridge: At The University Press, 1965.

Tillich, Paul. *The Courage To Be*. New Haven: Yale University Press, 1952.

_______. *Systematic Theology*. Chicago: The University of Chicago Press, 1951, 1957, 1963.

Torrance, Thomas Forsyth. *Space, Time and Incarnation*. New York: Oxford University Press, 1969.

Vail, L. M. *Heidegger And Ontological Difference*. University Park: The Pennsylvania State University Press, 1972.

Walker, William O. "1 Cor 11:2-16 And Paul's Views Regarding Women," *Journal of the American Academy of Religion* 94 (1975):94-110.

Walter, E. *The First Epistle To The Corinthians*. London: Sheed & Ward, 1968.

Welte, Bernhard. "God In Heidegger's Thought," *Philosophy Today* 26 (1982):85-100.

Wheelwright, Philip E. *Heraclitus*. Princeton: Princeton University Press, 1959.

Whiteley, D. E. H. *The Theology of St. Paul*. Oxford: Blackwell, 1964.

Williams, John R. *Martin Heidegger's Philosophy of Religion*. Waterloo, Ontario, Canada: Wilfrid Laurier University Press, 1977. Canadian Corporation For Studies In Religion Supplement #2.

Willis, Wendell Lee. *Idol Meat In Corinth: The Pauline Argument in 1 Corinthians 8 and 10*. Chico, California: Dissertation Series #68, Society of Biblical Literature, Scholars Press. 1985.

Wolfson, Harry A. *The Philosophy of the Church Fathers*. Cambridge, Mass.: Harvard University Press, 1956.

INDEX

References marked with Roman numerals signify chapter numbers while Arabic notations refer to page numbers.